OLD TESTAMENT WISDOM

—FROM KIRCHER'S *ARCA NOE*

THE TREE OF THE GENERATIONS OF ADAM

OLD TESTAMENT WISDOM

Keys to Bible Interpretation

By Manly P. Hall

THE PHILOSOPHICAL RESEARCH SOCIETY, INC.
Los Angeles, California 90027

ISBN NO. 0-89314-827-X
L.C. 87-19382

Copyright © 1987
By the Philosophical Research Society
Second Edition
Third Printing 1999

The Library of Congress Catalogued

Hall, Manly Palmer, 1901-1990
    Old Testament Wisdom : keys to Bible interpretation / by Manly P.
Hall. — 2nd ed.
    p. cm.
    Bibliography: p.
    Includes index.
    ISBN 0-89314-827-X
    1. Bible. O.T.—Criticism, interpretation, etc.   2. Cabala.
1. Title.
BS1191.H35 1987   87-19382
221.6—dc19   CIP

About the Cover
Head of Moses. Detail from the sculpure by Michelangelo.

Published by

THE PHILOSOPHICAL RESEARCH SOCIETY

3910 Los Feliz Boulevard, Los Angeles, CA 90027
Phone (323) 663 2167 Fax (323) 663 9443
Website www.prs.org Email info@prs.org

 PRINTED IN CANADA

FOREWORD

he first printing of my book *How to Understand Your Bible* has been unavailable for many years, and there have been numerous requests for a new edition. To bring the work up to date, considerable new material has been introduced derived from articles and lectures.

The nature of the present study is such that some will regard it as controversial, but every effort has been made to approach the convictions of Bible students and Bible leaders reverently and respectfully. It has long been my belief that devout persons of all denominations should understand, as completely as possible, those sacred Scriptural writings which have

1

inspired and strengthened the lives of Jewish and Christian peoples for so many centuries. My approach, therefore, is on the level of comparative religion, for it is no longer possible simply to divide mankind into believers and unbelievers. We all observe the growing importance of religion in the life of the average person; whether he be Christian, Moslem, Hindu, or Jew. It is therefore no part of my intention to write dogmatically or to compare the merits or demerits of the various faiths. It seems wiser to remind the thoughtful individual that it is more profitable, in terms of personal spiritual security, to attain a deeper and more satisfying appreciation for those great codes of morality and ethics which support and inspire the growth of civilizations and cultures.

The greater part of humankind shares a common religious instinct. Men naturally desire to worship a Creating Power, live according to its precepts, and serve one another as the final and factual evidence of their devotion. Such good will and generous intention are the most powerful available forces for the solution of individual and collective problems. Wherever possible, religion, as a total reality, should emphasize the essential unity of sects and creeds. We cannot have world peace on a political level unless men first unite in their hearts. While we remain divided on the level of theology, thus restricting good will at its source, there is little hope that we can wholeheartedly cooperate scientifically, economically, or socially.

Many years of research and thoughtfulness have induced me to believe that there is only one essential religion practiced among men. This has sometimes been called "the original religion" or "the natural religion" of mankind. It is enthroned in the human soul, and expresses itself through the irresistible desires to seek truth and to live constructively. At various times, illumined teachers, inspired prophets, and dedicated sages, have attempted to teach or preach this faith to their peoples, or to restore the purity of spiritual doctrines which have become corrupted by the ignorance and selfishness of mortals. Thus religions, as we know them, are human re-statements of eternal principles.

The great barrier between faiths has been the problem of language. We are not always able to recognize the identity of concepts when they are presented to us in strange or foreign terms. When one man speaks of God, and another of Tao, we may become confused and suspect essential differences in dogma. It is evident, therefore, that we cannot rightfully judge and estimate unless we are properly familiar with faiths other than our own. Comparative religion is a branch of knowledge which makes it possible for us to penetrate the barriers of terms, symbols, emblems, and allegories, and discover the true convictions of our fellow men. Without such knowledge, we are likely to fall into prejudice, which may in turn lead to intolerance. In religion it is especially true that most misunderstandings are due to lack of understanding.

The Jewish-Christian Bible is one of the great sacred books of the world. It is now the principal religious text accepted and venerated by nearly one third of the earth's population. Yet even with this vast following, we should not lose sight of the fact that two thirds of our fellow creatures belong to other faiths and cherish their own sacred books with equal sincerity. It is no longer wise or even possible to refer to the religions of non-Christian peoples in disparaging terms. They are our neighbors, and the rapid progress in communication and transportation results in a cultural intimacy which must be accepted and appreciated. We depend upon our brothers of other faiths to help us maintain a free world; support and defend our democratic institutions; aid and assist in planning the future of civilization; and share with us those commodities necessary for the preservation of our economic system. Sincere followers of many faiths must sit in our councils and leagues, our congresses and conferences, which have been created to preserve the peace, reduce crime, and distribute the advantages of scientific and industrial knowledge. Can we afford to allow a lack of common understanding to divide us psychologically and thus detract from the efficiency of those common labors by which we all so largely profit?

When we study anthropology, we discover that the races of mankind are like the branches of a great tree. Humanity is one family, and through the vast circulation of this tremendous organism, has moved an endless stream of arts and sciences, philosophies and crafts, and, most of all, of spiritual convictions. Sacred writings are intimately associated, and their descent can be traced from a common source. Factually, it is very difficult to distinguish clearly essential doctrinal differences between the Egyptian Book of the Dead, the Orphic Hymns of the Greeks, the Persian Avestas, and the Old Testament of the Jews. Apparent differences may at first alarm us, but they result largely from long cycles of interpretation, differences of environment, and the inevitable spiritual individuality of racial and cultural groups.

The study of sacred books reveals to us the beautiful story of man's noblest aspirations. These works form a wonderful literature set apart and dedicated to the love and service of God. If we are a truly religious people, we will be glad that Eternal Providence has provided all men with spiritual codes suitable to their needs. We may well find, if we seek sincerely, that many of these Bibles of other lands and other times can help us today to find our consolation of spirit. Sacred writings are part of the world heritage which is the precious birthright of modern man. We need not fear that we will be contaminated by writings that have brought comfort and understanding to millions, even hundreds of millions, of our fellow men. Inter-racial, inter-religious understanding will help us to come together in a kindly and gracious partnership of ideals. We shall respect our neighbor better when we know and appreciate the faith by which he lives.

It is in this spirit that our books of Bible studies have been compiled. We make no claim to infallible revelation. We do not say that these writings may not have other interpretations or other meanings. We ask no belief or acceptance, but invite consideration, and sincerely hope that the reader will be inspired to advance these studies in his own way and according to his own inclination. It is by thinking together with gentle patience that we advance our causes. Not through acceptance or rejection, but by sincerity of heart and purpose, we study to learn, and learn that we may come to understand.

Very sincerely yours,

Manly P. Hall

October, 1957

TABLE OF CONTENTS

OLD TESTAMENT WISDOM

CHAPTER I

THE DESCENT OF THE HOLY SCRIPTURES

The Holy Bible, consisting of two distinct works—the Old Testament and the New Testament—has often been called the most wonderful book in the world. Although widely venerated and almost universally respected, this sacred book has a long, strange history, much of which is obscure and uncertain. Even though the Bible, as we know it, is less than two thousand years old, the circumstances leading to its compilation have never been historically clarified. Many of the accounts relating to the origin and descent of the Old Testament writings have been compiled from legend and lore rather than from adequate records. If we choose to reflect upon some of the more abstract aspects of this religious and literary mystery, we shall not depart from a procedure which has gained traditional approval. It may be well, therefore, to summarize first such information as is generally available.

The Old Testament was anciently written in the Hebrew language, or in one of a related group of tongues which include Chaldean and Aramaic. There are sufficient historical and theological references to indicate that rolls or scrolls of the Old Testament, especially the Pentateuch, were in existence several centuries before the beginning of the Christian era. Yet up to very recent years, none of these original rolls was known to have survived. We have tablets of clay from the Valley of the Euphrates, and manuscripts on papyrus from ancient Egypt, which have withstood the vandalisms of both man and time. It is strange, therefore, that we should not have more source material in the case of the Old Testament writings.

The Dead Sea Scrolls recently discovered include a complete manuscript of Isaiah believed to have been written in Hebrew in the 1st or 2nd century B. C. This important discovery modifies older findings, as up to this time the earliest comprehensive manuscripts of the Old Testament in Hebrew date from the 9th or 10th century A. D., and are therefore only about one thousand years old. Even assuming that war, pillage, and the Diaspora resulted in the destruction of many ancient Jewish books, it would seem that some should have survived. It would be strange indeed if Jewish communities between the 1st and 9th centuries A. D. had not produced manuscripts for the use of their scholars and congregations.

The New Testament as a collected work is known only through early Greek manuscripts. Some have assumed that it was recorded in Greek, but this seems rather strange when we realize that during the first three centuries of Christianity the descent of the faith was largely in the keeping of Christians of Jewish origin. Greek was the language of scholars, and these were not numerous in the early historical descent of Christianity, especially in Syria. Little is known about the New Testament until the end of the 3rd or the beginning of the 4th century A. D. Three important manuscripts have survived from this period; they are the *Codex Vaticanus* (*Codex B*), *Codex Alexandrinus* (*Codex A*), and the *Codex Sinaiticus* (*Codex Aleph*). The first of these is in the Vatican Library, and the other two are in the British Museum. These manuscripts are called *uncils* because they are written entirely in capital letters. Incidentally, there was no punctuation or spacing between words. It was also customary to put as many words on a line as could be read conveniently without pausing for breath.

There was a second type of manuscript, also of Greek origin, known as the *cursive,* in which the writing combined capitals and small letters, and a running hand was employed. These are later than the uncils and are regarded as less important. Comparative value for scholars is based upon the important consideration that the uncils are the sources from which the cursive texts are taken. Less than one hundred uncil manuscripts of the Bible or parts thereof are known to exist, and only two—the *Vaticanus* and the *Sinaiticus*—are sufficiently complete to indicate the full scope of the original writings. There are about three thousand cursive manuscripts in Greek, dating from the 10th to the 16th centuries. These are sometimes useful to scholars, but do not solve the principal problem; that is, the determination of the original text of the two Testaments.

About the year 280 B. C., the most famous version of the Old Testament was prepared in Alexandria for the use of the Jewish colony in Egypt. According to the semi-legendary account, Demetrius of Phalera, librarian to Ptolemy Philadelphus, presented to his royal master a transcription of the Books of Moses as worthy of inclusion in the magnificent library of the Pharaoh. Ptolemy, pleased by the suggestion of his librarian, sent two ambassadors, Aristeas and Andreas, to Jerusalem to elicit the aid of Eleazar, who was then the High Priest. The Egyptian King was so anxious to impress Eleazar favorably that he personally bought and set at liberty all the Jewish slaves captured by his father, Ptolemy I. Eleazar was overwhelmed with these evidences of friendship and greatly impressed by the rich presents the King of Egypt had sent to him. The High Priest, therefore, chose seventy-two men who had the greatest reputation for learning among the Jews, six from each of the twelve tribes, and sent them to Alexandria. It is further recorded that these seventy-two men completed the translation of the Pentateuch in seventy-two days. Each of the scholars was locked in a separate cell so that they could not communicate with each other during the translation. Yet, when the work was finished, the versions were identical. The translation was then read in the presence of Ptolemy and numerous learned Egyptians.

This edition of the books of Moses is known as the *Septuagint* or the *Version of the Seventy*. By the 1st century A.D., this Version included the complete Old Testament. Two points in connection with this translation are of special significance. The Septuagint was originally prepared in Greek, which had become the common language of the Eastern Mediterranean area. Even more interesting is the fact that the Septuagint was the version of the Old Testament in general use at the time of Jesus and his apostles, and references to the Old Testament in the Gospels and Epistles are from this version.

Those parts of the Old Testament which occur in the Sinaitic, Vatican, and Alexandrian manuscripts, are according to the Septuagint version. It is assumed on reasonable ground that the translators and editors of the Septuagint made use of earlier Hebrew manuscripts which are not known to have survived. Unless further research in the field of Biblical archeology brings new material to light, it must be assumed, therefore, that the Septuagint is the source-work for existing versions and interpretations of the Old Testament.

The *Codex Vaticanus* and the *Codex Sinaiticus* were written in the first half of the 4th century A. D., and there has been speculation upon the possibility that the same scribes worked on at least parts of both manuscripts. The *Vaticanus* lacks the first forty-six chapters of Genesis, thirty-two of the Psalms, all of Hebrews after the ninth chapter, First and Second Timothy, Titus, Philemon, and the Book of Revelation. This manuscript has been in the Vatican Library since the 15th century, except for a brief period when it was brought to Paris by Napoleon I.

The *Codex Sinaiticus* was discovered in 1844 by Dr. Lobgott Friedrich Konstantin von Tischendorf. He found this important manuscript in the Convent of St. Catherine, at the foot of Mt. Sinai. Unfortunately, Dr. von Tischendorf arrived at the convent too late to prevent part of the manuscript from being burned as worthless parchment. He was able, however, to persuade the authorities of the convent to give him about forty-three sheets of the ancient vellum. His ill-concealed excitement and interest aroused the suspicions of the monks, who suddenly realized that the ancient writings must be valuable and decided to retain the rest of the manuscript. Dr. von Tischendorf returned to Europe and in 1846 published the fragments he had found, under the title, "The Codex Friederico Augustanus," in honor of the King of Saxony. This publication caused a considerable stir among the scholastic elect, and Dr. von Tischendorf was appointed Professor Extraordinarius. He carefully concealed the source of his forty-three priceless manuscript leaves and, realizing that the convent was in the Russian sphere of influence, he sought and secured the assistance of Czar Alexander II.

In October 1859, Dr. von Tischendorf, after many adventures and delays, was able to secure the Sinaitic Bible as a loan, and on the 19th of November, he brought it with him to Russia and placed it in the hands of Czar Alexander II. This monarch was so amazed and delighted that he caused immediate steps to be taken which resulted in the publication of an exact facsimile of the entire work for the use of the scholars of the world. The production was under the personal supervision of Dr. von Tischendorf. He was the first to suggest that one of the four scribes who wrote the text also wrote part of the Vatican manuscript. The Codex is of folio size, in Greek, four columns to the page. There are numerous corrections, dating from the 6th and 7th centuries. After the Russian revolution, the *Codex Sinaiticus* was acquired by the British Museum from the Russian government, part of the necessary funds being raised by popular subscription. As to the *Codex Alexandrinus,* it is also very defective. Its origin is unknown, but it is believed to date from the 5th or 6th century A. D.

The most famous Latin version of the Bible is known as the Vulgate, which intimates from its name that it was translated into the vulgar tongue, as distinguished from the Greek. The enormous task was undertaken by St. Jerome, at the request of Pope Damascus. Jerome was a scholar of outstanding ability, and had studied at Constantinople under Gregory Nazianzen. He began his work as translator about A. D. 384, and completed the project about A. D. 404. Apparently the original intention was merely to revise old Latin versions, but it gradually became apparent that a complete revision was necessary. Jerome was severely criticized for the changes which he made, but with the passing of time, the Vulgate increased in popularity. It underwent several

education were broadened. The laity, especially the sons of noble families, were encouraged to improve their minds in letters and the humanities. The demand for books increased, and this undoubtedly hastened the era of printing. Illiteracy was no longer considered synonymous with gentility, and royal fashions decreed the advancement of learning.

The invention of printing is closely associated with sacred books. Gutenberg and Fust are accredited with the first printing of the Holy Bible from movable type. Prior to this important advancement, however, forms of block-printing were known in various parts of the world. There is a supposed reference to printing in China as early as the 6th century, but this is regarded with suspicion. The earliest accepted examples of well-defined block-printing come from Japan, and are dated about A. D. 770. The oldest discovered complete printed book—in this case a roll—comes from China, and is dated A. D. 868. There is a tradition that a Chinese dignitary of the 9th century, who was later executed for political conspiracy, caused wood-carvers to cut inscriptions and writings on flat slabs of wood. These slabs were then rubbed with ink made of charcoal and oil, and impressions were taken therefrom on thin sheets of paper. This was a distinct improvement over the earlier fashion of making rubbings from inscriptions on stone. Block-printing spread rapidly in Asia, and the oldest known example of a book prepared by this method is the *Diamond Sutra* of Buddha, discovered by Sir Auriel Stein in the Caves of the Thousand Buddhas at Tun-Huang. This is officially known as the *Diamond Sutra of 868*.

In the 11th century, a Chinese commoner by the name of Pi Sheng, who may have been a smith by trade, conceived the idea of fashioning separate letters that could be used in any combination, thus creating a new and flexible means of perpetuating knowledge through the printed word. Pi made molds and cast in them clay characters, which he then baked to proper hardness. For the purposes of printing, he set them in a bed of resin and wax on a flat metal plate. When the letters had been properly fixed, the metal plate was heated, and as it cooled, the clay characters were firmly imbedded in the resin and wax. The surfaces were then carefully smoothed off. Any number of impressions could be taken from the clay type by the method commonly employed in woodblock printing. The plate could be re-heated, and the type removed and used again as need arose. This invention was conceived and executed about A. D. 1045, preceding Gutenberg by four hundred years. The heroic problem involved in Chinese printing can be better appreciated when it is realized that a font of type in that language required more than 10,000 different characters.

Paper had already reached Europe along the trade routes from the Near East. Prior to this, the Egyptian papyrus monopoly had resulted in the substitution of vellum, and the expense involved in the proper preparation of skins made paper a welcome commodity. Although the situation is not entirely clear, we know that woodblock printing also existed in Europe prior to the time of Gutenberg. It seems probable that printing reached Europe from Asia, at least as a tradition of method, and was not actually invented in Germany as is generally supposed.

To Gutenberg should go the credit for the construction of the first printing press, which greatly facilitated the otherwise slow and tedious process developed by the Chinese. As the first known printed book of Asia was a sacred Buddhist scripture, it was exceedingly reasonable that the first printed book of Western civilization should be the Holy Bible. This was issued between 1445 and 1450, and is one of the rarest printed works in existence. The original project was not entirely honorable, as the printers attempted to distribute this Bible as a handwritten work, at the fantastic prices that then prevailed for manuscripts. They were forced to reveal their secret methods, however, to escape the extreme displeasure of the Church, which developed the quaint notion that the Devil was behind the miraculous multiplication of sacred writ. The modern term "printer's devil" originated in the idea that the Prince of Evil operated the old handpress in his spare time.

The story of the Bible after the invention of printing is largely an account of early printers, their difficulties and tribulations and the extraordinary work which they accomplished with hopelessly inadequate equipment. Bibles of the 15th century are among the great incunnabula, or cradle books. This term is applied to editions made during the first 50 years of printing in Europe. Today these wonderful works are still accepted as the finest examples of the printing art. It has been affirmed by authorities in the field that printing is the only art which has never evolved. The first examples are still the finest.

In the beginning, printed Bibles were merely reproductions of older manuscripts, and closely resembled them, ornate initial letters being added by hand. As printing expanded into many fields, however, the level of scholarly thoughtfulness rose, and the human mind began to inquire into subjects previously ignored or forbidden. During the 16th century, there were handsome editions of the Scriptures in Greek, Latin, Hebrew, German, and English. By this time also, polyglots began to appear, in which several earlier versions were presented together as parallel texts. Even before the Reformation, these translations, in some instances, brought disaster to those involved in their production. In passing, mention may be made of the work of such men as Tyndale, Coverdale, and a man known as Thomas Matthew, whose real name may have been John Rogers. Later editions include the Cranmer Bible, the Bishop's Bible, and finally the Authorized Version, so named because it was undertaken by command of James I, King of England.

Although we hear much about various Bibles and their impact upon the periods in which they were issued, there is some misunderstanding about these works in the popular mind. A careful study would indicate that the differences between 16th- and 17th-century Bibles, such as the Erasmus and the Luther, are due either to their origin in previous variants, or to peculiarities of translation from one language to another. In many cases, they differ only in an occasional word and, except when typographical errors appear, there is slight change in meaning. It has been pointed out that more than 150,000 reading differences occur, but probably not more than 1% of these is worthy of consideration. The persecution which often accompanied new versions of the Scriptures were based not upon the texts involved, but rather upon the religious conviction held by the schismatic sects which sponsored the publication. In the case of Luther, the situation was somewhat more exaggerated, as he failed to include the Book of Revelation because he doubted its divine inspiration.

The Great King James Bible appeared in 1611. There are two issues or printings, which are referred to as the "He Bible" and the "She Bible," due to a typographical error. The editors and revisors of this work were already heavily burdened by the problem of popular veneration previously mentioned. King James was not a distinguished scholar in his own right, but was moved by a division within the Church of England. Two versions of the Bible were then in common use, the clergy favoring the Bishop's Bible, and the people, including the Puritans, preferring the Geneva Bible. The Puritans brought their case to the King, who called a conference at Hampton Court Palace, which convened on January 14th, 1604. This resulted in the selection of fifty-four outstanding scholars, of whom forty-seven actually carried on the project. In the instructions given by the King, and preserved by Fuller in his *Church History,* the first admonition is especially significant: "The ordinary Bible read in the church, commonly called the Bishop's Bible to be followed, and as little altered as the original will permit."

Examination proves that the editors followed the King's pleasure with the greatest care. As a result, the text of the Authorized Version has been polished but not materially altered from the older work. It is somewhat of an exaggeration, therefore, to assume that the King James Bible is an authoritative work of basic scholarship. There is a tradition that when the manuscript of the Authorized Version was completed, it was placed in the hands of Lord Bacon for editorial revision. His Lordship's extraordinary gifts in the use of the English language may therefore have contributed to the outstanding literary excellence of the book.

Recent printings of the Authorized Version differ to some degree from the original of 1611. The principal change has been the omission of the Apocrypha, and there have been a few changes in spelling and punctuation. The extremely interesting prologue, "The Translators to the Reader," no longer appears because of controversial elements involving the Church of England and the Roman Catholic Church. The principal typographical errors of the first printing were a repetition of three lines in Exodus 14:10 and the little difficulty which arose in Ruth 3:15. In the first issue, the last clause of this verse reads: "and he went into the city." In the second issue of the same year, this was corrected to read: "and she went into the city."

Incidentally, there have been many curious translations or errors that have crept into Bibles at various times, and

these have, in many instances, been used to distinguish printings or versions. The Geneva Bible is often called the
"breeches" Bible because of the translation of Genesis 3:7:
"and they sewed figge tree leaves together, and made themselves breeches." The "bug" Bibles gained their distinction
from a remarkable rendition of Psalms 91:5: "Thou shalt
not nede to be afrayed for eny bugges by night." The
meaning should have been "terrors" or "bugaboos," and not
insects. Gamblers will be interested in a curious mistake in
Matthew 5:9, where it reads, "Blessed are the placemakers"
instead of "peacemakers." The "balm in Gilead" got into
difficulties in the Douay Catholic Bible of 1609, where Jeremiah 8:22 reads, "Is there no rosin in Gilead;". Some other
versions have preferred "triacle," now spelled "treacle" and
more or less identified with molasses. The "Vinegar"
Bible of 1717 announces in the headline to Luke 20, "The
Parable of the Vinegar" instead of "Vineyard." We also
have appreciation for the improvement of Psalms 119:161,
where it says, "Printers have persecuted me" instead of
"princes." A high spot among these dilemmas is the
"wicked" Bible of 1631. In this version, Exodus 20:14 is
strongly revised to read, "Thou shalt commit adultery."
Such misprints are too numerous to describe them all, but
the printer of the "wicked" Bible was fined the sum of
300 pounds for his contribution to delinquency.

We are often asked by thoughtful students what version
of the Bible we advise for those who wish to have the most
correct translation. Perhaps the preceding outline answers
this question at least in part. Very little is to be gained by
attempting to choose between the available editions. They
are all revisions of each other, and for the most part, are
traceable to the great Codices. I have examined many of
these newer revisions, and the textual differences are not sufficient to clarify obscure meanings. It is doubtful that ef-

forts to modernize the King James Version will meet with enthusiastic response or support. The beauty, dignity, and poetic quality of the Authorized Version have became a part of the subconscious religious acceptance in Western man.

The only practical alternative is to read the Scriptures in the older tongues. The student of Greek, Latin, or Hebrew, can detect alternative rendering of words, and select such translations as appear most reasonable. He will realize, of course, that the Scriptural writings are richer and deeper than is generally understood. If, however, he is limited to the English language, or his knowledge of the classical idiom is slight, he may as well assume that the broad framework of morality and ethics in the Testaments is reasonably close to the original. Scholars are working constantly on controversial verses and sections, and their findings are available in their books or in learned journals. In the present volume, we shall attempt to unfold an interpretation of the Scriptures based upon comparative religion, an invaluable aid in the exploration of Holy Writ.

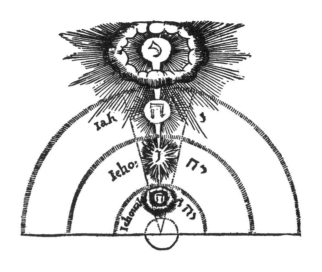

THE FOUR WORLDS OF THE DIVINE NAME

CHAPTER II
KEYS TO OLD TESTAMENT MYSTERIES

To those who are accustomed to accept the Bible as a religio-historical writing of divine or inspired origin, Bible study is restricted to mean reading, remembering, and accepting. It may not occur to these sincere and devout members of their respective faiths to consider the possibility that beneath the surface of the written text there may be secret meanings by which apparent inconsistencies are reconciled, obscurities clarified, and the philosophical content of the Scriptures strengthened, broadened, and deepened. All the great religions of the world have developed, within their own complex structures, schools of mystics and orders of sages unwilling to accept obvious forms of worship; men who have sought through inspiration and diligence to explore the hidden ground of traditional beliefs. They have assumed

26

it to the seventy elders of Israel. During all this time, the Cabala was never entrusted to writing, but was revealed lip to ear, in accordance with the instruction of God.

Historically, the descent of the Cabala is extremely obscure, as one would expect of a tradition so carefully hidden from the profane. It is believed that the first treatise on the Cabala to be prepared in written form was compiled by Rabbi Akiba, circa A. D. 120. This work is called the *Sepher Yetzirah,* or the *Book of the Beginnings,* or the *Book of the Formation.* Tradition ascribes the original of this writing to the Patriarch Abraham, and affirms that Akiba merely wrote down the ancient instructions.

The same flickering, faint, and uncertain light of history attributes the greatest of all the Cabalistic books, the *Sepher ha Zohar* or the *Book of Splendours,* to the celebrated Jewish Illuminist Rabbi Simeon ben Jochai. He was a disciple of Akiba, and was sentenced to death by Lucius Verus, co-regent of the Emperor Marcus Aurelius Antonius, presumably for philosophical and political heresy. To escape this imperial edict, Simeon fled with his son into the wilderness, and took refuge in a cave. They remained in this place of concealment for twelve years, undergoing extraordinary hardships. When their clothes wore out, the two men covered their bodies with earth, and most of their food came to them miraculously. Rabbi Simeon spent much of his time in a state of mystical trance, and, with the aid of his son, wrote down the whole body of the Cabalistic doctrine. He received visions of the prophets, especially Elijah, and his book, the *Sepher ha Zohar* is a remarkable compilation of obscure mystical and esoteric information. It has not been possible to trace the descent of Simeon ben Jochai's manuscripts, or even copies of them, but nearly twelve hundred years later, a book claiming to be a faithful rendition of the original was published under most curious circumstances.

Moses ben Schem Tob de Leon, who flourished in the first half of the 14th century, has long presented a variety of difficulties to modern scholars. He claimed that he had come into possession of an ancient manuscript of the Zohar in the autograph of Rabbi Simeon ben Jochai. After Moses de Leon's death, two distinguished scholars desiring to test the authenticity of the report, and knowing the widow of Moses de Leon to be penniless, decided to offer her a large sum of money as an inducement to secure the ancient writing. Both the widow and the daughter declared that such a manuscript did not exist, and that Moses de Leon had composed the Zohar himself. This seemed to settle a difficult question, and these findings have for the most part remained unchallenged. But the book itself is entirely inconsistent with the all too obvious explanation. If Moses de Leon wrote the work, he possessed a degree of scholarship, both physical and metaphysical, that would have justified his inclusion in that small band composed of the world's immortal thinkers.

The unqualified and factually unsupported statement that Moses de Leon wrote the Zohar and that therefore the work should be regarded as an elaborate forgery, is neither reasonable nor acceptable. The more thoughtful investigators, therefore, have been inclined to believe that the Zohar could not have been composed in its entirety by any one person or at any on time, but should be regarded as a complex compilation from many sources, most of them unknown. This would place Moses de Leon in the position of a transcriber or editor, who set down for the first time a metaphysical system of interpretation previously held secret. There is also a more liberal group of researchers who maintain that there is no reason to doubt that the Zohar could represent and embody the original teachings of Simeon ben Jochai, which may have been preserved by a direct descent of disciples.

There are certainly traces of Cabalism prior to the publication of the Zohar, but very little of the present form of the doctrine seems to have been in circulation earlier than the 10th century of the Christian era. Ancient Jewish scholars did not seem to be aware of the existence of the Zohar, even though their writings dealt with parallel matters. Further confusion could be due to the gradual absorption of commentaries and glosses into the body of the Zohar during those centuries when it was transmitted orally. It is quite possible that the historical uncertainties will never be entirely cleared away, and that the book must continue to stand upon its own internal merits. It has long been studied with favor and genuine interest by both Jewish and Christian scholars, and is certainly a monumental commentary on the deeper aspects of the Pentateuch. The formal school of Cabalists rose and flourished, and for the most part declined, between the 10th and 17th centuries of our era. Late writers upon the subject have been inclined to regard it as an ancient and curious tradition.

The first great Latin edition of the Zohar is included in the *Cabala Denudata,* published at Frankfurt in 1677, by Knorr von Rosenroth. This translation is the basis of most research into the Cabala since the time of its publication. The Zohar is so elaborate and complicated, both in structure and terminology, that only those long familiar with the deeper forms of the esoteric tradition can cope with its abstractions. It is the very obscurity of the basic text that has resulted in the numerous extravagant and fantastic interpretations of the Cabala which now burden the field of mystical literature.

It should be pointed out that the Cabala has been considerably influenced by the wanderings and migrations of the Jewish people. It went through remarkable modifications among the Jewish scholars in Arabia, and took on an entirely different coloring in Germany. The Spanish Cabalists developed a number of innovations, and with the Russians, the magical aspects were highly prized. In each case, the unfoldment of the basic formulas was due to the emergence of venerated masters of schools who gathered disciples about them, claiming to possess new interpretations of older interpretations. In most groups, however, the mystical experience, or the extension of consciousness through visions, constituted authority.

For practical consideration, the Cabala, as a compound structure, may be considered under five general headings or departments:

The Natural Cabala
The Analogical Cabala
The Contemplative Cabala
The Astrological Cabala
The Magical Cabala

Of course, all such divisions are in a sense arbitrary, but they will help to keep the subject matter within certain frameworks or comparatively reasonable boundaries.

The Natural Cabala corresponds closely with the modern concept of the sciences, and aims toward the organization of knowledge in all its departments. It further establishes a dependency of all physical learning upon the great metaphysical principles or laws governing the creation, preservation, and ultimate disintegration, of the universe.

The Analogical Cabala emphasizes the symbolical relationships which exist between all the energies and formal structures in Nature. It indicates the universal diffusion of fundamental designs or archetypes, and advances a system of analogies by which each structure in Nature explains all other structures, or at least provides the key by which explanation is possible. Thus the universe is regarded as the Grand Man, and man, in his turn, is represented as the little universe. Each grain of sand has locked within it the secret of all creation, and the universe itself is like a grain of sand in space.

The Contemplative Cabala is devoted to the rules by which the intellectual faculties of the human being may be extended and expanded so that consciousness may contemplate, by inward experience, the mysteries of the invisible world. The major purpose is the cultivation of the mystical experience, or a degree of cosmic consciousness.

The Astrological Cabala is not primarily a system of divination, but an effort to show that the form and structure of the solar system bear witness to a universal geometry and chemistry. It naturally includes the study of the laws governing the planets, their motion and relations, and even the substances of which they are composed. Thus it is possible to recognize in the outward machinery of the world the essential keys to the anatomy and physiology of God.

The Magical Cabala is that part sometimes referred to as practical. It contains the formulas for the binding and loosing of spirits, the making of talismans and amulets, the working of charms, and the adapting of universal knowledge to the personal advantage of the Cabalist. It is this last branch which resulted in much of the opposition of the Church and of the orthodox Jewish congregations to the subject of Cabalism in general. It came to be regarded as a highly complicated form of sorcery by those unacquainted with its real meaning.

All great systems of metaphysical and philosophical speculations must attempt in some way to define the nature of First Cause. Once the cosmic plan which resulted in the emergence of the universal form from its own source—the universal mystery—is organized into a rational concept, the whole plan of universal generation becomes comprehensible. All the creative processes are repetitions of one basic formula, on various levels and planes, and in the different degrees of matter. Obviously, the definition of absolute method must be conceptual rather than actual, but the concept is demonstrated and justified through reference to a concatenation of repetitions in the sphere of observable phenomena.

Before we proceed further, it should be emphasized that the entire philosophical concept unfolded by the Cabala is based upon the sacred books of the Old Testament. In the Cabalistic texts, these are constantly quoted and referred to, and it is assumed that the commentaries and interpretations are merely the enlargements and unfoldments of certain Scriptural verses and ideas. In studying the Old Testament, we must remember that an adequate comprehension requires proper orientation in terms of Jewish religion. This in turn implies that with the Jewish Scriptures we must note and examine a quantity of ancient legend and tradition through which we gain insight into the hearts and minds of these people. Such depth of insight is a subtle blending of the law of the Prophets and the lore of the people.

According to the Cabala, the eternal root of all existence is an incomprehensible quality represented by the word *Ain,* which means *boundless.* This boundless quality is the absolute equilibrium of all conditions, energies, principles, and laws. Equilibrium manifests as a state of universal suspension or non-action. By this concept, Absolute Being is essentially passive rather than active, but this passivity results from completeness and not from absence or privation due to deficiency of any kind. According to the Cabalists, therefore, such words as *negative* and *passive,* when applied to Absolute Being, must be understood according to philosophic context. We may think of these words as implying some kind of weakness, instability, or insufficiency. In the Jewish cosmogony, however, such terms imply a complete abstractness beyond positive definition or even positive conception. They signify the ultimate Sabbath, the perfect rest, the end of all striving, and the mergence of all states into a statelessness which is above and beyond the intellectual capacity of man to comprehend or even to sense.

The second quality of Transcendent Being is *Ain Soph,* meaning *boundless life.* By this concept, life is subordinated to existence. This part of the pattern requires careful thinking. The Cabalists contemplated existence as a condition without polarity and incapable of experiencing the absence of itself. Life, however, is not completely self-sufficient. It is an emergence, and is therefore susceptible of submergence. Life can be absorbed back into Being, or the boundless, but Being is not susceptible of further submergence, for it is of itself absolute profundity.

Boundless life is a revelation of the potential distributed without boundary throughout the substance of the boundless. Life, by extending outwardly in all directions from its own root and substance, causes the diversity of living things which come forth from it and are sustained by it and which absorb its power into themselves. All life bears witness to the ever-living, and living, in turn, bears witness to the ever-existing, but ultimately the ever-existing bears witness only to itself.

The third state of existence, or quality of Being, is *Ain Soph Aur* or *boundless light.* As life is the witness of Being, so light testifies to the presence of life. Light thus becomes the symbol of the concealed mystery. Light is the life of the outer world, even as life is the light of the inner world, and both restate, by revelation, the reality of the dark existence which is their sovereign cause.

In Hebrew the word *Ain* is composed of three letters, *Ain Soph* of six letters, and *Ain Soph Aur* of nine letters. By the Cabala, these numbers become the numerical equivalent of the powers of Being. As 9 is the last of the numbers before 10 (which is the restatement of unity), the whole mystery of Being is enclosed within this number. The formula is restated by adding the numerals of the three states; that is, 3 plus 6 plus 9, which equals 18. This again, reduced to 1 plus 8, equals the original 9. The number 9 is a 6 inverted, and this is also the number of generation, deriving its shape from the human sperm. We have seen that 6 represents life, and 9 represents light. Light is the inverted reflection of life. If the number of life, 6, be added to the number of light, 9, the result is 15. In turn, 15 is 1 plus 5, equaling 6, which restates life or the principle of spiritual generation. If the 6 and the 9 are combined to form a hieroglyph, their result is the constellation of Cancer, associated in the Cabalistic astrology with the symbol of generation.

Ain, the boundless, and its veils, *Ain Soph* and *Ain Soph Aur,* form the triune divinity, the one that is three, and the three that are one. The three-fold nature of the Eternal Cause is manifested in the three-fold constitution of all created things. Thus mankind has a body crystallized from light, a soul of the substance of life, and a spirit sharing the equilibrium of the eternal profundity. By further analogy, the revelation of the law which is according to the will of the Deepness, is of three parts: the *Torah,* which is the light of the law, the *Mishnah,* which is the life of the law, and the *Cabala,* which is the eternal profundity of the law.

We have already pointed out that *Ain* and its two qualifications are regarded as diffusions rather than as centers of existence. They are not beings as we understand the term, but rather states of being without dimensions or proportions. Creation, therefore, is not a motion from a center, but a motion to a center. As these principles must be explained symbolically if they are to be comprehended at all,

Ain may be represented by a circle, signifying an infinite area. Creation is a motion of forces in that area toward their own hypothetical center, which is diagrammatically the center of the symbolical circle. This motion causes a condensation toward the center, and a corresponding privation near the circumference. This privation, caused by the contraction of Being toward its own central ground, is the abyss, the *Ungrund* of Boehme, the Outer Darkness of the Gnostic mystics. The contracted essences of existence result, symbolically speaking, in the appearance of the dot in the center of the circle. This dot is the primordial creature, the first creation—unmanifested Being becoming manifested as a being. Thus we have the concept of oneness in its two recognizable aspects; one as all or wholeness, and one as first or beginning. To use a Rosicrucian axiom, "Eternity gives birth to time." By another definition, the Eternal Divine manifests as God.

One of the names for *Ain Soph* is *The Aged of the Aged*. Here age signifies not oldness in time, but that unaging time itself which is the forever of duration and which contains within its eternal essence the three-fold mystery of time— past, present, and future. From The Aged of the Aged comes forth by further contraction that which is called *The Aged*. Thus from eternity emerges by degrees the eldest of all things, qualities of oldness nearest to unaging time. As wholeness must precede division, and unity therefore is more aged than any of its parts, so the number 1 is the first-born of all, and the parent of diversity.

The name of the first-born is *Kether,* the *Crown,* and in the Cabala it has several names and symbolic appellations. It is the Crown because it is the highest of all things that are created. It is the Aged, because it is the oldest of all creations. It is the Primordial Point, because it is the ultimate contraction of the area of Being. It is the White Head, for it is the face of the Eternal. It is the Long Face, called *Macroposopus*, because it contains within itself the ten orders of generative existence. It is the Inscrutable Height, because it is suspended directly from that which is causeless. It is the Heavenly Man, because it is the archetype of all generation. It is the Smooth Point, because it is in all parts equal and without distortion of any kind. It is the Open Eye, because it is the first beholding of externals. It is the King of Peace, because it binds all striving in unity. It is the *Ehejeh*, or 'I Am,' because it is the first statement, the first witness, and the first word of power. It is in all creatures as potential, and encloses all creatures as potency.

Kether is the One, bearing witness to allness, and serving as a channel or medium for the dissemination of allness through manyness. The ultimate mystery of spirit is allness; the ultimate mystery of matter is manyness; and this manyness in turn is the eternal proof of the allness. The stick and the stone, the star and the man, are aspects of the manyness, but they bear witness to the all-potency. Each creature manifests one of the aspects of power, and all these aspects stand as proof of the completeness of the total parental principle.

In the Cabala, the Pythagorean law that division takes place within unity but unity is never divided, is everywhere upheld. The process of creation does not extend downward from Kether, but takes place within the Crown through the unfoldment of the internal patterns of diversity. Creation is therefore a tree, with its roots in the principle of *Kether*, or unity, and its branches extending downward within the Crown according to the descent of number from 1 to 10. This tree of the numbers, or of emanations, is called the *Tree of the Sephiroth*, and the early Cabalists declared the word *Sephira* (plural *Sephiroth*) to mean "to number" or "to bestow order according to number."

The ten *Sephiroth* were begotten of the Infinite, and are in themselves both infinite and finite. They are reflections of divine energy, and in turn are themselves reflected into the various levels and planes of creation. They are said, therefore, to be creators in that they image forth all form according to the archetypal likenesses which reside within them. From the spiritual *Sephiroth*, all spirits originate; from the intellectual *Sephiroth*, all intellects; from the formal *Sephiroth*, all forms; and from the physical *Sephiroth*, all bodies. Forms and bodies are not the same. A form is a pattern or an organization. Forms may exist in the mind as thought-forms. They are like the drawings on paper from which a house is built. The architectural plans are formal, but the house itself is material.

From this point on, the Cabalistic philosophy increases in complexity to become an elaborate psychological-mathematical symbolism which cannot be explained adequately in a brief space. We must therefore content ourselves with certain general conclusions and interpretations bearing especially upon the Bible. The interested student can advance in knowledge by recourse to one of the basic texts on Cabalism.

We have noted that the universe is conceived to be a vast tree, with its roots in eternity and its branches in time. This tree bears its blossoms and its fruit not only in the physical world, but also in the spiritual world. So vast are the proportions of this tree of life, that every electron and atom in space is like a tiny blossom upon one of its countless branches. In the winter of time, the leaves fall, and the tree seems to be dead. But with the return of the universal spring, its life is restored. Each of the countless suns in the heavens is one of the fruits of the tree, and each wild flower that dots the broad green meadows of the earth is a little sun shining with the divine power.

The three great branches of the tree are wisdom, strength, and beauty, and these sustain all the diversity of Nature. There is one life, fulfilling itself through its creation, as there is one energy in a tree, manifesting through all its leaves and buds. Each of the fruits of the tree can fall back into the dark earth and, in due time and in proper turn, become a tree. Thus creation is an endless process made possible by the fatherhood of light and the motherhood of moisture. As flowers of a hundred brilliant hues grow from one dark earth, each selecting appropriate nutrition according to the laws of its kind, so an infinite diversity of worlds, elements, creatures, and powers, are nourished from the immeasurable depths of Absolute Being. Who understands the mystery of the lilies of the field and how they grow, holds the key to the riddle of life. All is growing, flowering, and bearing fruit, fulfilling the admonition of the Lord, "Be fruitful, and multiply, and replenish the earth."

As the tree of life grows from the Crown of eternal mystery, so there is another tree which has its roots in the shadow, for the darkness of matter is only the reflection of the darkness of eternity. This second tree that grows from outer space, with its roots in privation, is nourished by "the great pain," by the longing in all things to be restored to their glory. This restoration is attained through the mystery of fruitfulness, for only that which gives life can know the giver of life. This tree which reaches up toward the sovereignty of the eternal sun is the tree of knowledge. It is the tree of the knowledge of good and evil, and those who eat of its fruit increase in wisdom, but must bear the pain which wisdom brings.

The *Cultus Arborum,* a term classically applied to the worship of trees as the symbols of the universal mystery, has flourished among all peoples. It has also been customary in the classification of various kinds of human knowledge to systematize the growth and order of man's achievements in the forms of trees. We speak of genealogical trees, trees of races and of laws, trees of religions and philosophy. This tree-form concept springs from the same conviction that led to the Cabalistic speculations. All types of life and all orders of thinking grow like trees from secret roots, and send forth their branches to shelter and comfort living things.

One of the primary considerations of the Cabalists was the interpretation of the early verses of Genesis. The old Jewish cosmogony was little more than an outline until the rise of Cabalistic mysticism. There was very little emphasis upon the mystery of the universal emergence, and the fragments that did exist were derived largely from the metaphysical speculation of the Chaldeans, Babylonians, and Egyptians. Genesis opens with the statement that in the beginning the order of creators, translated *God* in the Authorized Version of the Bible, divided existence into an above and a below; that is, into a superior and an inferior part. The above was the spiritual world of causes, and the below was the material world of effects. Then the creators moved upon the face of the inferior world and brought forth the order of generated things. That which was above the firmament was the vast ocean of Being; that which was below the firmament was the great sea of beings, and the creative powers moved in the middle distance, spinning the threads which, like the web of the spider, bind the opposites and unite the extremes. The creation was thus suspended between the superior and the inferior darkness and was the abode of creatures possessing spirits derived from above and bodies fashioned into habitations from the substances of the lower region.

All schools of philosophy derive some portion of their material from earlier traditional sources. In Cabalism we find evidences of the Pythagorean and Platonic systems, a generous borrowing from the Gnosticism of Syria and North Africa, and considerable material traceable to the Neoplatonic mysticism of Alexandria, Rome, and Athens. In some parts of the work, we are inclined to suspect that the Cabalists were actually using Pythagorean theories to interpret their own religion. It is even possible that Cabalism was affected to some degree by the philosophies and religions of Middle Asia.

Every religion has developed metaphysical overtones and magical undertones. The long history of Judaism records numerous mystical sects springing up among idealistic minorities not content to live by the letter of the law. There has always been a conflict between principle and practice. Manmade laws and concepts cannot be equally just to all men, and the human soul yearns after a higher justice. Also, all social orders include groups of scholarly men and women who desire to rationalize and integrate their beliefs in terms of logic and reason. These numerous groups may have little in common but their basic religious texts. Each school of interpretation differs from the others, resulting in endless conflict of cults. Yet even this conflict has a common denominator—dissatisfaction with the literal forms of accepted worship. But dissatisfaction is not a synonym for Cabalism, although the Cabalists certainly were among the dissatisfied. In fact, the dissatisfaction extended further, and even the Cabalistic schools were divided over points of belief.

We have mentioned undertones, for we must recognize that nearly all systems of human idealism have been subjected to intentional or unintentional corruption. When noble ideals suitable only to the most dedicated persons fall into the keeping of untutored masses, misinterpretation and actual perversion is inevitable. Nearly always, esoteric doctrines are corrupted in the direction of sorcery. The individual, gaining possession of a deeper or fuller understanding of the laws operating in and through Nature, may begin to consider how he can adapt his new knowledge to his own profit at the expense of the unenlightened majority. Knowledge is power; power is opportunity; and it requires a high degree of personal integrity to administer opportunity unselfishly.

Nearly all religions, therefore, consist of three parts or levels. There is a literal doctrine administered by the clergy; a metaphysical or mystical overtone in the keeping of scholars, seers, and transcendentalists; and a materialistic undertone which is exploited by semi-theologized opportunists seeking only the aggrandizement of themselves.

Like most systems of religious philosophy, the Cabala had to explain the primary circumstance of creation. As God was an eternal being without limitation and without fault, this sovereign power could not be the direct creator of a limited and imperfect world, nor could he populate this world with creatures deficient in wisdom, strength, or beauty, and capable of spiritual, mental, and physical corruption. Furthermore, Deity could not become the victim of Satan, for this Prince of Darkness was himself a fragment of the Divine Nature, and God cannot be evil in any of his parts. Hence, the Cabalists fell back on the Gnostic doctrine of emanation. Deity reflected from its own nature the ten radiant qualities called the *Sephiroth,* and this pattern of emanations, considered as an archetype, gave rise to the creation of the material universe. There are traces of Platonism here also. Inferiority is a matter of remoteness. Evil is not a principle in itself, but the privation of a principle. If the Divine Glory be conceived to be like a flame emitting light and heat, these qualities decrease in their intensity as they radiate toward a hypothetical circumference. By holding a book close to a candle, one may read words; but if the book is twenty feet from the candle, the light is not sufficient. Thus, as we depart from proximity to the source of light, we are enveloped by an increasing darkness which is the absence of that light. The Cabala is therefore a science dealing with the qualitative intervals which condition a series of emanations flowing sequentially from a center of light toward a circumference of darkness. Each center of emanations is less luminous than that from which it previously emanated, and reflects from itself other emanations still less luminous until ultimately all light ceases.

To make their concept still more rational, the Cabalists taught that each order of emanations was not an actual descent of principles, but rather a reflection of principles in lower planes of matter. As reflecting surfaces in each case absorb a certain part of the light, these reflections, or shadows, are less and less brilliant. There is nothing essentially original in this doctrine or in most of the other basic concepts of the School; rather it was the pattern formed by combining a number of concepts in a new arrangement that resulted in the Cabalistic philosophy.

These Jewish mystics also made free use of the Hermetic concept of analogy. All medieval learning emphasized analogy as a key to the universal procedure. The Hermetic axiom, "That which is above is like unto that which is below, and that which is below is like unto that which is above," served Cabalistic speculation in an admirable way. The universe was a descent of similars identical in qualitative pattern, but differing in quantitative magnitude and multitude. Here is another fragment of Pythagoreanism. Apparently the Cabalists chose wisely, for we know that today the smallest hypothecated units of matter bear resemblances to a minute solar system. Creation is one seal or signature, as Boehme called it, pressed upon the face of matter. The mysterious ten-branched tree of the *Sephiroth* reappears diagrammatically in all the departments of form and in the constitutions of all living creatures.

In the Cabala, it is further taught that souls are pre-existent, dwelling first in a spiritual abode, self-conscious and knowing good and evil. This was the state of paradise from which entities fell, first into forms, and then into bodies. The Cabalistic concept follows rather closely the Greek myth of Narcissus. This beautiful youth, seeing his own reflection in a pool, became so enamored of it that he cast himself into the water to embrace the reflection, and so perished. Souls, perceiving their own shadows or emana-tions in the world of form, and failing to realize that the original of the image is within themselves, hasten joyously toward union with the reflection. Having once become en-meshed in the illusion of form, the souls cannot extricate themselves, and are therefore drawn downward toward bodies, thus symbolically dying, or losing their own sense of identity. This is good Platonic and Neoplatonic teaching.

Because each soul originally contained within itself the model of perfection which it derived from the spiritual *Sephiroth,* its ultimate state must be that of re-identification through the conscious recognition of its own divinity. This was possible partly through experience, partly by the study of sacred sciences, and partly through virtuous works and obedience to the laws of Nature. If it were unable to ex-tricate itself in any one life, it would be born again; that is, reincarnated and given further opportunity. If, after many rebirths, it were still incapable of self-release, it might be attached for a time to a stronger soul for guidance, in-struction, and help. Christian Cabalists found in this belief an idea which helped them to explain their concept of a Messiah. The Messiah was the strong soul that saved the weak souls and brought them back with itself to the heaven-ly condition.

When all souls have been perfected and released from the illusion of matter, the paradisiacal state of the world will be restored. Satan will again become the Prince of Light, and acknowledge the glory of God. Hell and the infernal world will cease, and perfected souls will be united to the Divine Nature, will be ruled by God, and will rule with God. Some Cabalists went so far as to affirm that in this time these perfected souls can command even Deity, and Deity will obey. Here, then, we have a trace of the doctrine of Adepts, those initiated masters and teachers who have gained benevolent supremacy over life and Nature.

It was inevitable that such an elaborate and orderly concept of the origin and unfoldment of life should intrigue medieval scholars of many different faiths and beliefs. It was a period of scholastic thinking. Humanism had made few inroads into the structure of knowledge, and learning was still a matter of formulas. All mysteries were explained on paper. There was a further interest in that Cabalism claimed to interpret the Pentateuch, and the Old Testament was as sacred to the gentiles as to the Jews. Speculations based upon the Bible and upon traditional theological opinions were protected by a broad implication of orthodoxy.

The great Jesuit scholar Athanasius Kircher devoted a considerable part of his *Oedipus Aegyptiacus* (Rome, 1652) to a survey and examination of Cabalistical doctrines. The Christian mystical theosophist Henrici Khunrath transformed Cabalism into a mystic Illuminism, and illustrated his principal book with a number of figures strongly Cabalistic. Robert Fludd, often referred to as a Rosicrucian mystic, included a variety of Cabalistic speculations and diagrams in his *Collectio Operum* and his *Phylosophia Mosaica*. The field broadened to include such mystic visionaries as Jacob Boehme and such scientific pioneers as Paracelsus von Hohenheim.

The literature of the subject became extensive, and the heavy burden of perpetuating the Cabala was shouldered largely by Christian writers. Scholars were seeking some semblance of order in Nature. They were weary with the eternal fragmentation of knowledge due to the lack of scientific method. To them, the Cabala was a vital contribution to the concept of an integrated world. Here was a chance to apply mathematics, physics, astronomy, biology, and chemistry to problems large enough to challenge mature minds and at the same time justify the preservation of an over-all theological perspective.

Cabalism was to the 15th century what Einstein's theory of relativity has been to the 20th century—a magnificent formula susceptible of an infinite variety of applications. Naturally, these old Scholastics were able to discover the Cabala in every subject which they contemplated. They were reasoning from a conclusion, and not toward one, and they had been magnificently trained in this procedure by the whole program of scholasticism. We do not mean to imply, however, that the Cabalists were merely escapists, or that they had any basic intention of influencing the public mind along unorthodox lines. Many of them were truly noble dreamers, seeking to build a foundation upon which could be built a better world in which to live. But escapism did creep in, especially in those later centuries when the world was awaking to the challenge of natural phenomena.

Among Christian scholars who took a deep interest in Cabalistic speculation should be mentioned Raymund Lully, alchemist and Hermetic philosopher of the early 14th century; Johann Reuchlin (born 1445), distinguished scholar and orientalist and father of the German Reformation; Pico della Mirandola (born 1463), philosopher and classical scholar; Heinrich Cornelius Agrippa (born 1486), physician, divine, and transcendentalist; and Dr. Henry More (born

1614), English scholar and Platonist. All these men were distinguished for judgment, integrity, and scholarship. Through their efforts, the Cabala gained wide dissemination and drew the attention of leading thinkers.

The works of Reuchlin are worthy of special mention. He learned Hebrew from Rabbi Jacob ben Jechiel Loanz, a most learned man, and court physician to Frederick III. Having mastered the language, he immediately inmmersed himself in the metaphysics of the Jewish mystics, and in 1494 published his rare treatise *De Verbo Mirifico*. Then in 1516, after more than twenty years of additional research, he published a larger and more exhaustive treatise *De Arte Cabalistica*. Both of these works are in the form of dialogues between scholars of various sects. Reuchlin revealed a careful study of Plato, Pythagoras, and Zoroaster, and considerable acquaintance with the then little-understood teachings of the prophet Mohammed.

We have already mentioned the monumental work of the Christian scholar Baron Knorr von Rosenroth. To him, the intellectuals of the 17th and 18th centuries were indebted for the first comprehensive integrated text of the Cabala. Although the authors previously mentioned have written extensive treatises, none of them had translated or republished any portions of the Zohar or the important commentaries thereon. Baron von Rosenroth went so far as to include all the verses of the New Testament which appeared to contain Cabalistic implications. His work is significant not only for the text, but for the extraordinary plates and diagrams which unfold the doctrinal aspect of the subject more completely than any other work, previous or subsequent.

It also appears that the Contemplative Cabala requires additional consideration. The popular tendency is to intellectualize subjects of this kind, and to lose sight of the mystical implications. The Cabala, like alchemy, includes a

scientific method for extending consciousness internally toward the apperception of the divine order of the world.
It should be approached much as one should consider the
East Indian schools of Yoga. Its elaborate symbols are like
the Oriental mandalas, or meditation designs. The true Cabalist sought to accomplish a spiritual unity within his own
nature. Studies of this kind must lead toward some degree
of inward illumination. All religious and philosophical systems include mystical disciplines devised to bring about what
may be termed "the mystical experience of truth;" that is, a
direct personal participation in the divine consciousness.
Naturally, such doctrines languish during periods of intense
materialism, but they always have been and still are the natural end sought by idealistic scholars who recognize the impossibility of understanding metaphysical mysteries by intellectual energy alone.

The Cabala, then, can be summarized as a philosophic
mysticism, grounded in the Jewish religion, and serving as a
scientific approach to a spiritual way of life. Its end was
the reunion of the divinity in man with the divinity in space,
and its means were ceremonial arts and exercises, doctrines
and disciplines, intended to purify the body, refine the emo-
tion, and elevate the mind. The Cabala was one of those
many bridges built by religion and philosophy to span the
interval between the world of physical effects and the world
of spiritual causes. Nearly all schools that have attempted a
mystical or symbolical interpretation of the Scriptures, have
followed in some degree the methods and formulas inspired
by the study of Cabalism.

CHAPTER III

MOSES, LAWGIVER OF ISRAEL

The heroic figure of Moses, who delivered the children of Israel out of bondage in the land of Egypt, stands in the flickering light of uncertain history as the founder of the Israelite religion. Like most Biblical personages, the Great Lawgiver has been so completely traditionalized that his name and memory have survived principally in the accounts to be found in the Pentateuch. To the Jews, Moses is the most venerated of all religious teachers, and among Christians he is second only to Jesus as a messenger of the Divine Will.

Moses is generally regarded as the author of the Pentateuch, or the first five books of the Old Testament.* It

---

*The so-called Sixth and Seventh Books of Moses, dealing with ceremonial magic, are late forgeries.

should be mentioned, however, that absolute proof of authorship is lacking. The controversy which has naturally arisen cannot be solved from the original text. Even though much of the writing is in the third person, this is inconclusive, and it is quite possible that Moses could have written extensive parts of the Pentateuch. On this issue, there are three schools of thought, all sustained by sincere scholarship. According to the first school, the weight of evidence is in favor of Moses. The second group is convinced that he was not the author, and that the work is essentially a compilation. And the third group, occupying a conciliatory position, points out that according to the custom and propriety of the time, Moses undoubtedly would have dictated the works to professional scribes. Various secretaries might well explain certain editorial differences of policy and method of presenting material. It is also generally acknowledged that even if the authorship of the Pentateuch is conceded to Moses, there are certain sections and important elements of doctrine that were derived from older sources.

It would seem impossible to date the life of Moses, and the subject is avoided by most chronologists. He flourished about the middle of the second millenium B. C., lived to an advanced age, and died on the last day of his one hundred and twentieth year. He is not included among those patriarchs credited with phenomenal longevity. In the rabbinical lore, it is said that the soul of Seth passed into the body of Moses, and he became the liberator of Israel.

There is considerable controversy as to the race of the Prophet. According to some, he was a Levite, and according to others, an Egyptian. There have been further speculations but these have not been well sustained. The Biblical account supports the belief that Moses was an Israelite, but certain difficulties arise in reconciling this hypothesis with the known manners and customs of the Egyptians. Manetho, the Egyptian historian who was quoted by Josephus, said that Moses was a priest of Heliopolis, and that he took the name Mosheh, or Moses, possibly at the time of his sanctification. Josephus himself seems to imply that Moses was an Egyptian, born and brought up in that country, and employed in the service of Egypt in a war against the Ethiopians.

Sigmund Freud, in his *Moses and Monotheism,* presents a strong circumstantial argument to support the idea that Moses was an Egyptian prince or patrician who flourished during or slightly after the reign of Amenhotep the IV This wonderful man who is better known as Akhenaten, created a system of religious worship called *Atenism,* which emphasized the concept of one universal God. Although the cult of Akhenaten did not survive in the country of its inception, Freud believes that it inspired the extreme monotheism of the early Jewish faith, and may be the most reasonable explanation for the life and ministry of Moses. Freud also suggests that surviving records could well indicate that Moses was assassinated by those who rebelled against the austerity and severity of his teachings.

From all accounts, Moses was learned in the wisdom of the priests of Egypt, and such a report would imply that he had been initiated into their Mysteries. According to the precepts of the Egyptian religion, strangers—that is, those of other races—were eligible for advancement in the secret sciences of the temple only under certain extraordinary conditions. If Moses was a Levite, the simplest way of reconciling the conflicting accounts would be to assume that as a protege of the ruling house, he had become an Egyptian by adoption, or had in some way received full citizenship. Of course, honorary citizenship was conferred under exceptional circumstances by most ancient nations, but the Biblical account of the strained relations between the Israelites and the people of Egypt make such adoption the more remarkable.

At the time of Moses, the Egyptian religion was passing through a period of decline and corruption. This is altogether possible, for the history of all religions is burdened with the evidence of such deterioration. The increasing temporal power of the priesthood has always caused it to seek political advantage and to impose ecclesiastical authority upon the civil regulations of the state. Egypt was a theocracy, and the pharaoh was regarded as a divinity and as the head of the State religion. As long as selfishness and pride remain in the human composition, those in favorable positions will exploit others less favorably situated. This does not mean, however, a completely corrupt policy or the immediate appearance of a general tyranny.

In the terms of his time, the average citizen of the Double Empire of the Nile, enjoyed the advantages suitable to an advanced and enlightened nation. He was plagued by war and taxes, but by these discomforts he became one with the ages. Egypt was really a loosely integrated group of provinces or nomes, each of which enjoyed considerable autonomy. The citizens lived under a policy of what we might call "states rights," and their participation in the central government was to a degree voluntary. Each of the nomes had its own priesthood serving a hierarchy of deities who were the heavenly patrons and protectors of the province. This is why, factually speaking, it is uncritical to refer to the Egyptian religion. There were many religions, some of them native, others imported, and still others compounded of indigenous and foreign beliefs. It was not until the rise of the Osirian cult that an appearance of homogeneity was strongly evident among the faiths of Egypt.

It is remarkable, then, that a concept capable of assimilating many of the gods of strangers should have been so com-

pletely deficient in racial and religious tolerance toward the
Israelites. Egypt anticipated much of the liberality that was
later conspicuous among the Romans. Perhaps it would be
well to consider the Egyptian Sanctuary system as composed
of a complex of priestly colleges, each more or less independ-
ent and dedicated primarily to the dissemination of essential
learning. The arts and sciences were taught as essentials of
religious doctrine, and the patron deities themselves were the
guardians of knowledge as well as the protectors of their
people. Many of the sanctuaries were violated in times of
war when various provinces were invaded and occupied.
Under such conditions, survival was accomplished only by
certain compromises, but these were of the appearances rather than of the facts. The same arts and sciences were disseminated even though new theological forms were required
by the conquerors. It is not without reason that all ancient
nations regarded Egypt with a peculiar veneration, and held
its scientific institutions to be the highest in the Mediterranean area.

Most of the classical systems of the old world were influenced by the learning of Egypt. Lawmakers, scientists,
philosophers, poets, artisans, and geographers, visited the
Delta of the Nile, studied in the great libraries, observed the
policies regulating the State, examined the legal codes, and
were taught by the Egyptian artisans. These travelers returned to their own lands and were recognized as distinguished leaders of necessary reforms, and none, so far as
we know, seriously objected to the treatment he had received,
or found the Egyptians deficient in the generosity of their
assistance. If anything, the people of Egypt became over-
proud in their contributions to other nations, and took a
patronizing attitude toward the institutions of their neighbors.

From these considerations, it is quite possible that the
Egyptians were involved more symbolically than literally in

the trials and tribulations of the Israelites. To these shepherds, the land of Khem was a symbol of materialism, pride, and luxury. The same general method of interpretation was later applied to the relationship between the Jewish people and the Roman Empire. In the New Testament, the historical Rome becomes the embodiment of a concept of corrupt policy. The Empire of Rome is made to stand in opposition to the Kingdom of Christ. Early Biblical scholars sought out every corruption of the Roman state to justify this symbolism, and for the most part overlooked or rejected all the virtues of the Roman system.

Thus, the Egypt of the Exodus was not actually a country, but a condition of consciousness; not a place, but a way of life. This in itself helps us to understand why there is so much historical uncertainty over Scriptural events. The sacred narratives are loosely associated with certain areas and occurrences as a means of veiling esoteric import. "We must bear in mind," writes H. P. Blavatsky in *Isis Unveiled,* "that Pharaoh's daughter, who saved Moses and adopted him, is called by Josephus *Thermuthis;* and the latter, according to Wilkinson, is the name of the asp sacred to Isis ... " Throughout the world, the serpent was the symbol of a secret tradition and its initiates. Those overlooking the importance of proper names, have missed one of the most valuable keys to sacred writing. The asp was especially important in the symbolism of the Egyptians, and as it was associated with the cult of Isis, we may be sure that its appearance in the story of Moses is a veiled allusion to the Great Foster Mother, the sanctuary of the Mysteries.

When it is told that Pharaoh, through the visions of his priests, learned that a great leader was to arise among the Israelites, and is said to have commanded that the male infants of these strangers be drowned in the Nile, there is much to recommend that the account be considered as allegorical. It is too much of a coincidence to assume that this particular action should be literally and historically repeated a dozen or more times in the stories of sanctified persons and prophets. Sir James Frazer, in *Folk-Lore in the Old Testament*, analyzing the circumstances surrounding the birth of Moses, says that the story "presents features which may reasonably be suspected of belonging in the realm of folk-lore rather than of history." He then devotes considerable space to stories of extraordinary human beings who at birth were left in some remote place or exposed to providential preservation. Frazer includes in his list: Semiramis, Queen of Assyria; Gildanesh, King of Babylon; Cyrus, King of Persia; Perseus, King of Argos; Telephus, King of Mysia; Oedipus, King of Thebes; Romulus, King of Rome; Sargon, King of Babylon; and many others. The slaughter of the innocents occurs in the New Testament and is found in India in the birth legend of Krishna.

Folk-lore is a broad term which, as experience tells us, has often been applied to allegories and fables having their origin in the mystical rituals of ancient religions. Clemens Alexandrinus wrote that the parents of Moses called him Joachim, which is said to mean "the eternal has helped him and caused him to exist." His name in the Mysteries meant "the one who has been sent by Him." Such names are usual in the cases of persons predestined or foreordained. The name *Moses* is a Cabalistic rearrangement of the three Hebrew letters which form the word *Shemmah,* an ancient name for the sun. The sun is the natural and proper symbol of the eternal light, and the light-bearers, or the light-bringers, are nearly always endowed with solar attributes. The savior-deities, or the great prophets and religious founders, assume various aspects of the solar mystery. They are all sun-gods; that is, revealers of the mysteries of light and life. Their earthly careers are usually historically uncertain, and the legends and accounts which have survived about these heroes, are allegories relating to the annual motion of the sun and other astronomical phenomena. Moses, the Initiate, is so represented, and this in itself accounts for many of the parallels between his career and those of other great religious leaders. The Cabalists recognized this, and have referred to such parallels in their commentaries and interpretations.

Moses, surrounded by the twelve tribes of Israel, as Jesus was later accompanied by his twelve disciples, suggests the astro-theology of the Chaldeans and other ancient peoples. In China, the zodiac is called the *Yellow Road,* and the sun is called the *Emperor of the Yellow Road.* In the religious drama of Israel, Moses is subject to several interpretations. Astronomically he is the sun, the light-giver and the teacher. In the Hindu tradition, he might be compared to the Manu, the lord and leader of a race, and in many ancient rituals, he appears as the aged guide or conductor of candidates.

It has recently been suggested that Michelangelo placed horns on the brow of his statue of Moses by mistake. In reality, it would appear that the great sculptor was well informed. The horns are those of Jupiter Ammon, and they appeared later as ornaments on the corners of the Jewish altar in the court-yard of the Tabernacle. They are the horns of the celestial ram, Aries, the leader of the flocks of heaven. The symbolism traces from the fact that during the time of Moses, the vernal equinox took place in the sign of the ram, and the horned sun was the symbol of truth and divine authority. Ra, the solar god of the Egyptians, and the personification of universal mind, was often represented as wearing a helmet adorned with the curling horns of a ram.

There is a report that Pharaoh's wife was a woman of extraordinary attainments, one great of vision, and that she was the first to instruct the infant. This would be consistent with the matriarchal system of the Egyptians. Even this account, however, may have a double meaning, for the mother of the asp could be Isis herself. We thus have an appropriate setting for a discussion of a story at least allegorically associated with symbolical religious rituals. The real mother of Moses made an ark or boat of bulrushes and pitch, placed in it her babe, then three months old, and entrusted it to the water of the sacred river. This is the same stream down which floated the jewel-encrusted ark which contained the body of Osiris. The act of the mother entrusting her child to the waters so that he might escape the edict of Pharaoh, could signify the consecration of the babe in the stream of the Mysteries. Also, it does not necessarily mean that Moses was then a physical infant, but rather that he was one new-born in the Mysteries of the great goddess. Does it not seem strange that Moses should be accepted into the household of the very king who had decreed the drowning of the male children of the Israelites? Was Pharaoh unaware of the order which he himself had given, or would he be foolish enough to ignore the miraculous occurrence which might so easily bring about the fulfillment of the circumstance he most feared? Yet Pharaoh did not order the baby to be killed, but accepted it into his own household, in spite of the omens.

Later, according to one legend, when Moses was three years old, he approached Pharaoh and struck the crown from his head. The King, trying to find out whether the incident was accidental, caused jewels and a brazier of coals to be placed before the child to see if he had judgment and an understanding of his own actions. Moses instinctively reached toward the gems, which, had he touched them, would have resulted in his execution. In that instant, however, the hand of God deflected his arm, and Moses picked up a live coal and placed it in his mouth, thus burning himself so seriously that thereafter he had a defect of speech. Pharaoh was satisfied that the incident of the crown was without import, and continued to favor the boy.

Here again, the ideologies conflict. If the child was Jewish, Pharaoh must have realized this because of the difference in the appearance and color of the races. Yet if we are to believe the Scriptures, the King not only protected Moses, but also advanced him in the State Religion. Clemens Alexandrinus affirmed that the secret learning of the Egyptians was taught only to such persons as had been circumcised. For this reason, Pythagoras underwent the rite even after having attained maturity. It is said that Moses was born circumcised, and that this was regarded as one of the signs of his ministry. Philo Judaeus said that Moses was a prophet and theologian, and an interpreter of the sacred law. Several of the early Fathers have pointed out that the Israelites were without any formal religion in Egypt, and at that time had no written law. Ancient authors have always assumed that Moses was a sacred scribe and an interpreter of the secret doctrines taught in the temples of Egypt. He has been identified with Hermes, and regarded as the founder of one of those towns which bore the name Hermopolis.

If we wish to follow the direction of the Scriptures, we must assume that the elevation and spiritual authority of Moses were the result of the influence of Pharaoh. Perhaps the honors bestowed upon Joseph established a precedent for the honoring of Israelites possessing special talents or abilities. We might even hazard the speculation that certainly the more liberal and informed priesthood discerned the ministry for which the young Israelite was destined, and purposely aided and advanced him. The comparative independence of the different temples conceivably could have made this possible, even if the priests of other districts had opposed the action.

That Moses learned rapidly and remembered well what he had learned, is evident from subsequent events. In the formation of a faith for his own people, the lawmaker borrowed so generously from the rites and rituals of ancient nations that, like Buddha, he emerged as a reformer, a cleanser, and a purifier of older doctrines. Like Mohammed, he devised a program suitable to the requirements of his own nation, supplying the Israelites not only with spiritual conviction, but also with a code of civil law and a vital national-historical tradition. As a leader and legislator, he advanced the temporal state of his people and gave them both a racial and a national consciousness.

A wealth of legendry and lore about the early life of Moses is to be found in the rabbinical tradition. It is reported that he was a seven-month baby, and that his birth was accompanied by signs and wonders. In the Jewish account, the father of Moses was Amram of the tribe of Levi. This Amram was one of the four who were called "immaculate," and over whom death had no power. On somewhat more slender report, it is also told that at great cost, learned teachers, sages, and scholars, were invited to come to Egypt from neighboring countries to assist in the education of the remarkable child. Some of these wise men journeyed from far places, inspired by God to seek the boy who was to become the redeemer of his people.

Philo Judaeus, in his *Vita Mosis,* wrote that Moses received instruction not only in Egypt, but among the Greeks and other ancient nations. This presents difficulties for the reason that the spiritual and philosophical attainments of the Grecians of that time are matters of considerable negative speculation. Little has survived to indicate an advanced intellectual culture in the Greek states six hundred years before Homer. It seems possible that Philo was reporting only current tradition. Early writers sometimes refer to Moses as the first sage, and he is credited with having taught Hebrews the art of writing. Some more enthusiastic authorities include among the works of Moses the refinement of philosophy and medicine, the invention of numerous instruments, utensils, and weapons, the designs of certain hieroglyphical characters, the administrative division of Egypt into thirty-six districts, and the allotment of one district to the priesthood. On the syncretistic legends, Freudenthal has written learnedly in his *Hellenistische Studien.*

There is no doubt that Moses, like all other religious leaders who flourished at a remote time, has been invested with the attributes of several culture heroes. Usually the resulting biographical conflicts are reconciled syncretically. In other words, confusion is resolved by a process of clarification. By recognizing the accretions, and tracing doctrines and tenets to their proper sources, a larger reference-frame is created, suitable to enclose the difficulties without ignoring or denying them.

According to Josephus, the Egyptians, sorely oppressed by the Ethiopians, were told to appoint Moses as general over the armies of Egypt. He undertook the campaign after being persuaded by Pharaoh himself and Thermuthis. Moses showed his skill as a military strategist by devising a means of protecting his armies against venomous snakes and flying serpents that infested the territory. As one of the results of his brilliant victory, Moses married Tharbis, the daughter of the King of the Ethiopians. This account Josephus probably derived from Alexander Polyhistor, as it does not appear in the rabbinical sources.

There is also a tradition that immediately preceding the Exodus Moses searched for three days and nights for the coffin of Joseph, whom Pharaoh had made ruler in the land of Egypt. Without this sacred relic, the Israelites would not leave Egypt. Moses finally learned from Serah, the daughter of Asher, that the body of Joseph had been placed in a leaden coffin and sunk in the River Nile. The magicians had done this to bind the Israelites to Egypt. Moses took Joseph's cup and, cutting from it four pieces of metal, he engraved upon the first a lion, upon the second an eagle, upon the third a bull, and upon the fourth a human figure. These he cast into the water, and when the fourth talisman sank into the river, the coffin of Joseph came to the surface. It was carried in the midst of the tribes of Israel during the forty years of the wandering in the desert.

When it was time for Moses to lead the children of Israel into the wilderness, he sought the guidance of God. He cried out to the Lord, "I am slow of speech, and of a slow tongue." (Exodus 4:10). Thereupon, the Lord bade him to take his brother Aaron the priest as his companion when he appeared before Pharaoh. It is quite possible that when Moses complained that he was slow of speech, this does not refer to the episode of the burning coal, but to the obligation of secrecy imposed upon all who had taken the vows of the sacred colleges of learning. The Egyptian god Harpocrates, whose figure was placed at the entrance of the priestly schools, was represented with his finger to his lips, commanding silence. Aaron was therefore the voice of Moses, for he represented the priesthood, the anointed custodians of the old wisdom. It was the priests who clothed knowledge in fable, allegory, and symbol, that it might not be exposed to the profane.

The Pharaoh of the Exodus, as introduced into this account, becomes the embodiment or personification of the powers of the material world. He corresponds with Worldly Wisdom in Bunyan's *Pilgrim's Progress*. The proud ruler of the Egyptians is invested with the attributes of temporal power, pomp, and splendor. He is made to control a world dominated by selfishness, jealousy, and greed, those negative passions of the soul which keep man in bondage to the lower parts of his own nature.

After the Lord had ordered Moses to go unto Pharaoh, Moses asked by what name God should be known to his people, and the Lord said unto him, "I AM THAT I AM:" (Exodus 3:14). This is one of the most difficult to understand of Biblical statements. Innumerable interpretations have been given by various sects. Actually, the words form the most reasonable declaration of First Cause, revealing the impossibility of bestowing any qualifying or defining term upon truth or reality. To define God, is to defile God. Reality *is;* truth *exists.* Beyond these realizations, there must be silence. Perhaps this is the true meaning of "I AM THAT I AM." Further definitions must lead the mind into error.

So Moses went into the court of Pharaoh, and Aaron went with him, and at the command of the Lord, Aaron cast down his rod before Pharaoh, and it became a serpent. The magicians of Egypt did likewise, and their rods also became serpents, but the serpent of Aaron swallowed up all the other serpents. The magicians of Pharaoh's court may be likened to the materialistic scientists and scholars of today. By their wonderful knowledge, they have accomplished miraculous things, but the spirit of holiness is not in them, and they seek only physical dominion over the mysteries of Nature. The rod of Aaron represents the revealed truth of the Lord, for the serpent form is always the symbol of wisdom. Thus it is shown that the truth of the spirit, or the divine wisdom, swallows up or devours the lesser wisdom of proud men, which constitutes those forms of knowledge that have been perverted to the satisfaction of selfish desires.

But Pharaoh, the regent of the dark sphere of mortality, and the prince of this world, is not so easily converted. Like

all vain and ambitious men, he clings to his worldly possessions and rejects the testimonies of universal law. As infirmity and misery come to those proud and selfish mortals
who depart from the ways of righteousness, so the plague
descended upon the people of Egypt. Pharaoh remained
adamant until his own son was stricken. Similar occurrences
burden the way of modern life. Although the world is
filled with sorrow and pain, men think little of the ways of
the spirit, until their own personal possessions are in danger.
Pharaoh permitted his whole land to be laid bare, and he did
not relent. But when the affliction came to within his own
house, he cried out for mercy.

Thus it came about that Moses, the embodiment of wisdom, accomplished the release of his people through the help
of the Lord. And Pharaoh let the people go, and the Lord
(law) led them through the Red Sea and into the wilderness, and Moses took the bones of Joseph with him. The
Red Sea is an eloquent symbol for the sphere of human passion and desire. After man has overcome his material nature, and thus won freedom from Egypt, he must still conquer the intemperances of his emotions. The way of liberation leads to the conquest of negative qualities of character.
Wisdom led the people, and the sea opened and the children
of Israel passed through dry-shod. Pharaoh, still seeking to
enslave the hearts and souls of evolving humanity, went
against Israel with six hundred chariots, but the sea closed
upon them and destroyed them all.

The mummy of the Pharaoh of the Exodus is now preserved in the Cairo Museum. According to scientific opinion, this mighty Prince did not drown in the Red Sea, but
probably died of smallpox. Perhaps this terrible disease
was the mysterious deluge that engulfed him. There is very
little probability that the Exodus was actually opposed with
such extraordinary vigor by the Egyptians, or that any seri-

ous effort was made to hold the Israelites to their various tasks. We must therefore seek elsewhere than in history for the true meaning and circumstances of this account. It is doubtful if the historical aspect of the matter has any special value, and efforts to prove that the Red Sea actually divided would have very little constructive effect upon the problems of modern society.

After escaping the armies of Pharaoh, the children of Israel, representing collective humanity, went forth on their wanderings, and remained forty years in the desert of waiting. This forty year period has the same symbolic significance as the forty days and nights of the deluge, and the forty days of Jesus' fasting in the wilderness. This wilderness is the mortal span of man's existence, either individual or collective. The oases of rest and peace are few, and the hardships many. The search is always for the Promised Land — Canaan, the place of rest.

Gerald Massey was convinced that the key to the journey of the Israelites through the wilderness under Moses is to be found in the Egyptian account of the after-death travels of souls through Amenti. This may be considered, in turn, as symbolizing initiation into the State Mysteries. Amenti was a subterranean country, the abode of the nocturnal sun, and this strange land was hollowed out by Ptah, and his seven creating spirits (Elohim). (See, *The Natural Genesis* and *Ancient Egypt, the Light of the World*.)

The Exodus from Egypt, the wandering of the children of Israel in the wilderness, and the numerous adventures which befell them and their leaders, certainly include many references to what may be termed fragments of a Mystery ritual. In fact, the Pentateuch, as the Cabalists have indicated, is a veiled account of an esoteric doctrine. The opening chapters of Genesis, for example, are more than reminiscent of the dramatic presentations associated with the Mysteries of the Chaldeans, Egyptians, and Grecians. If we admit that the religious institutions of the Jews were based upon, or at least were profoundly influenced by, the Egyptian wisdom, and revealed by Moses, it is only reasonable that one should turn to the priestly institutions of the Nile for the key to this symbolism.

Although the Egyptian initiates, like those of other nations, were sworn to secrecy, and were obligated to abide by the rules of the temple in all matters relating to the dissemination of knowledge, it is completely erroneous to assume that the *Sodales* wished to keep the uninitiated in a state of ignorance. It was the method of disseminating knowledge that was controlled by these sacred councils. At the time of Moses, the genuine schools of initiation seem to have resolved upon an heroic experiment. The consequence of their resolution changed the entire course of religious descent.

The decision of the *Sodales* of Memphis is revealed through the immediate enlargement and intensification of the program for world enlightenment. These initiates were instructed to bestow upon the uninitiated the keys of the Lesser Mysteries as rapidly as possible. The immediate result was the instructing of non-priests and the emergence of schools of philosophy under the broad supervision of initiates or their disciples. Secrets never before revealed were entrusted to the ingenuity of poets and other literati, resulting in the appearance of a broad literature presenting the Secret Doctrine thinly veiled under fable and allegory. The temples had already instructed mankind in the arts and sciences, but the emphasis had been upon morality and utility. The *Sodales* decided to reveal the long-concealed fact that profane knowledge was merely the outer form of the Mystery sciences. Thus the ensoulment of learning came when the priestly colleges breathed the breath of life into the body of knowledge, so that it became a living thing.

The decision to prepare the uninitiated to become full participants in the secret tradition, seems to have been made by the Egyptian colleges about 1600 years before the beginning of the Christian era. From that time on, there was a rapid increase in the advancement of the human estate. The dangers which the more conservative priests had feared were also emphasized, however, and wisdom became a two-edged sword. Increase of knowledge among the so-called profane brought with it increasing personal responsibility and a larger direct participation in both spiritual and temporal government. Thus revelation set in motion the machinery of democracy, but released also the evils natural to the state of liberty. Once the secrets had been given, the use made of increasing knowledge depended upon the integrity of humanity. Divine right gave place to human right. It was a magnificent challenge, but for a long time the future of the world hung in the balance. Philosophy produced sophistry as its inevitable shadow, and the stronger the light, the deeper the shadow. Aristotle raised his voice against these prostitutions of truth, but long before his time, the decision had been made, and once the door had been opened, it could never again be closed.

An account has been preserved that Moses was entrusted by the priests with the task of releasing certain parts of the secret teachings of the temple from the strict pattern of the initiate system, so as to permit this philosophy to emerge through a highly specialized structure of religion. The old Mystery System was not strictly or exclusively religious; it was, more correctly, a confederation of schools or colleges of secret sciences. Men did not come to the temple schools to worship as we understand the term today, nor did they follow theological forms and customs. Religious services, as we know them now, did not exist, and faith, as the acceptance without question of the divine purpose by the devout, had not taken on the proportions of a formal concept.

Moses emerged, not only as the representative of the secret God of Israel, but also as a practical leader and reformer of the people. The twelve tribes were to become a microcosm of the democratic commonwealth of mankind, and Moses established among his people a system which was a repetition, or a recapitulation, of the form and structure of the invisible empire of the priestly institutions. Apparently he was chosen to lead his people—or, if we consider him an Egyptian, the people he had selected to serve—away from the highly formalized structure of the Egyptian social organization to a distant place, there to create a new religious-cultural entity. This was a step toward the ultimate purpose of the great philosophic experiment which was to form all humanity into one sacred college. In this way, Memphis of the White Walls was the archetype of the New Jerusalem, the universal city of God.

The House of Memphis was first rebuilt among the Jews as the Tabernacle in the Wilderness. This was designed directly from the classical pattern of the Egyptian sanctuary. The tribes of Israel were distributed around this Tabernacle like the signs of the zodiac, and the Egyptian astronomical sciences were revealed as supplying the archetype for the ultimate form of world society. The Tabernacle was a portable temple, divided into three parts, and its implements and symbols were foreshadowed in the carvings upon the walls of the temple of Philae. The building of the Tabernacle is therefore a symbol of revelation of the Mystery System operating on the level of uninitiated humanity.

Later, the distinguishing attributes of the Tabernacle were incorporated into the permanent structure of Solomon's house. By this time, however, religious interpretation had almost completely obscured the original design. Yet, as long as the symbolism was preserved without corruption, it revealed the truth to those who had the eyes to see and the mind to understand. To the orthodox, the temple might be a place of worship, but to those aware of the true meaning, it revealed, without exposing, the dimensions of the vast scheme. This, in substance, is the present state of theology, which is the outer form of the mystery which the world as a whole has not yet the wisdom to comprehend.

Moses ascended the holy mountain and spent a week in rites of purification. After he had reached the peak of Sinai, the day on which God revealed himself was twice the length of an ordinary day, for the sun did not set. Then God called upon Moses to come unto him, and a cloud was laid down before Moses. Suddenly the cloud opened like a mouth, and Moses walked on the firmament as though upon the earth. Then followed a wonderful experience among the angels, and there were strange mysteries which belonged to the world of spirit. Moses remained for forty days in heaven, in order that he might learn the Torah, which was placed in his hands by the angel Yefefiyah, the Prince of the Law.

When Moses came into the presence of God, he found the Divine One ornamenting the letters of the Torah with little crown-like decorations. God said that in later days there would be a man named Akiba (Rabbi Akiba, the Cabalist), who would base an interpretation upon every dot of these letters, and this interpretation would be like a great mountain. God and Moses studied together for forty days and forty nights, and in the days they studied the written teachings, and in the nights, the oral teachings. While dwelling with God, Moses beheld the seven heavens and the four colors which were later to ornament the Tabernacle, and he also saw the Celestial Tabernacle. When Moses departed out of the heavens, he carried the two Tables on which the Ten Commandments were engraved. They were created by God with his own hand in the dusk of the first Sabbath, and were made of a sapphire-like stone.

When Moses descended from the mountain and beheld the children of Israel worshipping the Golden Calf, he resolved not to deliver to them the Tables of the Law. So he turned back, but the seventy elders followed him and endeavored to take the Tables from his hands by violence. *But it was not thus that he had received them,* and during the struggle for the Tables, Moses saw the writing slowly vanish from them, and, beholding this miracle, he cast the Tables upon the ground and broke them.

In one of the lesser-known commentaries, it is reported that God disapproved of Moses for the breaking of the Tables of the Law. God said, "If thou hadst made these Tables thyself, thou wouldst not have broken them; make thou another pair of Tables, that thou mayst appreciate their worth." Adonai then showed Moses a sapphire quarry beneath the Throne of Glory, and here Moses made exact replicas of the original Tables. In the later Cabalistic teachings, Moses is caused to ascend Sinai three times, remaining forty days and forty nights each time. The first time he was given the Torah, which is the body of the law of Israel; the second time he was given the Mishnah, which is the soul of the law of Israel; and the third time, he was given the Cabala, which is the spirit of the law of Israel. The breaking of the original Tables, and the fading of the writing upon them, suggests a version of the "Lost Word" tradition.

The revelation of the law to Moses on Mt. Sinai, as reported in the Pentateuch, commented upon by the rabbins and interpreted mystically by the Cabalists, is certainly a veiled description of initiation. It is similar to the elaborate ritualism of the Book of the Dead, the account of Ishtar's descent through the seven gates, the vision of Hermes, and Mohammed's celebrated Night Journey to Heaven. These first prophets were generally regarded as having been in communication with the Great School, which accounts for the peculiar integrity of their revelations and the tremendous overtone of authority with which these revelations were given.

Only the Lesser Mysteries were entrusted at this time to the so-called profane. This is because the initiate himself is not immediately admitted into the sacred arcana, but has to approach the adytum, or Holy of Holies, through rites of purification and realization. The time had come when the whole body of humanity was to approach the sanctuary. Therefore, it had to walk collectively the same path as each of the individual candidates who had gone before. The secrets of religion were divided into three parts. In the Jewish mystical tradition, as it was perfected in Spain, these parts were represented by the Torah, the Mishnah, and the Holy Cabala. These correspond to the Court of the Tabernacle, the Holy Place, and the Holy of Holies. Exoteric religions are said to belong to orders of the Outer Court, for it was to this place that the children of Israel brought their offerings. The Inner Court, or the Holy Place, was reserved for those who had been consecrated; that is, who had dedicated themselves to the search for truth. The Holy of Holies was for the high priests, for within it was the Ark of the Covenant. This Covenant was the bond between the religion of Israel and the Universal doctrine. It was the true bridge across which the consecrated must pass to the place of initiation.

The personification of humanity as the candidate for the eternal rites has produced what has been called in symbolic ritualism the *folk-hero*. This is the true explanation of such characters as Siegfried and Gessar Khan. The hero of the world is the human being, considered either individually or collectively. Israel is the microcosm of humanity, and the limitation of this concept to a chosen people must ultimately give way to the deeper and broader realization that all people are both chosen and elected.

The adventures of Moses in the wilderness, and the various reverses with which the Israelites were afflicted, are all traceable in the pageantry of the Mystery Schools. This pageantry, in turn, is a revelation of the internal journey of man in his quest of reality. Therefore, one must assume that these experiences are intended to represent the trials and tests which lead to the collective human initiation. The crossing of the Red Sea, the wandering in the wilderness, and the final arrival at the Promised Land, represent the three degrees of the symbolical "journey" of the Israelites. While there may be historical elements involved, these should not be allowed to confuse the deeper spiritual intent of the account. Religiously speaking, one may say that the eternal doctrine released itself through a diversity of faiths, and these, in turn, through the gradual unfoldment of their essential principles, will ultimately be reunited and restored as the parts and members of one vast spiritual organism. This final union is the restoration of the Mysteries, not as privileged institutions, but as the great commonwealth of truth.

In the 17th chapter of Exodus, there is a brief account of a battle between Israel and Amalek. The armies of Israel were under the leadership of Joshua (symbol of intuitive faith), and Moses (the rational power) did not go into battle, but retired with Aaron and Hur to a high place nearby. Moses stood on a hill with the rod of the Lord in his hand, and whenever he raised up his arms, the armies of Israel were victorious, and whenever he lowered his arms, the forces of Amalek gained advantage. Moses was old, and it was difficult for him to hold up his arms continuously throughout the long day of the battle; nor could he stand for so great a length of time. A stone was brought for him, that he might sit, and Aaron stood upon one side of him, and Hur upon the other. And they held up his arms until nightfall, and the armies of Israel were victorious.

Aaron, the priest, was of the tribe of Levi, and Hur, the great general, was of the tribe of Judah. In Jewish mysticism, as we have already suggested, Israel did not necessarily signify merely the Israelitish tribes. The battle was the same as the great Hindu war between the powers of light and the forces of darkness upon the plain of Kurukshetra. Moses is the embodiment of the universal law, and he is upheld on the one hand by religion (Aaron), and on the other hand by the statehood (Hur). If the arms of the law are permitted to fall, Amalek, the adversary, gains advantage in the battle of life. Here is an interesting and seldom mentioned Biblical story, highly symbolical in the philosophical sense. We should also remember that Joshua, the son of Nun (the fish), is a Messianic figure in the Old Testament, and that he led the children of Israel into the Promised Land, where it was not lawful that Moses should enter.

The Promised Land, which Moses was permitted to behold from afar, signifies the complete experience of truth. In the Gnostic *Hymn of the Robe of Glory,* this is the homeland to which the wanderer returns after his long exile in the darkness of materiality. Thus Canaan is the symbol of fulfillment, the reward, the ultimate goal, the end which justifies the long and difficult disciplines of self-unfoldment. There is an Oriental subtlety in the allegory that Moses could not enter Canaan. The Lord of all things, when he fashioned the world, created fifty gates of wisdom. Moses, the servant of the Lord, passed through forty-nine of these gates, but through the fiftieth gate he could not pass.

The aged lawgiver is in this way revealed as a personification of the human mind. Growing wise in wisdom, the mind may approach the mystery of "I AM THAT I AM," but it is not given to the reason or the intellect that it may

possess truth. Greatness of learning makes it possible for
man to stand upon a mountain and look across toward the
substance of the eternal promise, but final union with the
Supreme Mystery is beyond even wisdom. As Plotinus explained to his disciples, man ascends from opinion to knowledge, from knowledge to wisdom, from wisdom to understanding, and then, by a dynamic experience beyond understanding, he attains that illumination which is union with
the blessed God.

Moses ascended the mountain Nebo, which was in the
land of Moab. Then the Lord spake unto Moses: "And die
in the mount whither thou goest up, and be gathered unto
thy people; as Aaron thy brother died in mount Hor, and
was gathered unto his people: (Deuteronomy 32:50).
Mount Nebo is now identified with the mountain El Neba
in Trans-Jordan. The association of the word *nebo* with
the idea of wisdom and learning can be traced to the Babylonian religion. Nebo was the god of wisdom, the patron
of the scribes, and the protector of the Mystery Schools. He
was called the Lord of the Writing Table, and had many of
the attributes of the Egyptian Thoth and the Greco-Egyptian
Hermes. Mount Nebo is therefore identical in meaning
with Lord Bacon's Pyramid of Pan, the ladder of learning,
the upper end of which—that is, the summit or crest—approaches but does not reach the mystery of truth.

According to the Biblical approach, Moses was not permitted to enter the Promised Land because he had become
angry and smote the rock as described in Numbers 20:10-12.
At that time, the Lord rebuked Moses and decreed that he
should not bring the congregation of Israel into the Promised Land. The commentaries say that the Angel of Death
came to Moses in the lonely hill of Moab, and the great lawgiver sought to drive away the Angel of Death with the
staff upon which was written the name of the Most High.

Then the Lord came unto Moses and promised his servant that he should not be delivered unto the Angel of Death. And the Lord kissed the soul of Moses, and the liberator of Israel went to sleep in God, in the valley of Moab. And Moses was taken unto the Lord on the Sabbath, the seventh day of Adar, and the call of the angels could be heard for twelve miles about the place.

The Bible says that the place where the physical remains of Moses were buried was unknown, even in ancient times. Popular tradition, however, associates the site with a building which still stands and is shown to tourists. It is believed that the tomb was connected by subterranean tunnels with the cave of Machpelah, which had been set aside by Abraham as a burial place. Here, incidentally, legend reports that the bodies of Adam and Eve were placed. The site was long sacred to the followers of Islam, who greatly enriched both the building and the legend.

No consideration of the life and work of the lawgiver of Israel would be complete without a survey of the consequences of his mission. The incorporation of the Old Testament into the compound of the Christian Scriptures vastly enlarged the influence of Judaism among non-Jewish people. The Mosaic law, as summarized in the Ten Commandments, is probably the most widely disseminated ethical-moral code in the world today. Moses is no longer regarded by Christians as a Jewish legislator, but as a great spiritual teacher. Among those less theologically minded, Christianity is still sometimes referred to as reformed Judaism. Naturally, the two faiths are in some variance on this delicate question, but Jesus himself declared that he had come to fulfill the law and the prophets, and not to overthrow or destroy them.

Broadly speaking, the Ten Commandments have refined and ennobled all peoples who have accepted and applied them as rules for living. While it would be unfair to say that Moses actually invented the code associated with his name, he is certainly responsible for much of the modern regard in which these commandments are universally held. Through him, the Jewish people have exercised a sphere of moral influence far greater than the numerical or political strength of the congregation would otherwise have made possible. Strengthened and united under the Mosaic Dispensation, the Jews were also largely responsible for the preservation of essential learning through the long and dark centuries of the medieval world. Refusing to be incorporated into the then prevailing Christian society, they perpetuated arts and sciences, philosophies and ethical concepts, and priceless heritages of tradition, until the Renaissance and the Reformation made possible the restoration of learning.

THE ROLL OF THE LAW WITH ITS ORNAMENTS

CHAPTER IV
THE FIVE BOOKS OF MOSES

The English word *Bible* is derived from the Greek through medieval Latin, and simply means "the Books." Specifically it is that collection of sacred writings which forms the basis of the Christian faith, together with the account of those circumstances which constitute the basis of the Christian religion. The Bible is divided into two major sections, which are called the Old Testament and the New Testament, of which the first is composed of the principal sacred writings of the Jews, and the latter of the Gospels and other works peculiarly and completely Christian.

The essential relationship between the two Testaments has been a subject of profound consideration, for it is not usual to find the Scriptures of two distinct and separate religions combined in this way. For Christian people, the Old

Testament forms a background, or a framework, to support the Messianic revelation, a spiritual dispensation consummated in the life and teachings of Jesus Christ. Obviously, this could not be the viewpoint of the orthodox Jew, who regards the Old Testament as a complete work. He may be willing to admit that the Prophetic Books in the Old Testament contain intimations of the coming of a Messiah, but he does not accept the New Testament as the fulfillment or continuation of the older work. As the Christian points out, however, the combination of the two Testaments is historically and ethically fortunate.

The greater part of the New Testament deals with the life of Jesus of Nazareth as unfolded through the four Gospels, proceeds to the delineation of the Acts of the original apostles, passes through the Pastoral Writings, and terminates with the Apocalypse. It is a powerful moral work, with magnificent statements of mystical faith, admonition and instruction. It is, however, deficient in one particular when compared with other sacred books of the world. It lacks a theogenesis, cosmogenesis and anthropogenesis. Therefore, the weight and strength of its teachings depend in some measure upon a concept of the divine will and the divine works, as these are unfolded through the Old Testament. Actually, the New Testament, in its presentation of the cultural descent of a people, covers less than a century. The need for a broader perspective—religious, philosophical, and historical —was recognized at an early date.

The Old Testament answers many questions concerning the race and nation from which Jesus came, the beliefs of his forebears and also his contemporaries, the unfoldment of their religious and political psychologies, and the rise and fall of their national existence. Nor can it be forgotten that many of the words of Jesus are derived from the Old Testament, and are given special authority by this fact. It is now generally assumed that Jesus himself was conversant with the Septuagint version of the Old Testament, and that most of the original converts to Christianity were orthodox Jews.

Although the Old and New Testaments were written originally in different tongues, the oldest comprehensive versions of both that have been discovered, are in the Greek language, thus strengthening the tie which binds the works together. It therefore does not seem unreasonable, from a Christian point of view, to accept the obvious and inevitable conclusion that the two Testaments reveal the gradual unfoldment of the will of God through his prophets, patriarchs, saints, and apostles. In the light of accepted tradition, it is also proper, when studying the Bible, to begin with the Old Testament. The student should attempt to bear in mind that he is here dealing basically with the sacred writings of the Jewish people, which merit proper respect and consideration.

The Old Testament, as presented in the Christian Bible, consists of thirty-nine books of various lengths, written at different times, and essentially dissimilar in many respects. To simplify our approach, we may follow the ancient practice of dividing the books of the Old Testament into three groups or classes. Ben Sira, who flourished about 200 B. C., refers to the sacred writings of his people as the *Laws,* the *Prophets,* and the *Other Books of our Father*. That part of the Old Testament referred to as the *Laws,* or the *Torah,* consists of the Pentateuch, attributed to Moses and identified as the first five books of the Holy Scriptures, from Genesis to Deuteronomy in the present order. When the Book of Joshua is included with the Pentateuch, the collection is called the Hexateuch. According to Jewish tradition, the Prophetic Books are divided into the Early and the Later Prophets, and the Later Prophets are further divided into three major and twelve minor prophets. In the Hebrew

Canon, the minor prophets, from Hosea to Malachi, are combined into a single book. The remaining books of the Old Testament are grouped under the general heading of the "Sacred Writings." These are in three parts: the Poetical Books, the Five Scrolls (or Megilloth), and the Chronicles.

At the time of the first Greek translation of the Scriptures, the order of the books had not been permanently established, and the translators rearranged the books into three sections: Historical, Poetic, and Prophetic. The early Chistians followed this order, since the Prophetic Books, with their intimations of a coming Messiah, logically led to the New Testament as the fulfillment of these prophecies.

THE HOLY SCRIPTURES
(According to the Jewish Canon)

TORAH: (THE PENTATEUCH)
    Genesis
    Exodus
    Leviticus
    Numbers
    Deuteronomy

PROPHETS:
    EARLY PROPHETS: (Historical)
        Joshua
        Judges
        I. and II. Samuel
        I. and II. Kings

    LATER PROPHETS: (Messages and Sermons)
        MAJOR PROPHETS:
            Isaiah
            Jeremiah
            Ezekiel

MINOR PROPHETS: (The Twelve)
Hosea; Joel; Amos; Obadiah
Jonah; Micah; Nahum; Habakkuk
Zephaniah; Haggai; Zechariah; Malachi

SACRED WRITINGS: (HAGIOGRAPHA)

Psalms

Proverbs

Job

Song of Songs)
Ruth   )
Lamentations   )   The Five Scrolls (Megilloth)
Ecclesiastes   )
Esther   )

Daniel

Ezra

Nehemiah

I. and II. Chronicles

THE OLD TESTAMENT
(According to the Septuagint and Early Christians)

HISTORICAL BOOKS:

The Pentateuch

Joshua

Judges

Ruth

I and II Samuel)
I and II Kings   )   Basileion

I. and II. Chronicles

Ezra

Nehemiah

POETIC BOOKS:

> Esther
> Job
> Psalms
> Proverbs
> Ecclesiastes
> Song of Solomon

PROPHETIC BOOKS:

> Isaiah
> Jeremiah
> Lamentations of Jeremiah
> Ezekiel
> Daniel
> Hosea; Joel; Amos; Obadiah
> Jonah; Micah; Nahum; Habakkuk
> Zephaniah; Haggai; Zechariah; Malachi

The names of the five books of the Pentateuch (the Five-Volumed Book), as they are found in the Authorized Version, are according to the Septuagint. The word *Genesis* signifies generation or origin. In Hebrew, the name is *Bereshith,* which means "In the Beginning." *Exodus,* signifying departure, refers to the principal event in the book—the departure of the Israelites from Egypt. The name of the book comes from the Greek through Latin. The Hebrew title is *Shemoth* ("Names"), or *Eleh Shemoth* ("These Are the Names"), from the opening words of the first chapter. *Leviticus,* also from the Greek through Latin, means "Belonging to the Levites." The emphasis is upon the code of holiness, the consecration of priests, and religious observances. The rabbinical name for the book is *Torath Kohanin,* "The Law of the Priests." The customary Hebrew title is *Vayikra.* The fourth book is called *Numbers,* derived from the Greek

Arithmoi, rendered *Numeri* in the Vulgate, apparently because it contains mention of two censuses of the people. The second verse of Chapter I reads: "Take ye the sum of all the congregation of the children of Israel, after their families, by the house of their fathers, with the number of *their* names, . . . " *Bemidbar* ("In the Desert") is the generally accepted title in modern Hebrew editions of the Bible. *Deuteronomy* is from the Greek *Deuteronomion,* and means broadly "Repetition of the Law." The early Hebrew name *Mishneh Torah,* used in Talmudic times, was replaced by *Eleh Hadebarin* ("These are the Words") from the first verse of the book. This name has again been shortened to *Debarin,* the ordinary Hebrew term now in use.

The five books which constitute the Torah are not actually separate writings, but the sequential sections of one story, including a prologue (Genesis), and an epilogue (Deuteronomy). Between these two are placed the remaining three books in their usual order, and in a sequence acceptable not only to the historian, but to the psychologist and sociologist. Though somewhat obscure with historical involvements and the broad emphasis upon genealogies and the descent of families, and further heavily concerned with the wanderings of the tribes of Israel, their wars and other difficulties, the essential story unfolds in a simple and direct way. The great danger is that details will obscure the essential structure and cause the mind to disregard or overlook the broad pattern of the work.

The Torah of Moses conveys much more than a literal interpretation of the Word itself. It certainly presents a legal code applicable to the moral and physical lives of a people, but it extends beyond this limitation to include the entire concept of religious instruction and spiritual guidance. The Torah is one of the three principal pillars supporting the Jewish world; the others are worship and benevolence. It was anciently taught that God, in his infinite wisdom and love, offered the Torah to all the nations and races of the earth, but they rejected it, and therefore it was placed in the keeping of the Jews as their greatest wealth and heritage. Thus it is appropriate to examine most carefully those five books which unfold the Mosaic Dispensation.

The purpose of Genesis is not primarily to present the story of creation, for this account is limited to a few chapters. The true purpose is to establish the conceptual integrity of the Pentateuchal Dispensation. It presents to the reader the circumstances which led to the setting apart of a Chosen People, peculiarly and wonderfully provided for and protected, so that through them and through their works a dispensational law might be revealed to the world. The entire weight of the Pentateuch is upon the unfoldment of this dispensational law. Certainly, this statement does not exhaust the wealth of wisdom and beauty contained within these books, but it is the great thread running through and connecting them.

It was entirely proper, therefore, that the first book should deal primarily with the answer to the question: "Why is there a special dispensation?" We see the gradual representation of a certain selectivity on the part of the Creating Power. This is not a unique procedure, for it is to be found wherever sacred books have come into existence. Through its scriptures, the culture of a race explains itself, telling the story of its own psychic entity, and presents its claim to an individual psychic existence. The deepest motivations which can be comprehended by a people and experienced in the inner life of that people are set forth in scriptures. In Genesis, we have a moral or spiritual situation established by means of which the rest of the Pentateuch becomes necessary. In other words, a concept or pattern is revealed, and this concept becomes the basis of a precept, the code or way of life and redemption, which must actually and inevitably follow. In this case, Genesis sets forth not only the basic premise of the Jewish religion, but also, to a large measure, that of the Christian doctrine which was to arise much later.

The opening chapters of Genesis present us with the story of a divine creation, a disobedience, and a fall. We observe the individual establishing a moral or spiritual interval between himself and his God. This is the interval which must be bridged by repentance, by a life of virtue, by obedience to law, and by the gradual maturing of an ethical and religious life. Had not the fall been established in the early chapters of Genesis, there would have been no justification for Exodus, Leviticus, Numbers, or Deuteronomy. There would have been no need for a Messianic redeemer unless there had been original sin. The Pentateuch attempts to explain the obvious imperfection of man's present state, and sets forth a concept which is a symbolic statement of man's deepest and most enduring requirement. Thus is defined the enormous spiritual necessity upon which the works of religion depend.

In this particular instance, disobedience causes the departure of man from a paradisiacal state, and forces him to take upon himself the burden of original sin. He is exiled from his native land, and deprived of the conscious power to apperceive and know the presence of his God. After he has been exiled from the paradisiacal garden, he is forced to wander in the world, dependent increasingly upon his own resources, and sustained only by his inward faith. These powerful chapters seem to have a direct dependency upon the Sumerian account of the Genesis, and suggest that they originated in the remote oral tradition of that region.

In Genesis, also, we see the concept strongly arising that true religion is actually obedience to divine law. Man, therefore, must worship his Creator by keeping a covenant or a

code bestowed upon him by God. The admonition to observe the Torah inevitably implied that there must be a revelation of the law to man. We cannot be certain to what
degree our own judgment, acceptance, and rejection, of codes
and creeds are true. The need for the revelation of the law
is fulfilled in the lawgiver. There is little to indicate that the
divine plan was so vividly written upon the surface of the
ancient world that primitive man could read and understand
the sacred language of symbols and fables. In fact, even
modern man is without the positive assurance of religious
certainty. That. which is intimated, determined, and ordained in Genesis, gradually unfolds its own inevitable pattern. This unfoldment moves in conformity with the social
and cultural changes which mark the descent of the Jewish
people.

Exodus, the second book of the Pentateuch, reveals the
gradual unfoldment of the Torah. It opens with an historical
perspective. It develops through time and circumstance,
especially under the emergency of a great and pressing need.
The consolation of the spirit comes most rapidly to those
who are deprived of other means of security. To borrow
an old saying, "Man's emergency is God's opportunity." So
Exodus carries the children of Israel along the difficult road
which leads to their integration socially, nationally, cultural-
ly and religiously. We note them slowly building the sanctuary of their own existence; not a physical house, for this
was still a period of wandering, but a shrine of convictions,
a sacred place of social and psychic values. Exodus is one
of the most powerful psychological documents in the entire
Bible. It supports the general belief of modern sociologists
that the only way revelation is possible is through the gradual
development of the native psychic potential of a people.

A race must bring forth from itself that which is necessary to its own cultural survival. Revelation is therefore re-

lease; it is knowledge, wisdom, and understanding, moving through a people, ensouling them, uniting them, and molding them gradually into an integrated pattern. The study of Exodus reveals the Jewish people growing into a nation—a strong cooperative unit—thus forming a body for the perpetuation of a powerful conviction. As the body of man must pass through infancy and growth before it is capable of sustaining the soul within it, and before that soul itself can move through that body to the revelation of its own glory, so in the story of Exodus we find an account of the gradual integration of both the collective and individual psyche and its motion toward a state of sufficiency from within itself.

The Book of Leviticus is concerned principally with the immediate unfoldment of the Levitical ministry as such. The body of the law is slowly integrated to become the instrument of its own psychic overtones. We are introduced to the mysteries of the Tabernacle. We see with inner vision the spirit of the Lord hovering over the Mercy Seat between the wings of the cherubim. We come to understand the presence of the Shekinah's glory. We sense the worship of the Archangel Michael, the psychopompos of heaven and the secret god of Israel. In Leviticus we find the more complete revelation of the law, so far as the Levitical code could be supported and sustained by the people. The priesthood is consolidated in Israel, the soul within man is his anointed priest, and the maturing collective soul of a people chooses to appoint and anoint its religious counselors, setting them apart and dedicating them to the service of the mysteries of the Lord. So in Leviticus, the Old Dispensation— the law of the Pentateuch—is ensouled and becomes a living thing. The breath of life, in the form of rich religious overtones, is bestowed. The people are consecrated and united as one body in the Lord.

As man's psychic life integrates, does he immediately find happiness, and peace of mind? Unfortunately, this is not usually the case. The moment an individual takes control of his own spiritual life, and acknowledges a divine destiny from within himself, he faces the greatest challenge that can ever confront him. He passes through a long cycle of uncertainty, as one wandering in a desert region. Like the young man or woman who suddenly accepts the weight of maturity, he is heavily burdened by the sense of inner psychic change. He is no longer a child, nor has he yet the wisdom of years. He becomes one with those wanderers who, through all ages, have sought the consolation of the spirit.

Thus Leviticus leads inevitably to Numbers, which deals essentially with the eternal story of sorrow in the wilderness. Here is represented the great struggle against worldliness, the struggle between the rising power of internal life and the enveloping darkness of environment. Only when the soul is enlightened is it aware of the conflict or contrast between itself and that which is not itself. The story of Numbers, therefore, is much like the initiation ritual of one of the old Mysteries of Greece or Egypt. It is reminiscent of the wanderings of Ulysses, searching for his own far-distant native land. Always the wandering in the wilderness of ignorance is the inevitable prerequisite to the attainment of wisdom and security. The Biblical account of this journey is comparatively abridged, but there is much more to be found in the old Jewish commentaries bearing upon this tradition than has ever been brought to the attention of non-Jewish scholars. It is in this section of the Pentateuch that Moses receives the Tables of the Law on the thundering peak of Sinai.

In Deuteronomy is set forth, in the form of three great discourses, the fullness and purity of the law as revealed by Moses to his people. The lawmaker unfolds his concept of the divine will as it operates in the world of men. The law

is revealed on the one hand as firm and even relentless, and
on the other hand as all-embracingly kind and gentle in
spirit. There are stern passages binding the children of
Israel to the letter of the Covenant, and there are deeply
beautiful parts, rich with solicitude and tender consideration.
Thus the pattern revealed in Genesis is consummated in
Deuteronomy. The Torah is complete, and the ministry of
Moses is finished. It remained for Joshua, the son of Nun,
to lead the children of Israel into the land of milk and
honey. So Moses, full of years, went to sleep among the
hills of Moab, and the earth knew him no more.

If we have the inner power to experience the majesty of
universal law, and can recognize its inevitable power within
ourselves, we understand the Pentateuch. We discover this
law through the patriarchal dispensation within ourselves.
The great prophet of old is a part of our own internal spiritual being. We also accept the account of the law as a
descent of personal and collective experience. It is a heritage enriched by the passing of time and interpreted from
generation to generation by men seeking after truth. In
each of us, there is an archetypal pattern, bearing witness to
the operations of the divine will. The law comes to us
through the voice of the folk. We live and die within its
deep mysterious design. It moves through our blood stream.
First it was the law of the jungle, the plain, and the desert,
which both man and animal must obey. In those days, the
rule was simple: Keep the law and live, break the law and
die. Sometimes it is called the old law, but it is forever
new, for it can never be violated without penalty. All these
deep truths have been conveyed to us by the patriarchal instinct in our own souls.

But as men grew in knowledge and understanding, it
was inevitable that they should meditate upon the verity of
the ancient way of life. In their hearts, they sought to tran-

scend the letter of divine legislation, and transform the Old Dispensation by the inner experience of God, into a new statement of divine love in a mystery. Here are the roots of the New or Messianic Dispensation, not only among Christians, but also among Jews and the peoples of other races and faiths. The law leads inevitably to the prophets, those wonderful men of vision who transcended the outer forms of things in the search for an eternal indwelling spirit. The prophets were the ones who had the vision of strength perfecting itself in beauty, of obedience glorified by simple faith. It was the contemplation of these eternal verities that led to the visions of Isaiah and the sad, gentle story of the tribulations of Job. This light of mystery touches us directly in the meditations of Ezekiel, and blazes forth in the inspired songs of Ruth and Esther. So it is that the law must lead always to the prophets, whose primary concerns were the liberation of Israel and the dream of a better world to come.

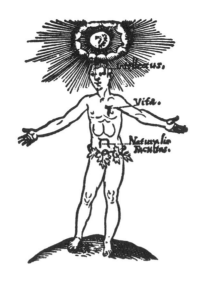

THE DIVINE NAME ON THE BODY OF ADAM

CHAPTER V

THE BIBLICAL STORY OF CREATION

Cosmogony and anthropology, as unfolded in the Old Testament, are principally set forth in the first ten chapters of the Book of Genesis. The word *Genesis* itself, from the Greek, means literally "beginning" or "birth," and also implies "becoming," or "emerging," into a state of being or existence. It suggests also the source of historical tradition and the state of the world in primordial or antediluvian times. It appears to set forth the creation of the world and the first pair of human beings. It then proceeds to describe the origin of sin, outlines the rise of civilization, and emphasizes the decline and regeneration of primitive mankind and the destruction of the greater part of humanity by a deluge in the time of Noah. It explains the confusion of languages and the division of the human race by the dramatic story of the Tower of Babel.

The origin of the Book of Genesis is difficult to trace. Certain parts seem to have been derived from ancient Babylonian sources such as the Chaldeo-Babylonian tablets in the British Museum, which were translated by George Smith in in his work, *The Chaldean Account of the Genesis.* It is also quite possible that the spiritual and ethical traditions of the early Egyptians were drawn upon. Reflections in this direction are hampered by insufficient knowledge of the deeper phases of Egyptian religio-philosophical concepts. It would appear certain, however, that the religious overtones of Genesis are more highly advanced and essentially more mature than earlier sources in the Mediterranean area, and suggest an indebtedness to the philosophical institutions of the Far East. There are strong indications of that powerful originality and clear pattern of morality by which the early Jewish writings can be immediately distinguished from other works of a similar nature.

The extremely abridged form of the account of the creation in the book of Genesis further suggests that the work was supported by, or suspended from, a large structure of religious tradition. It is known that Genesis was among those books which were destroyed and then re-transcribed or restored from memory by priestly writers and scribes. In the course of time, much may have been and almost certainly was lost, but even in the face of this deficiency, it is possible to broaden the foundations of research. With the aid of Jewish and Cabalistic commentaries, Genesis may be amplified into a rational account of the beginning of the universe—a story far more vital, significant, and impressive, than the generally accepted theological version.

Much has been made of the impossibility of reconciling the opening chapters of Genesis with the findings of modern science and archeology. This immediately leads to a deep and bitter controversy. One school affirms that the Biblical account must be accepted as a divine revelation, and all inconsistencies be ignored because they are beyond human understanding. Another school approaches the subject on a psychological-historical level, and takes the attitude that the work unfolds the traditional convictions of the time at which it was compiled, and must be regarded in this light. A third school, addicted to mystical speculations, has consciously or unconsciously assumed the Cabalistic point of view and believes that the inconsistencies can be bridged by interpretation. On this premise, the conflict between the old writings and modern knowledge will disappear if the ancient records are correctly understood. There is much to recommend the last position, especially when the rich tradition of the early Jewish scholars is carefully examined. The present treatment of the subject is in this spirit.

It is not possible in a general survey to exhaust all the potentials of any theme. Certain parts of the work can be examined, however, to indicate a general direction, and the serious student can extend his researches to any degree that he considers useful or profitable. We should always bear in mind that Near Eastern peoples were not especially addicted to a critical or scientific approach to knowledge. The men of this region have always been poets and story-tellers, and their literary productions have been colored by their natural tendencies toward fantasy and imagination. Their knowledge of the world in which they lived, and their moral reflections upon the larger verities of time and space, were a combination of bright-tapestried tradition and their instinctive reaction to the challenging experiences of daily living.

The Book of Genesis opens with a simple and dramatic statement which has been anglicized into the most impressive sentence in the English language. In Hebrew this reads: "ALEIM BRA BRAChIT AT EChIM UAT EARTz." In the Authorized Version, this is simply translated: "In the beginning God created the heaven and the earth." At first reading, this verse seemingly presents no problem, but the more carefully it is considered, the more fully the Bible student will realize that into these ten English words has been compressed a cosmic process involving hundreds of millions of years of time and innumerable complicated factors and elements. Only an elaborate commentary can make this verse even partly intelligible to a human mind entirely ignorant of divine procedures and not too certain of universal unfoldment even on a physical level.

It has been said that the first chapter of Genesis covers some vast immeasurable period within the absolute nature of duration, when a series of successive attempts were being made by the Creating Power, operating through its immutable law, to form universes or vast bodies in space. This is the concept advanced in the Zohar, where it is written that there were old worlds called *sparks,* which perished even as they were fashioned. These sparks could not continue because the Sacred Aged One had not yet assumed its geometric form, and the Master Architect had not yet been called to his work. (See the *Idra Suta*).

Before the creation of the world, the greatest of the mysteries were established within the Divine Nature itself. The first of these mysteries was the Torah (the Law), which rested forever in the lap of God. The second was the divine throne, which was erected in heaven and was the establishment or the foundation of foundations. The third and fourth were paradise and purgatory, which were placed on the right and left sides; and the fifth was a celestial sanctuary, which was placed before God, having upon its altar a jewel with the name of the Messiah graven into its surface.

The Mighty One, whose name is Blessed, wore the twenty-two letters of the alphabet upon his crown, and when he was about to create the world, the letters descended from their radiant dignity and gathered about him. Each asked that it have the dignity of being selected to bring forth the creation, and the Lord finally chose Beth because it was the letter of blessedness. Before he began the fashioning of any creature, God consulted with Torah, and she assured him that a mighty ruler should not be without a kingdom of creatures to do him homage and discover the secrets of his infinite wisdom and love.

Let us first examine the word *God* as it is used throughout the first chapter of Genesis. The word in Hebrew is not *God* or *Jah,* or *Jehovah,* but *Elohim.* The Anglo-Saxon word *God* is a reverent but entirely insufficient term with which to convey the true meaning of *Elohim.* In Hebrew, this is an androgynous term strongly implying a combination of male and female attributes, and also, by its termination, the word is plural. It would be more correct to say, therefore, that *Elohim* means "The Male-Female Creators," representing a host, or at least a group, of powers, symbolically described as a septenary, and not under any condition a single personal deity.

The words *heaven* and *earth* are also misleading, through inadequate translation. They actually signify two conditions, one superior and the other inferior. Fabre d'Olivet, whose scholarship was profound, in translating this verse, says: "Elohim created in principle;" that is, fashioned a potential existence, an archetype, of two states or primordial differences. Thus we have a separation of causes, and not a division of place. The average reader might think of heaven only as the firmament scattered with constellations of stars, and the earth as the planet on which he lives. Such an interpretation would destroy utterly the significance of the verse. It would be better to interpret heaven and earth as spirit and matter, or as subtle and gross qualities in the sense of vibrations, or as conditions of activity and passivity.

The words *in the beginning* also present difficulty. The old and wise scholars chose to interpret these words as "from that which is first," or "from eternal principles," or "of that which was in the beginning." This is important, for it solves the very present dilemma of how something or anything can come from nothing, unless we understand *nothing* as standing for *no-thing*. It is not so confusing, however, to contemplate the generation of a conditioned state from its own inevitable unconditioned source. Fabre d'Olivet translates "In the beginning" as "At-first-in-principle," which seems to imply an internal experience in the Divine Consciousness prior to the fashioning of any external uiversal structure.

This leaves only the word *created...* The human mind customarily conceives creation as the making of something new, but deeper thinking leads to the realization that in the generation of physical things, creation is only the fashioning of a new pattern or combination, composed inevitably of already existing elements or factors. Thus a man may create a picture, but he requires the aid of paint, brush, and canvas. Creation is truly the inward inspiration or impulse to express, and the expression itself is made possible by the availability of the necessary instruments and means. *Creation* in this verse thus implies formation, manifestation, the revelation of things from their roots and sources, and the arranging of ever existing elements into new patterns to serve as vehicles for the revelation of will, mind, and consciousness.

Bearing these thoughts in mind, the first verse of Genesis may be restated or expanded as follows: "From the eternal principles and essences which are the substances of the beginnings of existence, the forces, makers, or fashioners of the world, the androgynous creator-gods, molded, sculptured, or carved, and thus brought into manifestation, the substances of the superior and the inferior creation, or released archetypally the positive and negative aspects of eternal Being."

Obeying an eternal cyclic law, resting forever in the lap of God, space periodically caused to emerge from its own being, primordial unity. From this unity, in turn, there descended a septenary of cosmic beings. These are the seven vowels, released by the divine pronouncement of the *fiat,* or the *word* of creation. According to the Cabala, these cosmo-creators were the Elohim, the formators and the great builders. They brooded over the deep, and their motion in the depths of space brought forth the will-born universe over which they ruled, and around which they continued to circle under the symbolism of seven sacred invisible planets. Although they are regarded as the creators of the mundane world, it is not to be understood that the Elohim directly fashioned the physical universe as it is known today. Rather, they brought forth a vast metaphysical system of energies and powers of which the physical creation is the seventh and lowest part. This first manifestation or agitation is known in Hindu philosophy as "the churning of space." It is the *primum mobile,* or the first motion, of the Divine Power. Also, according to tradition, the Elohim sowed the seed of creatures in the dark field of space, and from this seed grew all living things, bearing witness to the universal life which sustained them.

Comparison with other religious systems supports and justifies these speculations of the old Jewish mystics. In the Northern Tibetan system, the meditations of Adi Buddha, or universal consciousness, produced the seven Dhyani-Buddhas, or the seven modes of conditioned consciousness, by which the world was formed. In the teachings of the Persians, the Su-

preme One, Ahura Mazda, manifested forth his glory through
the Amesha-Spentas who became the foremost of the manifested world. In the Egyptian Hermetic teaching, the Elohim
were the governors, the keepers of the gates, the guardians of
the dawn. In the more ancient Egyptian system, they were the
Ammonian Artificers, the servants of Ptah, the master builder and the potter-god of Memphis who fashioned the egg
of the universe on a potter's wheel. The Elohim are also
the seven Cabiri of Samothrace, the seven rays upon the
golden crown of the Gnostic lamb, and in the Gnostic Mysteries, we have the Leonocephalic Cronus, ornamented with
the seven sacred lights, the unwritten vowels which together
make up the name of the manifested deity. The Elohim are
also the seven colors of the spectrum born from the white
light of eternity. They manifest through the seven days of
creation, and are symbolized on the seven seals of Revelation. They are the eternally recurring septenary by which
art, music, and physics are bound together. They are the
seven breaths which, moving upon and within the deep,
caused the great design of the world to flow into objectivity.

In the Authorized Version, the second verse of Genesis
reads: "And the earth was without form, and void; and darkness *was* upon the face of the deep. And the Spirit of God
moved upon the face of the waters." Interpreted according to
the mystical tradition, this verse could be amplified as follows: "And the below, the passive aspect of Being, was form-
less and devoid of manifested life, and darkness or oblivion
filled the whole expanse. The spirit of Elohim moved, impregnated, and enlivened the essence of the universal negation." Two words are introduced in the original text: *Tohu,*
which has been translated *Form;* and *Bahu,* which has been
translated *Void.* *Tohu* is a band encompassing the creation,
from which flows darkness; and *Bahu* is an abyss of stones

from which water is produced. We can see how far such meanings are from the generally accepted renderings.

The seven modes of creating intelligence are the personifications of the seven primordial laws of Nature, which, in turn, bear witness to the seven wills or the septenary determinations of the world spirit. They are described as releasing or bringing into manifestation the pattern or archetypes of the inferior universe. They are first described as vortices, called in the *Sepher Yetzirah* (*The Book of Formations*) "the whirlwinds." In one form of this theogenic narration, it is declared that the universe was created by the outpouring of a sacred word which is the secret name of the Eternal. In the North Asiatic tradition, the seven sons of the Infinite are described as establishing their foundation in the deep, and building their thrones in the six directions of space. Six of these builders surround the seventh, who is placed in the center and is called the *Immovable*. In the Cabala, this center is called the *Holy Temple,* the Sabbath of eternal rest, around which move the six days of creation.

The higher powers do not descend into the lower elements to ensoul the mundane diffusion, but rather cast their shadows upon the deep, or into the lower elemental regions. In the teachings of Lamaism, we have a somewhat similar concept. The meditating Dhyani Buddhas dream themselves into the illusion of matter, causing a certain part of their own consciousness to accept or assume the shadow of existence, even though as vast spiritual beings they are forever meditating from a plane far above this illusional state. The shadows of the Elohim, cast into the depth of matter, result in the formation of four levels or planes of transitory existence, which the old Jewish philosophers called worlds. These planes correspond approximately to the theological concept of the levels of spirit, mind, soul, and body, both in the universe and in man. In each of the four worlds, the

seven Elohim establish their reflectional images, to become
in all twenty-eight. This has caused them to be associated
in symbolism with the lunar month and its four weeks of
seven days. The ancient Jewish priests had peculiar veneration for the moon, and were therefore associated with the
descent of the lunar cult.

Only the lowest of the four worlds was involved in the
mystery of the physical creation. This lowest or fourth
world was again made up of seven parts or planes, also the
shadows of the seven Elohim. Of these seven planes which
make up the mundane sphere, six are superphysical, and
only one, the lowest, is physical. The six superphysical
planes are called causal, and are the source of the patterns
and energies which flow into and through the seventh. It
is this seventh, or lowest, part of the fourth world with
which the creation story in Genesis is usually identified.
This is not correct, however, unless we are willing to assume
that this is the least or lowest part of creation, and therefore
is a material symbol of a larger spiritual mystery. The final
unfoldment of the physical plane follows closely the pattern
broadly known as the Chaldean system of cosmogony. Always, physical procedures are but the shadow of spiritual
activities taking place in the higher dimensions of space-
spirit.

In the theogeny of the Greeks, the material universe is
brought into being by seven gods, each of whom rules over
one of the seven spheres of the mundane world. In the
Greek system, as unfolded by Orpheus, these deities are, in
order: Phanes, Ouranos, Chronos, Rhea, Zeus, Poseidon, and
Hades. The seven concentric spheres of the mundane world
consist of the bodies of these divinities, in the form of seven
inter-penetrating zones of which six are superphysical, and
only the lowest, or seventh—the zone of Hades—is physical.
According to this system, the physical plane is therefore ruled

over by Hades, a subterranean god. The Greeks believed that the physical plane is that part of the universe furthest removed from the source of divine energy.

Thus the description given in Genesis 1:1-31, must be understood to represent the gradual development of the physical universe from its spiritual root. Most of the account deals with conditions prior to the formation of the material planet and its creatures. The Elohim, the gods of the dawn, finally mold the negative substances of Being into the forms and patterns of the solar system. Having brought the planets, including the luminaries, into objective existence, the Elohim then take up their thrones in the bodies of the seven wanderers (planets), and, according to the Chaldean creation myths, circle about the earth in their orbits. These orbits are the "wheels filled with eyes" that turn age after age upon their immovable axes, governing with celestial splendor the creatures of the lower worlds.

The pattern for the creation of the solar system with which we are most familiar applies to all others in our universal plan. This same pattern also governs all forms of life within the solar system, from the sun and planets to the grains of sand, atoms, and electrons. This is the Cabalistic concept of the macrocosm and the microcosm, or the greater and lesser creations, each patterned according to the other, and each supplying the perfect key for the interpretation of the other.

This led the Cabalists to say, when comparing man (the microcosm) with the universe (the macrocosm), that "man is a little universe, and the universe is the grand man." This does not mean that the universe actually resembles man in his physical form, but rather that the same internal system of geometry which patterned the world also patterned man, and that the same essences, principles, and forces, exist in both, and that both are equally responsible to keep the great laws which govern existence. The Elohim say, "Let us make man in our image." That is, let the lesser creation be patterned after the greater creation, and be similar to it in all essential principles.

Medieval theologians insisted that the seven creative periods called "days" in Genesis made up together a veritable week similar in length of time to a week of mortal calculation. This, the wiser of the ancient philosophers always denied, insisting that the term *day* in Genesis referred to an age, cycle, or great period of time. In the Chaldeo-Babylonian tablets, Ishtar, the great goddess, speaks: "Six days and nights the wind, deluge, and storm overwhelmed. On the seventh day, in its course was calm the storm, and the deluge."

Science makes use of such terms as *period* or *age* to signify one of the major divisions in the unfoldment of the earth and of the living creatures evolving upon it. Thus we have such terms as the *Miocene age,* or the *glacial period.* It is not profitable to attempt to summarize the scientific position, as this is subject to almost constant revision. According to present opinion, it is not inconceivable that the earth has existed for from 500 to 1,000 million years. Recent discoveries would indicate that animal life has existed upon the earth for many millions of years. When these figures are compared with the older theological opinion that the earth was created by the arbitrary will of God in the fifth millenium B. C., it is apparent that these schools of thought have come to a parting of the ways.

The modern Bible student, if he is acquainted with the old commentaries on the sacred books, finds, however, ample grounds for reconciliation. The trouble does not lie on the level of understanding, but on the level of misunderstanding and, to a degree, is due to the limitations of ancient language. There is much confirming testimony to indicate that the account of the genesis given in the Bible was originally intended to describe how the creating powers of Nature, obeying the will of God, brought forth sequentially the superphysical bodies of the solar system, and then the material planets. Finally, shifting perspective to the earth itself, the account describes the unfolding of life upon the earth to its present state.

The descent of the Elohim, with their hosts of attending spirits, into the swirling mists of primordial substance, and their molding of these mists into the sidereal patterns and bodies which we can recognize and understand, constituted an involuntary process, or the descent of the qualitative spirit into the substances of matter. The unfolding of the world through the manifestation of ever improving types of life, or, religiously speaking, the release of consciousness through a concatenation of improving vehicles, corresponds, at least to a degree, with the Darwinian statement of evolution. There can be no real argument between science and religion on a philosophical level. The difficulty is principally due to the extremely compressed description of the creative act as given in Genesis. If the reader can take such a statement as "and God created," and understand it to mean, "the universal spiritual energy, operating through the forces of Nature, brought into manifestation over a vast period of time," most of the difficulties will be overcome.

It should be clearly realized that the ancients understood their gods as creative hierarchies or vast archetypal images, and not personal deities performing strange sorceries in space. The aspects of creative conscious intelligence gradually unfolded through their own creations, revealing the divine plan through the geometry of growth. In the Egyptian rites, it was said that the gods impregnated space with themselves, and that the seeds of these divine natures grew and unfolded, and that this growth was the universe. It was held that the Divine Power is forever unfolding in and through the universal formations. Evolution is really internal life ideating or shining through material organisms much as the light which shines through the glass of the lantern. Evolution is also, therefore, the process by which the spiritual internal of things ever builds more perfect forms through which to express or reveal its own potentiality.

In Genesis, the anthropological sequences are unfolded in some detail. Cosmogony is a framework to explain the appearance of man and the means of his formation or generation. There are two distinct accounts of what at first appears to be the production of the human being. The first is contained in 1:26-28. The first part of verse 26 reads: "And God said, Let us make man in our image, after our likeness: . . . " The wording in the King James Version is rather confusing. That the Creating Power was not a single being, but the Elohim, is evident from the use of the pronouns "us" and "our." It is not safe to assume that the royal plural is intended, considering the antiquity of the language. If, in reading this passage, the plural word *Elohim,* which appears in the original, is substituted for *God,* the inconsistency is entirely clarified.

The word *said* is not to be understood as speech in the human sense; it means *to will,* to inwardly determine, or to pronounce as an edict. The same thought is implied in the Tibetan creation myth, where the worlds are formed by the meditations, or the internal mental determination, of the Dhyanas. In the Gnostic and Hermetic writings, the Elohim or builders gave to man a certain part of their own natures so that when the human being was finally completed, he participated in all the universal powers, and in addition possessed the life-essence of the Eternal Father.

Verse 27 reads: "So God created man in his *own* image, in the image of God created he him; male and female

created he them." This further confusion of pronouns indicates the trend to emphasize a monotheistic concept of
Deity. Yet in the original, the creating power is still called
Elohim, and the old text definitely implies the likeness, similitude, or universal archetype, of man, and not a person.
In the second chapter of Genesis, there is another description
of the human creation. The context indicates definitely that
this second process of generation is not merely a restatement
of the first, for it occurs after God has blessed the seventh
day, and the first creation took place on the sixth day. At
the end of verse 5, it is clearly stated " . . . and *there was* not
a man to till the ground." Obviously, then the man created in the first chapter was not of the earth-earthy. The
7th verse of chapter 2 reads: "And the LORD God formed
man of the dust of the ground, and breathed into his nostrils
the breath of life; and man became a living soul."

It is further noteworthy that the translators now introduced the term *Lord God* or *Jehovah Elohim,* translated by
d'Olivet as *He-the-Gods.* It can be suggested, therefore, that
one of the creating powers became especially associated with
the ensouling of man. It is also interesting that the first
man described in Genesis 1:27 is not called Adam; in fact,
is not named at all. There is another curious implication
in Genesis 1:28 where Elohim are made to say to the man
they have fashioned: "Be fruitful, and multiply, and replenish
the earth, . . . " This certainly sustains the concept in the
Zohar that there were worlds and orders of life prior to the
account given in Genesis, and that the creation was actually a re-creation following a period of universal sleep or
darkness.

According to the old commentaries, this first man of
Genesis 1:27 is the Heavenly Man, whose parts and members are composed of the ten *Sephiroth.* This is the Grand

Man of the Zohar, with his head in heaven, one foot upon the earth, and the other upon the sea. This being is reminiscent of the great image of Nebuchadrezzar's* dream, with head of gold and feet of clay. This is the Idea-man, the archetypal man of Plato, and the Protogonas of classical speculation. The explanation of this account is that man in his human form is the most perfect of all generated symbols of the universal plan. Mortal man was fashioned in the image of the heavenly man, and embodies within his human structure the proportions of the entire order of the universal scheme.

This idea of man, which exists in the higher worlds as a thought in the Divine Mind, is a restatement of the heavenly unity on one of the planes of Nature. This concept of unity divides within itself, but is itself not divided. Thus, the one archetypal man contains within its nature the mystery of all races, tribes, clans, and brood-families that have populated or will populate the earth. This archetypal being, the first un-named man, of Genesis 1:27, is that vast mystery "whose body Nature is, and God the soul."

The second man, of Genesis 2:7, is said to represent the human species as we know it, and in the 19th verse, he is called by the name *Adam*. This is from the Hebrew *ADM*, which is still a collective term meaning a species, a type, or a kind, and which certainly was not intended to signify merely an individual or one person. In the Cabala, this man is called *Adam Kadmon*, or "the species formed of the red earth." The meaning of *red earth* in this sense is most obscure, but certainly has no reference to physical soil of that color. It has been suggested that the universe was fashioned of a fiery nebula or whirlwind, that the planet was once in a state of violent volcanic upheaval and combustion, and that

---

*Preferred spelling. Usual Biblical form is *Nebuchadnezzar*, notable exception being the Book of Jeremiah, where *Nebuchadrezzar* is used.

the whirling fire-mists of that time were the red earth. There may also have been legends that primitive man was of a reddish hue, with reference to his Mongolian progenitors.

According to the Zohar and other commentaries, the Heavenly Man emerged from the highest primordial obscurity and created the earthly Adam in his own likeness and image. Originally, this earthly man dwelt in a luminous atmosphere above the surface of the earth. His body was composed of a kind of radiance like the world in which he lived. He dwelt with the angels, but he was by spiritual potential superior to them. The sphere of luminous ether or energy in which Adam resided was the paradise, the heavenly garden, the abode of immortal beauty, and the sphere of wisdom, truth, and happiness. It was while in this paradisiacal condition that Adam attended the school of the Cabalistic Mysteries in the eternal temple, and became inwardly informed, or received into his own nature all the branches of the sacred sciences.

Adam was greater than the angels because in him converged all the laws, principles, and images of the heavenly archetype. The process of man entering into physical existence, or of his birth as the terrestrial Adam, was preceded by an elaborate evolutionary program. Strange forms were fashioned by the forces of life striving together in the prehistoric world. These forms have vanished away, and only myths relating to them have survived. They were not habitable by creatures possessing minds, and they endured only for a time in the alchemistical laboratory of evolution. It was only after millions of years of growth and development that forms were generated suitable to manifest the power of the man who had been fashioned by the Elohim. The forms which could not be used were called the mindless, the shadows, and the monsters, and are described by Berosus in

his *Chaldean History* as composite beings made up of animals, birds, and fishes, some with many heads and arms.
They are also referred to in the Cabala as the *Kings of Edom,*
the terrible giants who perished in the void. Genesis 6:4
states: "There were giants in the earth in those days." In
the secret writings, Adam is described as the perfect microcosm, fashioned in the image and likeness of the heavenly
man. One of the reasons why he was greater than the angels was because in the angelic order the principles of physical creation had not been perfected or unfolded.

The parable of the Prodigal Son is supposed to conceal
the Cabalistic account of the relationship existing between
the angelic and human life-waves. The virtuous sons, who
remained at home, signify the angelic order, and the prodigal son, who went forth in pride and arrogance to waste
his substance in riotous living, signifies the human order.
After descending to the lowest and most corrupt condition
of mortality, which is referred to as the "flesh-pots of Egypt,"
the prodigal son repents of his sins and returns, weary with
worldliness, to his father's house. For him, the feast was
prepared because he had been lost and had been found
again; had died and was alive again. In spite of his numerous sins and failings, the estate of the prodigal was higher
than that of his virtuous brothers, for he had gained experience, wisdom, and understanding, and had chosen to restore a virtuous way of life while his brothers had remained
secure in the house of their father—their heavenly home.

Most of the ancient philosophies of the world have
taught that life descended onto the physical planet from a
sphere of superphysical energy which encloses the earth.
Curiously enough, this old opinion survives, and recent researches have revealed the existence of living spores in the
stratosphere. Some scientists have come to the conclusion
that space may be alive with these spores, which, like drops

of condensing water, ooze out of the etheric field of the solar system. It may not be proper to suggest what ultimate findings will be, but it is possible that the ancient sages and mystics were essentially right when they taught that life comes to planets from the atmosphere.

Boehme, the German mystic, describes the celestial man who dwelt not upon the earth, but in some heavenly place —a generality which may imply this etheric diffusion. The ancients believed that even the process of human incarnation involved the descent of the superphysical principles of knowing from a humid region outside the earth. This humidity is described by the old mythologists as a river dividing the material world from the spiritual universe. To the pagan Greeks, this river was the Styx, and to the Christians, it is the Jordan, with the host of the redeemed gathered upon the distant shore. It is the same mysterious ocean across which the Ship of the Doctrine bears the faithful, according to the Pure Land Sect of Northern Buddhism. The Greek poets wrote of the herds of souls floating in the mist which divides the world of the living from the world of the dead. By the world of the living, we generally imply the physical plane, and by the world of the dead, the subjective superphysical universe. But as Plato points out, it might be more correct to reverse this concept, for it is those who are bound in physical bodies who are most truly dead.

In the Biblical story, the paradisiacal sphere where Adam dwelt before his fall into the mysteries of generation, is called a *garden,* and it has been variously located by religious enthusiasts on many parts of the earth's surface. Eden is not, however, on the earth's surface at all, if we are to believe the old account. It is above the earth, in the higher etheric element which encloses the planet in a globe of translucent energy. The four rivers which flow out of Eden are the four streams of ether or energy which sustain the four kingdoms of the physical world as these were understood by the ancients: the mineral, vegetable, animal, and human. Man is physically nourished by the vital ethers of his nature. These ethers now work through his body, but in pre-Adamite time he possessed no physical body, and these ethers formed his only vestment.

Many Eastern sages believed that the Garden of Eden was located in the area of the North Pole or, more correctly, in the air above the Pole. The study of cell life shows that impregnated cells develop first from their north polar caps, and it was believed that the same was true of planets with all their planes and orders of life. The first connection between the etheric world and the physical globe was said to have been established at the Pole. Physical life, moving downward from its etheric over-state flowed toward the terrestrial poles, which were the first parts of the physical earth's surface to crystallize or harden.

It is therefore stated that in the beginning of time upon the earth, the gods brought forth the seeds or germs of life in the area of the earth's north polar cap. This descent of the gods is described in Genesis 6:2: " . . . the sons of God saw the daughters of men that they *were* fair; and they took them wives of all which they chose." The cooling of the earth's surface resulted in the gradual liberation of the elements. These elements, moved by the will of the gods, were assembled into forms and patterns, even as the impregnated cell gradually builds an organism capable of sustaining individual and even intelligent existence.

The first bodies were fashioned of air, mist, and water, for these respond most easily to the impulses of the creating will. When these vehicles, first fashioned of the more subtle parts of the world-substances, had sufficiently developed, the grosser elements of matter were introduced, and "the soft forms hardened." It was then that the spirits, fashioning and directing the development of form, and still residing in the etheric region above, entered into the bodies which they had prepared. In the Bible, these spirits are called the "sons of God," and the bodies which they had resolved to inhabit were called the "daughters of men." So the spirits, seeing that the bodies were fair—that is, were capable of sustaining consciousness—descended to them and took "wives" of all which they chose.

The daughters of men were, more correctly, the daughters of Manas, or mind, for in its oldest form, the word *man* literally means *mind*. While dwelling in the paradisiacal state, the entities which we now know as human were androgynous, as it is explicitly stated, "male and female created he them." These entities possessed inwardly the potentiality of both positive and negative manifestation. The Edenic Garden contained not only the rudiments of human existence, but also the other kingdoms which were to be manifested. It was therefore a kind of superior earth in which forms of life developed and prepared themselves for physical embodiment. The old mystics also remind us that the wise who live in this world are building superphysical bodies in which to function when the race that we know has finished its physical evolution.

Philo Judaeus declared the air to be full of souls. Those nearest the earth were drawn into bodies and, becoming tied to mortal forms, lost their spiritual perception, and desired to remain in the material sphere. So complete was their absorption into the physical state, that they then prayed not to die; that is, not to be separated from their bodies. The mystical sect of the Essenes held that there was a storehouse of souls, and that from this reservoir of lives those seeking birth descended from the pure air, and were chained in vehicles composed of the elements. It is worth noting that Plato believed that human souls descended into matter as drops of luminous substance falling from the milky way, the heavenly seed-ground of lives. To descend into the illusion of the earth's humidity, was to be intoxicated with darkness and to drink of the waters of Lethe, which flowed from the fountain of forgetfulness.

Adam was given dominion over the magical etheric garden and all the seeds of the several kingdoms which existed together in paradise. The power was given to the intellect of Adam so that he was able to "name," that is, to know and understand, all the creatures in their essential natures. It is said that when Adam was only one hour old, God assembled the animals before him and the angels. When the angels were asked to name the many kinds of animals, they could not do so, but Adam spoke without hesitation. Then it was that God asked Adam what his own name should be, and he replied that he should be called Adam because he had been created out of *Adamah*, the dust of the earth. On this occasion, also, God asked the man he had fashioned to name his own creator, and Adam replied that the name of God should be *Adonai*. It is also reported by legend that Adam invented the art of writing and devised the seventy languages.

The creation of woman represented a division within the body of Adam. By this separation, the androgynous creature was prepared for the laws governing the sphere of generation. The Cabalist doctrine, however, does not lead inevitably to the popular belief in soul-mates; rather, the androgyne or asexual creature became male-female, or bisexual. The cleavage was psychological—another division within unity. Thus Adam became the father of generations, and all the races which make up the children of Adam became races of male and female creatures. In the Authorized Version, the Creating Power is said to have caused a deep sleep to descend upon Adam, and from his side, Eve was created.

This was first a polarization of the psyche, which was divided into its male and female aspects, now referred to in psychology as the *animus* and the *anima*. In man's internal life, this polarity is clearly revealed under psychological analysis. It is written that the true companion of man must be of his own body and being: "Only when like is joined unto like the union is indissolvable."

There is an interesting psychological fable bearing on a phase of this concept. Prior to the creation of Eve, it was said that Adam created within himself a mate from imagination. This imaginary or magical complement was called Lilith, the projection of the neurotic instinct of the Adamic creature. Lilith is referred to as the "demonic wife" of Adam, and from this union was born a progeny of monsters. The mystery of Lilith is intimately involved in the circumstances of the symbolical "fall."

The fall of Adam was essentially the extension of certain parts of the Adamic being into the material state. The human soul remains androgynous, and only appears to be male and female when it descends into the sphere of generation. The old mystics accepted the doctrine of reincarnation, and in their philosophy they described the periodic descent of souls into the abyss of illusion. During this process, the unity of the invisible and superior parts of consciousness was obscured.

The third chapter of Genesis opens with a description of the serpent, and contains the account of the temptation and fall of the first man. In the original Hebrew, the serpent is distinctly associated with the volative power of man himself, so that the temptation comes through man and not to man. It was believed in the magical Cabala that the serpent was the symbol of the power of Samael, the Archangel of Mars and the master of subtle arts. In ancient Scriptural writings, serpents are frequently used to represent currents of energy or waves of force moving in space. They are also frequently associated with the processes of generation, and are symbolic of the sexual urge in living creatures. No symbol is more diversified in its meanings or implications than the serpent.

The Midgard snake of the Nordic *Eddas,* and the Orphic serpent twined around the egg of the year, are symbols of the zodiac, the serpentine course of the sun, or the nodes of the moon. The erect serpent of Egypt and the hooded naga of India and Cambodia signify the human spinal column. The winged serpents of the Gobi, and the Taoist dragons of China, represent the psychic forces within the human soul and also the great initiate teachers, sometimes called the *sky-men,* who possess the secrets of human regeneration. The Amerindians of the Southwest have serpent symbols of similar meaning, and Quetzalcoatl, or the Feathered Snake of Central America, is symbolic of the initiated high priest or teacher of mankind. The Druid priests of the British Isles and Gaul called themselves serpents, and these are probably the snakes that St. Patrick is said to have driven from Ireland.

The Bible student should be acquainted with these accounts, for it is only by the aid of comparative religion that the average person can interpret in a satisfactory manner the serpent symbol in Genesis. The astral light, or the sphere of imagination and desire, was believed to be under the dominion of Samael. In the older commentaries, Samael appears as the adversary. Yet, in the Authorized Version there is no explanation for the existence of the tempting serpent, or why the all-wise Creator should have placed in the Garden this evil creature to corrupt the noblest of the divine works—man. The Persian poet Omar sounds this complaint when he asks why the Deity "with paradise devised the snake."

After the creation of Eve, Samael appeared to her in serpent form, and tempted her to eat of the fruit which the Lord had forbidden her to touch. Samael, the angel of poison or death, is sometimes presented in the Bible under the name of Satan, although there were Cabalists who distinguished between these two beings. It is said in the Talmud that Satan, the angel of death, descends and seduces, ascends and accuses, and then descends again and kills. Cain, the fratricide, was believed to have been the son of Eve and Samael. A part of the key to the riddle lies in the metaphysics of the Persians, whose philosophy, in turn, was derived from the most ancient religious mysteries of both the Near and the Far East.

In this system, good and so-called evil are but the aspects or qualities of one principle. Creation brings into manifestation the innumerable hosts of lives which lie asleep in the infinite. In this respect, creation is release or expression, and therefore good. But creation also implies certain limits and boundaries placed upon the duration of space. Thus the very world which is man's sphere of opportunity is also his living tomb, and in a sense, therefore, it is evil and adverse to that luminous inner self that must dwell so long in bondage to matter. Every action of the Creating Power is understood as releasing or bringing into manifestation not only a good angel, but an evil spirit which is its adversary.

There is a simple example of this in the modern problem of invention. Whenever a man invents something new and useful, or improves some old device to make life more secure and comfortable, abuse inevitably follows. Good laws are perverted by selfish men; great ideals are compromised and applied to numerous purposes inconsistent with the original intent. Primitive man realized this, and the earliest sacred writings described the universe as a battlefield of good and evil impulses, usually personified as gods and demons.

Even as God was the chief and lord of all the benevolent forces, so the evil agency, or negative reactive attributes, were personified as offending beings under the leadership of Satan, Lucifer, Yama, Loki, Hades, or Kali. In the third chapter of Genesis, therefore, this eternal adversary is Samael, who, like Mephistopheles in Faust, is "a spirit of negation; part of the power that still works for good while ever scheming ill."

In the formulas of Buddha and Pythagoras, unity alone abides in perfect wisdom, for wherever there is division, desire is born. Desire is possible only under the concept of diversity, and possessiveness is one of the first of those illusions which flow from desire. This, in turn, leads to an innumerable array of other ills, and is itself rooted in ignorance, which is substantially man's inability to perceive the sovereign wonders of all things. Thus division is the source of a kind of darkness which obscures the spiritual life of the world.

The third chapter of Genesis further explains that there were two trees growing in the Garden of Eden. One is the tree of the knowledge of good and evil, and the other is the tree of life. The symbolism of these trees requires some explanation, for it belongs to one of the oldest phases of man's religious understanding. The world-tree is the earth's axis in nearly all ancient mythologies. Trees are also symbols of evolution and unfoldment because all life, tree-like, emerges from one root and seed. The Cabalistic tree of the *Sephiroth,* with its ten symbolic blossoms, is based upon the tree of life in the midst of the Garden of Eden.

Special trees have particular symbolisms, as the pine tree of Atys, which has become the modern Christmas tree. The "Cedars of Lebanon" was a veiled reference to an ancient order of Syrian priests dwelling in that region. According to one derivation, the word *druid* means *tree,* and these

British sages were called the "men of the oak trees" because they performed rituals in groves of oaks and gathered mistletoe therefrom. The dryads were the tree-spirits of the classical Greeks. All these interpretations are significant and interesting, but there is another example of such symbolism more immediately relevant.

Early anatomists recognized two great systems in the body of man: the arterial system, which they likened to the tree of life, with its roots in the heart; and the nervous system, which they associated with the tree of the knowledge of good and evil, with its roots in the brain. These two trees bear witness to the physical manifestation of a complicated network of energies and forces essentially superphysical. In the old diagrams, the tree of life was often represented as inverted, with its roots in heaven, or in the divine substance, and the tree of the knowledge of good and evil was depicted as growing upward from the earth. This total concept signified that grace or spiritual reality comes from God, whereas knowledge and wisdom grow upward through the unfolding experience of mortal life.

In medieval art, it was customary to represent the tree of the knowledge of good and evil in the form of an apple tree. This fruit has been concerned with two important episodes in the history of man: first, the apple eaten by Eve; and second, the apple that fell on Newton's head. Both incidents, of doubtful historicity, have certainly modified the course of history. The older mystical writings seem to suggest not an apple, but a pomegranate. The Greek statues of Demeter and Persephone frequently depicted these fertility goddesses holding pomegranates. This fruit also had a place in the rituals of the Eleusinian Mysteries, and seems to be the original of the Chaldean "apple."

It may be mentioned at this point that there is a strong possibility that the opening chapters of Genesis, like the com-

plicated mythology of the Egyptian Book of the Dead, were
originally part of a ritualistic drama representing initiation
into the higher grades of a secret school or a system of State
Mysteries. This is further substantiated by the legend that
primordial humanity attended a celestial academy while still
abiding in the heavenly region, and that the wisdom so ob-
tained was preserved by an unbroken hierarchy of initiated
priests after the symbolical fall into a physical state. Subsequent to the creation of Eve, the angel Raphael visited the
Garden and discoursed with the progenitors of mankind concerning the mysteries of the soul. Thus, one key to the fall
of man, brought about through the disobedience of Adam
and Eve and the eating of the forbidden fruit, is that it was
a veiled representation of the effort of mankind to secure the
keys to the mystery of life without being duly and truly
prepared and properly initiated. It was, in other words, an
effort to storm the gates of heaven in violation of the laws
of the secret school. For this violation, primitive humanity
was exiled and caused to wander in the outer world.

By another interpretation, equally useful, the serpent-
tempter, Samael, is caused to personify the intellectual principle. That such a concept is not extravagant is evident from
the admonition of Jesus, "Be ye wise as serpents." The intellectual principle leads to the experience of conscious self-
responsibility. This results in an exile from the Edenic
Garden of innocence, the state of spiritual infancy. The
evolving intellect of primitive man brought with it a gradual
extraversion. From an inward contemplation of spiritual
principles, man came to recognize an external life. Slowly,
the inner senses were dimmed and the perceptive powers
correspondingly strengthened. The result is man's present
state, in which he has slight awareness of an internal existence, and has become overly conscious of the significance
of outward circumstances. Thus the outer life is the re-

lapsed or fallen state, and the inner life is the paradisiacal or Edenic state. The resurrection promised by the Messianic Dispensation is the restoration of the inner life and the conquest of the external or sensory sphere. This is clearly revealed in the teaching of Buddha, and is an essential part of the dicta of Plato.

The Creating Power, manifesting through its aspect as natural law, then pronounced a curse upon the disobedient mortals. They were doomed to the cycle of birth and death; they were no longer supported and sustained by inward understanding and could not speak with the gods who walked in the Garden. They were required to work out their salvation with diligence, in a universe of doubts and fears. Ixion was bound to his wheel, and "the cycle of necessity" gained dominion over the divine sparks—the host of Edenic souls. In Genesis 3:21, it is explained that the Creating Power fashioned for Adam and Eve "coats of skins." The Zohar describes these coats as a kind of firmament or sky surrounding and enveloping the microcosm or little universe. These coats gradually became physical bodies, the mortal vestments of immortal life. Man's memory of his heavenly state was obscured by these material forms, and he was cast forth from the abode of peace.

At the gate of Eden, the Creating Power placed cherubim and a flaming sword to guard the sacred Garden so that Adam and his progeny might not be able to return to it again until the day of the resurrection. It is interesting that Solomon, when he built the Everlasting House, placed upon the doors of the temple cherubim with a flaming sword. This strengthens the belief that at least part of the mystery dealt with old temple rites. Eden was the first Holy of Holies, and as such was identical with the adyta of ancient temples. It is also the heart, the Sacred Place, the Pyramid of Hermes, and the Buddhist Cavern of Seven Rooms. To enter the sanctuary, really meant to attain to a state or condition of sanctity. Temples are not only buildings, but symbols of an exalted level of consciousness to be approached by the disciplines of meditation and realization. One who attains this exalted state within himself gains entrance to the Holy Place, which is guarded from the profane by the appointed keepers of the gate—the testers or initiators. Philo Judaeus declared the cherubim to represent clouds or obscurations which concealed Eden from the profane. These clouds are mortal ignorance or perversion, which must forever obscure sacred things until regeneration dissolves illusion.

In Chapter 4:1 of Genesis, Eve says: "I have gotten a man from the LORD." Some of the commentators have declared that this indicates that Cain was not the child of Adam, but of the archangel Samael, the old serpent, that mysterious luminous power at the root of all human perplexities. In the Authorized Version, the translation is so obscure that both the Lord and Adam are referred to as the fathers of Cain, but the old scholars and rabbins should have known their Scriptures better than the 17th-century theologians of another faith. The ancient commentaries insist that Cain was the son of Samael, and Abel the son of Adam. Cain was therefore the embodiment of the power of cosmic fire, the Martial principle, and Abel, the son of water, the agrarian principle. It was for this reason, the Chasidim explained, that the offering of Cain was not acceptable to the Lord, leading to the first crime, the murder of Abel.

After the fall or descent into the material state, two orders of human beings are therefore reported. Cain, the son of the angel of fire and death, became the progenitor of those who built cities and went forth to conquer the world. In the sons of Cain ambition ruled all other emotions, for in them were the seeds of rebellion against the laws of the creating life. That this story also relates to Mystery rituals is suggested by the words of Voltaire when he wrote that the Samo-thracian Mysteries were the account of a brother slain by his brethren. Early efforts were also made to identify the drama of Osiris and Typhon with the Abel-Cain story.

If, by Adam, is also to be understood the *anthropos,* or the collective and individual overself of man, there is an analogy with the incarnating human ego, the one father of all the bodies that are manifested by an entity during its cycle of rebirth. The fall of Adam would then depict the descent of this egoic vortex into the sphere of generation. By union with the humid principle, or the psychic power of Eve, the ego begins its generation of bodies, a mystery cunningly concealed under the genealogies or descents of the patriarchs. In the process of generation, polarity must first be established. In the Chinese cosmogony, which by proper interpretation is also a version of anthropology, creation arises from the endless striving of two principles called Yang and Yin. In the Greek system, ether and chaos are the polarities from the minglings of which the cosmos is fashioned. As the physical universe is engendered from the opposing of polarized forces, so in like manner the human soul arises from the strivings of the polarized will, and by an alchemy within consciousness itself.

Jacob Boehme depicted this striving within the self by a series of symbolic figures showing the eternal battle between light and darkness, action and inertia, wisdom and ignorance. Johann Gichtel later illustrated Boehme's principles with a series of curious engravings, now extremely rare, which provide a valuable key to a mystical interpretation of the Scriptures.

Cain and Abel can represent, therefore, the first discord or confusion arising in the superphysical psychic organism of man. It is evident that the allegory has a universal application; otherwise it would not be part of the Mystery rituals of so many ancient religions. Furthermore, it is known that all these rituals relate primarily to the unfolding of the human soul. It must therefore follow that Cain and Abel represent two parts of man's inner consciousness. Boehme created the terms "self-will" and "divine will" with which to designate the two parts of man's internal nature which are ever in a state of mutual contention. The allegory of Lucifer and his battle with Michael the Archangel, has similar interpretation. War in heaven means conflict within the soul or the superior inner nature, as contrasted to wars on earth, which relate to the body and the inferior outer nature.

By this allegory, Cain represents self-will, the active principle. His descendants become builders of cities (bodies) and workers of metals (the sense perceptions). Cain may also be understood as a symbol of the human mind, which, rebelling against limitations, seeks to gain dominion over life through the powers of thought and reason. Tubal-cain, a descendent of Cain, described in Genesis 4:22, who later occurs prominently in Masonic allegories, was the first to pound swords into ploughshares. He therefore represents self-discipline as an aspect of self-will by which the destructive emotions are refined and tempered.

If, then, Cain and Abel are the divided halves of the human will, born like Castor and Pollux from a single golden egg (the ego), we can understand why the Greeks symbolized the soul as a sphere composed of gold and silver hemispheres joined together. Abel, in the Biblical account, brings his offering, the "firstlings of his flock," to the Lord (Law). By old symbolism, this means that he brought the animal propensities of his own nature, for such is always implied by the burnt offerings referred to in the Scriptures. Because he brought "the animal," his offering was accepted.

Cain, on the other hand, brought the fruits of the ground (material substances), and these were not accepted. The fruits are here used to represent not the principles of the soul, but the consequences of action. Cain gave of what he had, his accumulations or possessions, but Abel gave of what he was, the "firstling," his own transmuted animal nature. Cain, incensed because the Lord favored the offering of Abel, slew his brother. This is reminiscent of the words of the Indian classic: "The mind is the slayer of the real." The allegory, therefore, has extraordinary significance, for it is the very key to the mystery of worship. It explains why most faiths are deficient in their deeper parts. As long as ceremonialism obscures the inner perceptions, and words and formulas are regarded as more important than deeds, so long will the creeds of the world continue in useless conflict on a theological level.

The fifth chapter of Genesis is devoted to the genealogy of the patriarchs from Adam to Noah. It will be observed that in this chapter there is no mention of either Cain or Abel. Seth is established as the founder of the races of the earth, begotten in the image of Adam, his father, even as in his turn Adam was begotten in the image of the Lord, the creative hierarchy. Seth therefore became the symbol of the heart doctrine which would attain reunion with the spirit by mystical atonement. From the children of Seth came the shepherds (the wise teachers) and those who lived in simple ways and rejoiced in the goodness of God and were humble in their hearts.

In the invisible atmosphere to be found only in sleep and trances, the demon children of Lilith continued to dwell in the sphere of imagination, the false paradise. They became the temptresses of subtle ambition and discontentment, luring those who long to improve their physical estates but have not the strength of character to build better lives for themselves. Today, in a strange way, the sons of Cain and Seth continue as the workers and the dreamers of the world. The descendants of Cain created the state, and the descendants of Seth fashioned the church. Like fire and water, these elements have ever striven against each other, but in the end they must be reconciled if the heavenly world is again to be manifested upon the earth.

Much has been made by Biblical students of the extraordinary length of life attributed to the patriarchs. In Genesis 5:5, Adam's age is given as 930 years, and in verse 27, Methuselah is recorded as living 969 years. In the old legends, it is told that the Lord allotted one thousand years to the life of Adam, but because of the strength of his inner vision, Adam knew that one was to come whose name was David, and he would be King of Israel, but the Lord had allotted him only one year of life. So Adam gave to David seventy years of his own life. It should be understood that all such references and the numbers of years are Cabalistic symbols. They refer not to the span of historical individuals, but to the duration of families, clans, and orders of blood descent, for it was believed in those days that a man continued as long as his progeny endured. Also, in the Jewish system of metaphysics, each of the numbers is symbolic of certain Hebrew letters. These letters, in turn, form words, according to the hieroglyphical system attributed to Moses. Proper decipherment of these symbolic ages reveals the astronomical and cosmological import of the patriarchs and their lives.

Realizing that in the original work Adam was not an individual, but the human life wave, it follows that his children and their children unto the ninth and tenth generation signify the branchings and forkings of the racial tree, and also the differentiation of the cyclic currents of energy by which the life of man and of his world is sustained. This explanation solves such problems as arise in Genesis 4:17, where the wife of Cain is mentioned although the Scriptural accounts imply that at that time Cain and Abel were the only progeny of Adam, supposedly the only man in the world. Also in the same verse, Cain builds a city which he names after his son. One man could scarcely build a city, nor could the abode of one man and his son be properly termed a city. But when we realize that Cain is a race, we then understand that the story of Cain's wanderings is also an account of racial migration.

By Seth is to be understood a new generation, one that takes the place of an earlier creation that has failed. There is an Hermetic legend that the first creatures who inhabited the earth were destroyed by the gods. Among these were the *Sheddai,* the antediluvian kings recorded in the Zohar. The third of the children of Adam, which was Seth, may well represent the third race, known in legend as the Lemurian. It was in the later sub-races of the Lemurian race, according to Asiatic tradition, that the human being we now know as man was fully differentiated from the animal prototype. Thus, in Lemuria, the true man came into being. The concept that man was formed as the vehicle for the embodiment of the "thinker," provides the explanation for the opening verses of chapter 6. Thus Seth can stand for the physical archetype of man, even as Adam represents the spiritual archetype of humanity. By this interpretation, Adam as the complete psychic entity, is polarized or divided, and these divided parts are called Cain and Abel. Seth is established between them as the reconciler, and in all creatures descended from him, both the conflict and the reconciliation must exist.

THE LUNAR ARK ON THE FACE OF THE WATERS

CHAPTER VI

FROM NOAH TO THE TABERNACLE

The fourth and fifth chapters of Genesis are concerned with the generation of Adam. It will be noted that in chapter 5 no reference is made to either Cain or Abel, and it is stated only that Adam begat a son in his own likeness, and called him Seth. The ten Biblical patriarchs of the ancient line, therefore, according to the Sethite descent are: Adam, Seth, Enos, Cainan, Mahalaleel, Jared, Enoch, Methuselah, Lamech, and Noah. There is also an alternate genealogical table, called the *Kenite,* which places Cain in the position occupied by Seth in the Sethite line, and changes several of the other names, making Tubal-cain occupy the tenth place in the descent. There is much to indicate that these patriarchs are identical in meaning with the *Pradjapatis* of the Hindus and the *Sephiroth* of the Jewish Cabalists. It is also believed that the ten patriarchs are associated with the ten signs of the zodiac according to the ancient system which preceded the division into twelve signs.

In the Sethite table, Seth occupies the most important place after Adam in the order of the patriarchs. He is referred to as "the first of the perfect men." According to old commentaries on Biblical lore, there were thirteen men born perfect. The Christian inference based upon this concept is that in the end, these thirteen will appear as the Messiah and his twelve disciples. There appears to be at least an indirect reference to this mystery in the words of Christ: "Before Abraham was, I am" (John 8:58) and "Ye have been with me from the beginning." (John 15:27). The thirteen perfect men represent the flowering of the ages. In each order of descent of the patriarchs, there is one who is perfect. The first was Seth, and the second was Noah.

In the Kenite genealogy, or the line of descent from Cain, every fifth patriarch was a murderer. In the case of Lamech, because he was blind, he used to hunt with the aid of his son, a small child. This boy, perceiving a strange object at a distance, and thinking it to be an animal, pointed his father's arm so that Lamech shot the creature, and it fell dead. But upon approaching, they discovered they had killed a human being. The little boy explained to his blind father that the man who lay dead before them had a horn in the middle of his forehead. Thereupon Lamech fell on his knees in great anguish and cried, "I have slain my own ancestor, Cain!" For the Lord had placed a horn upon the forehead of Cain, that every man should know him.

THE "ROYAL ARCHES" OF ENOCH

In Genesis 5:18-24 it is stated that Jared begat Enoch, and that when Enoch was sixty-five years old, he begat Methuselah, and that all the days of Enoch were three hundred and sixty-five years. Then Enoch walked with God and was not, because God had taken him. According to a curious work describing the ascension of Enoch, he was carried through the seven heavens in a manner reminiscent of the Apocalypse of St. John and Mohammed's Night Journey to the celestial regions. He then returned to earth for thirty days to instruct his sons. When this time was ended, the Lord sent a darkness upon the earth, and in this darkness, the angels carried Enoch away so that he passed into the divine abode without death.

Accounts differ greatly as to the exact time at which Enoch lived. According to some opinions, he flourished before the deluge of Noah, and inscribed the wisdom of the pre-historic world upon pillars which survived the destruction of the Atlantic empire. The Greek philosopher, Solon, visiting Egypt in the sixth century before Christ claimed to have seen and examined these pillars in a subterranean temple near the banks of the Nile. In the Cabalistic writings, Enoch, the second messenger of God, was one of the Messianic descent, or perfect men. He is said to have departed from the earth because of the wickedness of mankind. God so loved Enoch that he transformed him into a celestial being, and he was called *Metatron,* or the Angel of the Lord, and he is said to have been reborn on earth as Jesus, the son of Mary.

One of the most interesting legends associated with the story of Enoch is the apocryphal account of the building of the "Royal Arches." With the aid of his son, Methuselah, Enoch is said to have created a subterranean temple. This consisted of seven rooms, one above the other, each with an arched ceiling. Descending from one room to another in the heart of the earth, Enoch placed in the lowest of the arched chambers a golden delta, or triangle, with the secret name of God inscribed thereon. After the translation of Enoch, the site of his temple was lost, and for centuries men sought in vain for the secret rooms. Later, when Solomon resolved to build the Everlasting House upon Mount Moriah, his workmen, while digging the foundations of the temple, discovered the sealed vaults of Enoch. Solomon's temple, therefore, was built upon the site of the mysterious structure contrived by Enoch, the ruler and teacher of men.

In modern Freemasonry, much of the symbolism of the "Royal Arches" of Enoch is carefully preserved. Again we are in the presence of an astronomical mystery. The seven rooms, one above the other, represent the orbits of the planets. Thus, we have another ziggurat, but this one inverted and descending into the earth. The golden triangle concealed in the lowest room is a symbol of the divinity, or tri-form creative energy, locked in the deepest parts of matter. In man's nature, the golden delta may also stand for the three-fold structure of consciousness, with its attributes of will, wisdom, and action, locked or hidden within the deep substances of man's material nature. By another interpretation, Enoch is the human spirit itself, the builder of the seven-bodied or seven-fold corporeal constitution. For the spiritual part of man is the only part which can walk with God and cannot know the mystery of death.

NOAH AND HIS WONDERFUL ARK

There is an ancient legend that Noah was born with white hair, a strange, prematurely aged creature. This so vastly amazed Lamech that he hastened to his father, guide, and counselor, the wise Methuselah, saying: "What manner of offspring or son is this?" Methuselah replied: "He is the one who is to bring the oblivion, therefore thou shalt name him 'Rest' or 'the Suspension that is to hang above all things.'" Because of these words, the child was named Noah, which means "rest" or "that which moves not and is suspended above the oblivion."

Chapters 6-9 of Genesis are devoted to the story of Noah and his ark. In order to understand this story, it is again interesting and useful to have recourse to some of the early Jewish commentaries. Noah is the second Adam, and he becomes the foster-father of the human family, according to the Jewish metaphysical system. The parallels between Adam and Noah are numerous. Adam ate of the forbidden fruit, and Noah drank of the fruit of the vine, which was not lawful. Both Adam and Noah became aware of their nakedness, and both had three sons who were to be the progenitors of races.

As Noah saved his family and carried it over the darkness of the deluge, he was also regarded as a prototype of the Messiah. According to Christian mystics, Noah preserved the just from destruction because he was obedient to the will of the Lord, and it was early believed that the Messiah would carry the souls of just men over the Armageddon in that time to come when the world would be destroyed by the divine wrath. Noah was associated with the zodiacal sign Pisces because this sign is the end of the great cycle and also heralds the coming of a new order of existence. In Chinese mysticism, there is a similar account of the good man, his wife, their three sons and three daughters, being preserved in a ship to become the progenitors of a new human race. It is obvious, therefore, that the story relates to cosmic occurrences.

In most of the ancient writings, Noah's ark did not actually or literally mean a boat. Its name signified rather some peculiar form of enclosure, a superior place to which men could go for refuge, and the idea of a boat floating on the waters of the universal night was a poetic form developed by later theologists as a symbol of the ship of salvation. Philosophically speaking, the ark symbolizes a spiritual sphere or over-state, above the material world, which survived the disintegration of the physical universe. Briefly, then, the ark of Noah, with its three decks, represents the three parts of the divine world, or the archetypal region. The ark, as its symbolism develops, is evidently a miniature of the universe.

According to astro-theologists, the ark is shown to be the zodiac, the grand body or sidereal being containing within itself the seeds of all living things. The astronomical key to the symbolism is revealed through the Ptolemaic system of astronomy. In the night of the cosmic oblivion which follows the day of manifestation (the Hindu days and nights of Brahma), the seven spheres which make up the lower creation are dissolved one by one and absorbed back again into the cosmic substances from which they originally emerged. The first sphere to be absorbed is that of the physical earth. After that comes the Lunar sphere, then the Mercurial, the Venusian, the Solar, the Martial, the Jupiterian, and lastly, the Saturnian. This order corresponds with the orbits of the seven planets in the ancient cosmic theory. As explained in Greek mythology, Saturn, or Chronos, the last and highest of the planets, ultimately devours all of his children. This means that during what the Hindus called the *Pralaya*, or *Cosmic Night,* the lower world sleeps, and everything that is below the zodiac rests in a state of non-manifestation. The lives which have manifested in the solar region (solar system) are preserved in their spiritual or seed natures in the ark (arc) of the zodiac, which turns securely around the face of the oblivion.

According to this same interpretation, the mundane universe is enclosed by a crystalline sphere of stars called the angelic world. This sphere also is divided into three parts, according to a rule familiar to the ancient astronomer. There was a northern hemisphere of stars and a southern hemisphere, and these were separated by the equatorial belt called the zodiac. These three parts of the heavens may also be

likened to the three decks of the ark, and are further personified as the three sons of Noah. The mast, which Noah
placed in the center of the ark, is the polar axis.

We learn from the Talmud that Noah took into the ark
three hundred and sixty-five kinds of reptiles, and thirty-two
major divisions of animals. Since the serpent was often used
as a symbol of the year (consider the Aztec calendar-stone),
the three hundred and sixty-five reptiles could significantly
stand for the days of the year. The thirty-two major divisions of animals correspond suspiciously with the thirty-two
paths of wisdom described in the Cabala. These paths consist of the ten *Sephiroth* and the twenty-two letters of the
Hebrew alphabet.

Some fragments of the mythology of Noah and his ark
are not well known to modern Bible students. According to one of these, there was an animal called the *reem,*
which was too large to get into the ark. In order that it
might also be saved, Noah tied a rope to the animal and
allowed it to swim behind the vessel. This legend seems to
have been derived from the same source as the Hindu account of the fish Avatar of Vishnu. This describes how the
god Vishnu assumed the form of a great fish and pulled the
ark of the Hindu Noah through the sea by a rope fastened
to its back.

As all the principles of life had to be enclosed within the
ark, it was necessary for the archetypal image of the material
world to be there also; otherwise the great form of the world
could not again come into being. Therefore, we learn
from the ancient writings that in the days of Noah, there
was upon the earth a very good and wise giant who was
named Og, King of Basham. As Og was too large to get
into the ship, he is described as seated astride the roof, being fed by Noah through a small hole or window.

It was most necessary that the deluge should accomplish precisely the purpose for which it was intended. For this reason, the ancient writers go into considerable detail in describing how the oblivion was brought about. As the accounts are all intended to symbolize the processes of cosmic night, apparent contradictions or inconsistencies are not especially important. Each legend must be analyzed only in terms of its own context. There were giants upon the earth, and if the waters of the deluge came from below, the giants were strong enough and sufficiently numerous to close the fountains of the earth. If the waters came from the heavens above, these same giants were so tall that even if the earth's surface should be inundated, they could still escape. These giants probably represent the lower mental powers of man by which he is enabled to preserve himself against physical disasters. To solve this problem, the divine powers caused the substances of the deluge to flow first through the sphere of Gehenna, the place of subterranean fires, and thus to flow forth as a blazing deluge upon the places of the world, destroying all things. It is obvious, however, that Noah's wooden ship could not have floated on a sea of fire, nor could the kindly reem have endured such combustion. From these accounts, it is evident that the old scholars did not consider the deluge to have actually consisted of water or of fire, but the terms are used to imply substances of oblivion.

The same old philosophical commentators describe the waters of the deluge as both male and female. This is because part of the water descended from above the firmament and part came up from the abyss. The two streams then mingled in Gehenna, and flowed forth upon the temporal earth. The male and female waters are those described in the first chapter of Genesis as the waters which were above the firmament and the waters which were beneath the firmament.

To release from the firmament the upper waters which were to bring about the deluge, the Lord God removed two stars from the constellation of the Pleiades, and to stop the flood he replaced them by taking two stars from the constellation of the Great Bear. The two stars borrowed from the Great Bear belong to the constellation which guarded the pole, that is, pointed the way to Polaris. This account certainly veils those cosmic processes contributing to the re-establishment of the material creation by the restoration of the polar axis.

When the flood subsided, the ark came to rest upon Mount Ararat. This is the polar mountain, the Olympus of the Greeks, and the Meru of the Hindus. Thus the story implies that the higher or superior parts of the physical world were the first to be restored. This would correspond to the orbit of Saturn which is directly beneath the zone of the fixed stars. Saturn corresponds with the first of the Elohim, because he is the eldest of the seven planets, or Chaldean gods. It is this same Saturn who said in the beginning, "Let there be a firmament in the midst of the deep." When the first day of the re-manifestation began, the creation began to awaken from the sleep of solar night. The Saturnine principle of crystallization re-awakened to mold space, and a firmament was manifested.

Mount Ararat, upon which the ark finally rested, thus symbolizes the foundation of the new creation. It is the first sphere of the renewal of life, and because of its exalted quality it is represented as a high peak. But the old mystics would hardly have identified it with the physical mountain of that name in Syria. When the ark had come to rest, and the Holy Spirit or Breath of Life in the form of a dove was sent forth, the new day of manifestation began. From these suggestions and commentaries from various sources, it becomes evident that the story of Noah is much deeper and far more significant than would at first appear from the Biblical account. It may be proper, therefore, to discuss other legends bearing on the subject.

The ark of Noah, under its symbolism as a box or container, occurs in the religious teachings and sacred rites of many ancient peoples. The Ark of the Covenant with its holy relics was carried by the Jews throughout their long wanderings in the wilderness. A similar ark was venerated by the Egyptians, who depicted it in bas-relief on the temple of Philae. In the Egyptian legend of Osiris, the body of this god was sealed in an ornamental box or ark and cast into the River Nile down which it floated to Biblos. Deluge stories are to be found in the mythologies of most ancient civilized nations of both the Eastern and Western hemispheres. For the most part, these accounts have been either completely rejected by modern science as fabulous, or entirely accepted by theology as actual. The possibility of a secret or allegorical meaning has been generally ignored.

In Jewish metaphysics it is taught that superior principles reflect themselves into the material world, casting their shadows, so to say, into the substances of the deep. This is in agreement with the Hermetic law of analogy, which declares that those things which are below are like those things which are above. By an extension of this law, it was long believed that the spiritual body of man is reflected in his corporeal structure, the physical body being the lengthened shadow of the soul. Every part and member of the human body, every function and process taking place within it, bears witness to cosmic laws eternal in the heavens; that is, existing forever in the spiritual region.

The ark has been called the symbol of the sea. Metaphysically, this sea, in the case of man, is represented as a spiritual vortex containing within it the germs or life-principles of man's mental, emotional, and physical natures.

This archetypal sea, being reflected downward, became by Hermetic analogy the physical body itself within which, as within an alchemical vessel, the processes of generation and life take place. Physical man is therefore a unity, one living creature suspended from a unity—one spiritual entity. The body is a physical manifestation of recondite and invisible agencies, and is fashioned like its cause, and bears witness to the immutable workings of universal law.

Plato refers to the physical body by likening it to the shell of an oyster, and in another place, he calls the body "the sepulchre of the soul." This sepulchre, sarcophagus, or burial chest, is associated with the ark of Noah. The thoughtful student will therefore realize that the account of the deluge has several widely different meanings. One relates to the sphere of causes, and another to the lesser sphere of man's human life. We can never cease admiring the rare skill with which the ancient Scriptural writers incorporated many meanings into a single story. The Bible itself, therefore, like the truth for which it stands, may well be "all things unto all men."

Great wisdom was needed for the building of the ark, for all living creatures had to be provided for. Noah acquired the necessary knowledge from a book which had been given to Adam by the angel Razael, in which all earthly and heavenly knowledge was recorded. Later the angels, fearing that Adam would become all-knowing, stole the book and cast it into the sea. Adam fasted many days, and God appeared to him and instructed Rahabab, the angel of the sea, to recover the book and restore it to Adam. After the death of Adam, the holy book disappeared, but later the cave in which it was hidden was revealed to Enoch in a dream. From this book, Enoch became so wise that his wisdom exceeded the wisdom of Adam. After he had committed the book to memory, Enoch hid it again so that it might not fall into the hands of the profane.

When the Lord resolved to cause the flood upon the earth, he sent the Archangel Raphael to Noah, bringing the holy book, which included full instructions for the building of the ark. Noah took the book, which was made of sapphire, with him into the ark, having first encased it in a golden casket. During the time he was in the ark, the book acted as a timepiece, for it distinguished day from night. After the death of Noah, the book was entrusted to Shem, and he in turn bestowed it upon Abraham. From Abraham it descended to Jacob, then to Levi, Moses, and Joshua, and finally to King Solomon, who learned all his wisdom from it, including his skill in the healing arts and his mastery over demons.

According to the Biblical account, the deluge continued for forty days and nights. This is a round numerical term standing actually for the significant number forty-two, just as the number seventy in the Old Testament actually implies seventy-two. It is written that seventy elders were selected, six from each of the twelve tribes. It is obvious that six times twelve cannot be seventy. In the Apocalypse it is said that it was for a time of forty-two months that the gentiles trod over the outer court of the temple. It is also stated in the same work that for forty-two years (that is, periods or eras of time), the seven-headed serpent shall have power to blaspheme. Jesus fasted for forty days and nights in the wilderness, even as Noah is said to have floated for forty days and nights through the deluge. This numerical symbolism implies that Noah and Jesus have certain symbolical parallels on the archetypal level. Ciphers are frequently rejected when interpreting the meaning of numbers. Thus the 144,000 in Revelation, the number of the redeemed, may be read as merely 144, which is twelve times twelve and

refers to the zodiacal cycle. The forty days of Noah, therefore, can also represent four cycles or vast periods of time.
This might hint an association with the Atlantean or fourth
race, which is supposed to have perished in a deluge.

It is recorded that Noah carried the body of his ancestor,
Adam, with him into the ark, and when the deluge had
subsided, he re-interred the body on the hill of Golgotha.
Adam, of course, represents a type or life-principle which
lives eternally in its progeny or creations, and is the true
germ of fertility by which its descendants are made fruitful.
The Greek mythology gives a descent of deities from the
first and eternal principle, which is denominated "unaging
time." In the mundane order of gods—that is, the hierarchy
controlling material creation—unaging time, the primordial
principle, is manifested through Zeus, who is termed the
son or offspring of First Cause. If we consider the primordial Adam to be a symbol of the eternal principle of life,
then Noah, like Zeus, becomes the mundane manifestation,
or direct descendant, of First Cause. This explains why
Noah is sometimes called the second Adam.

If we see the ark as a figure of the physical universe, we
can understand how all living things are grouped together
in one small vessel of three decks, the measurements of
which are entirely symbolical. We can also understand why
this strange ship should have but one window, a problem
that has greatly perturbed agnostics. The Chinese have a
patriarchal family which they regarded as the ancestors of
mankind. This family is an ogdoad, or a pattern of eight
principles. These are Khwan and Kheen, the male and female potencies, and their six combinations, which are called
sons and *daughters*. These eight principles were instructed to
fashion an ark in order to escape the universal deluge.

Plato used the story of the lost continent of Atlantis to
veil the secret of man's descent into oblivion or the mortal

state of ignorance. There can be no doubt of the direct relationship between the story of Noah and the lost Atlantis,
but most writers have been unable to clarify the original tradition. Noah, born with white hair and prematurely aged,
is easily recognizable as the symbol of mind, or that which
is above the confusion of matter or can attain to this state
of security by being attentive to the instructions of the creator-
gods. Noah is therefore the Knower, or the intellect, and
Og, King of Basham, the good giant, is the personality or
body-consciousness, as can be learned from the Cyclopes
myths of the Greeks. Like the Cyclops, Og can also be recognized as the over-soul, or anthropos, the one-eyed giant
who is too great to be contained within the body, but sits
on the roof; that is, dwells in the upper parts of the magnetic field which envelops man, and is fed through the one
small window, the pineal gland, or third eye, of the soul—
the "eye-single" of Scripture.

There is also a legend to the effect that a baby was born
in the ark. This is the psychic being, or divine infant, born
within the chemistry of the body, and destined to achieve
the redemption of flesh. It is identical in significance with
Harpocrates, the infant god of the Egyptians described in
the Osirian rites. This infant is the celestial self—the Christ
Within—born amidst the animals, for the ark of Noah and
the manger of Bethlehem also have a common meaning.

The ninth chapter of Genesis describes a covenant between Noah and the Creating Power. In Genesis 9:13, the
Lord is made to say, "I do set my bow in the cloud, and it
shall be for a token of a covenant between me and the earth."
Among ancient peoples, the rainbow was regarded as a
bridge connecting heaven and earth. In the Norse mythology, this is the *Bifrost,* the arc of light upon which the Aesir
climbed to the royal palace of Asgaard. The seven colors
easily distinguishable in the rainbow have always been sacred

to the creating gods; in this case, the Elohim. And from the earliest times, priesthoods distinguished their ranks and offices by the color of their garments. Even in the Christian church, certain colors are associated with the saints, with the persons of the God-head, and the various ranks of the clergy. The Gnostics related color and sound, assigning one of the notes of the scale to each of the spectrumatic colors. As the white light of the sun contains within it all the colors of the spectrum, so the divine effulgency, the eternal light of God, though in itself colorless, contains a spectrum of powers, creating principles or gods, which emerge from it and become the formators of the world. When these gods blaze forth and their colors are revealed, it is a sign that the vast processes of universal formation have come into manifestation.

It cannot be supposed that ancient peoples were entirely conversant with our modern scientific concepts of light and color. But they did associate the seven colors with the planets, the worlds, the invisible heavens, and the orders of angels and celestial beings which embody the numerous aspects of the Divine Nature. Thus, the rainbow is an appropriate symbol of the restoration of the orderly procedures of Nature. In it were visible together, in their proper sequence, the colors and energies of the seven worlds which are to be reborn from the oblivion. The appearance of the rainbow at the end of the deluge therefore appropriately symbolized the restoration of the energy of the Logos through its seven principles—the builders of the cosmos.

The reborn universe, according to the old accounts, was divided among the sons of Noah, who thus become symbolical of the reappearance of the creative trinity on the level of material generation. To Shem was given the center of the world or, said the Chaldeans, the central band of constellations—the zodiac. To Japheth was assigned the northern part of the world and the northern constellations; to Ham, the southern extremity of the heavens and likewise of the earth. Of the parts and members of the Grand Man of the Zohar, Shem received, therefore, the heart as his throne or dominion; Japheth received the brain; and to Ham was given the generative system, symbolizing the power of growth.

Through consciousness (Shem), intelligence (Japheth), and force (Ham), the creative triad came forth again after the oblivion. Ham is called the *Dark One,* because he represents the physical universe and the dark earth which is its most appropriate symbol. From Shem, Japheth, and Ham, descended the races of humanity, and to this newly established humankind was given the collective term *Israel.* The word *Israel* signifies not the Jewish people alone, but all humanity, and the evolution of humankind in the period subsequent to the deluge is symbolically described by the wanderings of the twelve tribes of Israel. These tribes are twelve orders of human beings, a constellation upon the earth analogous with the twelve signs of the zodiac in the heavenly band above.

THE TOWER OF BABEL

It came to pass that during the lifetime of Noah, princes were appointed over the descendants of Shem, Ham, and Japheth. One of these rulers bore the name of *Nimrod.* It seems that when Noah entered the ark, he had taken with him the coats made of skin which the Lord had bestowed upon Adam and Eve before they were cast out of paradise. When Nimrod reached his twentieth year, his father, Cush, gave these garments to him, and when he wore them, Nimrod was an invincible man. Not knowing the source of his strength, his followers regarded him as superhuman, and it was said of him: "Since the creation of the world there has been none like Nimrod, a mighty hunter of men and beasts, and a sinner before God." A great throne was built for Nimrod, and when he sat upon it, all the nations came and paid homage to him. The most godless of the acts of Nimrod was his resolution to build a tower in Babylon, which was to be a monument to rebellion against heaven.

It is reported that six hundred thousand men labored upon the great tower, which was built in Shinar, and the workmen were of three kinds, according to the nature of their resolutions. The first resolved to ascend to heaven and engage in war against God; the second intended to set up their own idols in the firmament; and the third resolved to destroy heaven with arrows and spears. The construction of the tower was crude, and it took a great deal of time to make the bricks, but these rebellious workmen labored with great zeal, and at times they shot arrows against heaven, and when these fell, they were red with blood.

Most early representations of the Tower of Babel show it to be constructed in the form of a Chaldean ziggurat, or astronomical observation tower. The ziggurat was a kind of artificial hill or tower with a circular stairway ascending in a spiral around the outside. Such buildings were either circular or square, and examples of both types exist in various parts of the world. Ruins of such ancient structures have been found in Egypt and in the Valley of the Euphrates. Reconstructions of the Hanging Gardens of Semiramis, Queen of Babylon, included among the seven wonders of the ancient world, invariably show this type of architecture. About fifteen miles southwest of the ruins of Babylon, rises the Mound of Birs-Nimrud, marking the site of the ancient city of Borsippa. There are two large mounds of ruins in this area, and excavations were first attempted by the French in 1852. The southwesterly of these mounds, usually called the *Birs Proper,* is actually a ruined ziggurat. Modern ar-

cheologists are of the opinion that the original structure had
never been completed, but that Nebuchadrezzar had faithfully attempted to fulfill the work of some illustrious prede-
cessor. The ziggurat stands upon a hill about a hundred
feet high, and rises as a jagged spike of riven brickwork,
vitrified by some terrible fire—probably the result of a war.

Sir Henry Rawlinson learned, through his excavation at
Birs-Nimrud, that the original structure had consisted of six
distinct platforms, or terraces, each of which was about
thirty feet high and forty-two feet less in horizontal length
than the one below it. The entire arrangement constituted
an oblique pyramid, the terraces in the front being thirty
feet in depth; those at the rear, twelve feet; and those at the
sides, twenty-one feet each. On the sixth story of the pyramid, stands the vitrified mass which was once the sanctum
of the temple. Built into the corners of the walls of each
terrace were the cylinders of Nebuchadrezzar, which referred to the complete structure as "The Stages of the Seven
Spheres of Borsippa." Each level of the pyramid was dedicated to one of the planets, and had been stained with the
color usually atttributed to that planet according to the
teachings of the Sabian astrologers. This system is still traditionally preserved in the Chaldean theory of planetary influences.
The lowest stage was colored black in honor of Saturn; the second, orange for Jupiter; the third, red for Mars; the fourth,
yellow for the Sun; the fifth, green for Venus; and the sixth,
blue for Mercury. It is likely that the temple which sur-
mounted the pyramid was colored white to represent the
Moon. From present calculations, the ziggurat was about
two hundred and seventy-two feet square at the base, and
about one hundred and twenty feet high, not counting the
temple on its summit.

The references to the Tower of Babel in Genesis are believed to refer to such a building as that described by Sir

Henry Rawlinson. The word *babel* is merely the native name of Babylon, and literally means "gate of God." Apparently, the Hebrews associated this word with their verb *balal,* "to confuse or confound." This would be natural as the result of the Babylonian debaucheries which led to the condemnation of their culture. It is evident that ancient towers or ziggurats, like the minarets of Mohammedan mosques, were symbolically intended to signify a link between heaven and earth. The astronomers, ascending their towers, studied the heavens from which they derived their prophecies and predictions, and were therefore believed to have communed with the gods and to have received from them all wisdom and knowledge.

The Tower of Babel, as described by the learned Jesuit father Athanasius Kircher, was also the prototype of Jacob's ladder, which led up to the seven worlds or orbits of the planets to the sphere of the zodiac. This is the same ladder described in the Apocalyptic vision of St. John. It is also the "ladder of silken cords" upon which Mohammed ascended through the seven gates of the world. In the sacred language of symbolism, the Tower of Babel has many meanings. It is a form of world-mountain—Asgaard, Meru, Olympus, the axis mountain of the ancient Egyptians—and the symbol of the North Pole of the earth. It is the *escalier de la sage,* or the philosophical ladder of the Mystery Schools, the rungs of which are the degrees of initiation. A pyramid of seven steps was used in the sacred rites of Mithras, celebrated both in Persia and in the catacombs under Rome. Man, climbing upward along the seven stations of the initiatory rites, was declared to be ascending toward the gods. This is intimated in the Homeric account of the Cave of the Nymphs. The levels and platforms of the Babylonian ziggurats were appropriate symbols of the planes of consciousness through which the human soul ascends toward reality.

It is the seven-runged ladder of the Neoplatonic disciplines, ascending from ignorance, through the levels of knowledge, to illumination. The ancient Table of Cebes is arranged in the form of a ziggurat, with humanity ascending toward the temple of the deities upon the cloud-capped summit. This is also Lord Bacon's *Scala Intellectus,* which he also called the *Pyramid of Pan,* through which he diagrammatically unfolded the gradual ascent of the sciences.

The Tower of Babel can also represent the physical earth itself. Nearly all the ancient observatory towers had seven steps rising from a broad foundation. The foundation in this case signifies physical matter, and the ascending platforms are the superphysical parts of the earth's septenary constitution. An abridged form of this symbolism is preserved in the Calvary of three steps which supports the cross or crucifix when it stands on the altar of the church. The Tower of Babel is furthermore man's seven-fold constitution, through the perfection of which he rises from the darkness of materiality until he attains to the apex of his own nature. This regeneration or restoration brings him into closer proximity with the Divine Principle, so that he is said to become "as a god, knowing good and evil."

In the Biblical account, Babel is man's monument to pride, and before it was finished, the creator-gods confused the tongues of men and prevented the completion of the tower. In Genesis 11:7, the Lord is made to say: "Go to, let us go down, and there confound their language, that they may not understand one another's speech." Thus, the word *babel* has come to mean a confusion of tongues or a chattering of persons who do not understand each other's words. Commenting on the confusion of tongues, Louis Ginzberg writes: "Thenceforth none knew what the other spoke. One would ask for the mortar, and the other handed him a brick; in a rage, he would throw the brick at his partner and kill him. Many perished in this manner, and the rest were punished according to the nature of their rebellious conduct. Those who had spoken, 'Let us ascend into the heaven, set up our idols, and pay worship unto them there,' God transformed into apes and phantoms; those who had proposed to assault the heavens with their arms, God set against each other so that they fell in the combat; and those who had resolved to carry on a combat with God in heaven were scattered broadcast over the earth. As for the unfinished tower, a part sank into the earth, and another part was consumed by fire; only one-third of it remained standing. The place of the tower never lost its peculiar quality. Whoever passes it forgets all he knows." (See, *Legends of the Jews*).

When the time came that God resolved to confound the builders of Babel, he called upon the seventy angels who surrounded the throne (the seventy-two names or powers of God in the Cabala), giving them the power to punish the arrogant generation who labored upon the works of Nimrod. He did not destroy the people because he had made a covenant with Noah to preserve the races of mankind. It is also noted that this is one of the occasions on which God descended upon earth, and it is written that he comes down only ten times between the creation of the world and the day of judgment. After the confusion of the tongues, God and the seventy angels cast lots for the various nations, and the lot of Israel fell to God. Also, the Hebrew language was given to Israel because it was the language which God used in the creation of the world. Such legends indicate the trend of mystical Jewish thinking.

The confusion of tongues is symbolical of the perversion of the ancient Mysteries, and also of that intellectual darkness which descends upon man as punishment for the misuse of his God-given powers and faculties. In pride and arrogance, human beings were resolved through the increase of arts and sciences to attack heaven and take over the management of the world. As self-will grew within them, their intuitive faculties were darkened, and they were no longer able to speak or understand the universal language. Thus it came about that the secrets of the inner wisdom were lost, and it was said that the gods punished mankind for its presumption and vanity. The same story occurs in Greek Mythology, and underlies part of the myth of Prometheus. Outwardly, there are many languages, but within the soul there is one mysterious symbolical alphabet of archetypal patterns and designs. When man departs from a simple way of life, burdens his intellect with false doctrines, and ceases to venerate the spiritual source of his own nature, he loses his ability to share in the divine wisdom.

It is said that while studying the stars from the heights of their ziggurats, the Chaldean astronomer-magicians discovered the sacred alphabet of the constellations, which is referred to again in the account of the handwriting of heaven which appeared on the wall at Belshazzar's feast. The Hebrew alphabet, with its tiny flaming points, is said to be composed of letters derived from the forms of star groups. For details concerning this sacred alphabet, consult *Unheard of Curiosities Concerning the Talismanic Magic of the Persians*, by James Gaffarel, Counselor to Cardinal Richelieu.

Melchizedek, King of Peace

The Book of Genesis is divided into two general sections. Chapters 1-11 cover the creation of the world, the flood, and the dispersion of peoples. Section 2, extending from chapters 12-50, is devoted to the history of the patriarchs, beginning with the life of Abraham. The Biblical narrative names Abram, later Abraham, as the ancestor of the Hebrews and the first of Israel's patriarchs. Following the command of God, he departed from his home, which was in Ur of the Chaldees, and, sustained by the divine promise that he would become the founder of a mighty nation, he journeyed to Canaan. Genesis 14 describes a battle during the course of which the cities of Sodom and Gomorrah were pillaged, and Lot, the son of Abram's brother, was taken prisoner with all his goods. When Abram learned of this, he armed his servants, pursued the conquering kings, defeated them, and rescued Lot and many other captives. It was on his return from this victorious expedition that the King of Sodom came forth to meet Abram, and with him also came Melchizedek, King of Salem.

Although the reference to Melchizedek, beginning Genesis 14:18, is extremely brief, it has held great fascination for both Jewish and Christian writers. It may be useful, therefore, to approach the subject first from the Christian viewpoint. In the Epistle of Paul to the Hebrews (7:3), this ancient Priest-king is described as: "Without father, without mother, without descent, having neither beginning of days, nor end of life; but made like unto the Son of God; abideth a priest continually." In the same chapter, verses 17 and 21, Jesus is likened to Melchizedek. The entire chapter should be studied, for it gives a summary of beliefs that must have been current at the time of St. Paul. In chapter 7:15-17, the Apostle acknowledged Melchizedek to be of a priestly order apart from the patriarchs and the prophets, and assumed his association with the Messianic Dispensation. St. Paul writes: "And it is yet far more evident: for that after the similitude of Melchisedec there ariseth another priest, Who is made, not after the law of a carnal commandment, but after the power of an endless life. For he testifyeth, Thou art a priest for ever after the order of Melchisedec." The last part is directly taken from Psalm 110:4: "The Lord hath sworn, and will not repent, Thou *art* a priest for ever after the order of Melchizedek."

According to the account in Genesis, Melchizedek brought bread and wine, thus instituting a sacrament which is preserved in Christianity in the account of the Last Supper and the Sacrament of the Eucharist. Because of this, the name of Melchizedek is placed in the Canon of the Mass. Early in the rabbinical mystical tradition, a supernatural origin was associated with Melchizedek. Philo Judaeus regarded him as "the logos, the priest whose inheritance is the true God." St. Paul suggested that Melchizedek, like Jesus, was immaculately conceived, but the account is also susceptible of another interpretation. When the strange King of Salem became the priest of the most high God, it is supposed that he renounced all worldliness for a lonely existence in which he accepted neither parent nor kin, having been born again as a new being in the spirit.

Some early writers have attempted to identify Melchizedek with Shem, the son of Noah, which would, of course, conflict with the tradition that he had no earthly parents, and support a mystical interpretation of the statement. St. Jerome, the Church Father, speaks of Shem-Melchizedek, and there are legends that this great Priest was the only man then alive who had lived before the deluge and therefore possessed the secrets of the antediluvian world. Later Christian authors preferred to consider him a descendant of Shem, a view held also by Moslem writers. Abram is said in ancient lore to have studied in the Academy of Shem-Melchizedek at about his 51st year. There is also a stray legend to the effect that Melchizedek, like Adam and Seth, was born circumcised, and that he spoke immediately after his birth, praising the mysteries of God. It is not remarkable, therefore, that an heretical Christian sect, called the *Melchizedekites,* should have come into existence. They regarded this ancient Priest as a heavenly being superior to Jesus.

Melchizedek is said to have assisted David in the writing of the Psalms. Later, this eternal Priest offered bread and wine upon the altar at the center of the earth near the place where Shem and the angel had deposited the body of Adam. This legend makes Melchizedek a descendant of Shem. On the occasion of the meeting of Melchizedek and Abram, the Priest blessed the Patriarch. In so doing, however, he named Abram first and then God. (Genesis 14:19-20). Because he named Abram first, God was offended at Melchizedek and took from him his priestly dignity and bestowed it upon Abram and his descendants. This account is ignored in the New Testament, where it is the obvious intention of St. Paul to preserve intact the descent of the spiritual authority of Melchizedek. When it is said that Melchizedek visited the center of the earth and was later buried there, it is assumed that the site of Jerusalem was implied.

In his *American Antiquities,* Josiah Priest refers to Melchizedek as the "Adam of God." By this is implied a divine order of spiritual leaders, created, not generated, fashioned by the divine will as the archetype of sanctity. Under this concept, Melchizedek, King of Salem (Peace), represents universal wisdom, the eternal and dedicated servant of the living God. He also personifies the various sources of knowledge and binds the early Jewish lore to the great Mystery School systems of surrounding nations. Gesenius translates the name Melchizedek as meaning "king of righteouness." Josephus identifies Salem with Jerusalem, implying an earlier community on the site of the sacred city. The name of this ancient "Prince of Peace" invites further careful examination. Melchizedek can also be translated as "hail to—" or "honor to - " or "power to Sedek." Therefore, the name can be freely translated, "the authority of Sedek" or "Sedek is king." Thus Melchizedek, King of Salem, really means "Sedek, King of Peace." The word *Sedek* is Egyptian. Sedek was the father of the artificer gods of Egypt. Faber, in his great work, *The Cabiri,* says that in the Phoenician and Samothracian rites, the seven Cabiri—that is, the seven planetary gods that turn or move about the sun—are the children of Sedek. Melchizedek, therefore, is the Lord Sedek, the father of the planets, and the master of the Cabirian artificers. Sedek, like moses, the red-haired man, and Melchizedek, the King of Salem and the first priest of the Eucharist, are all solar symbols.

As the great orb of heaven, Melchizedek was his own father and mother, and a priest forever. Later, Christ was called "the light that lighteth every man that cometh into the world." Christ is therefore a type of the spiritual sun, the light-bearer, the Prometheus, or the light-bringer. The sons of the sun, the *Hershesti,* the children of Horus, are the light-bringers, the prophets, the teachers, and the army of the Lord under Michael, Archangel of the sun. As the physical sun dispels the darkness of night, so the prophets dispel the darkness of ignorance, and are honored and revered as the servants and messengers of the light of truth.

FROM ABRAHAM TO ISRAEL

In Genesis 17:1-16, it is written that the Lord appeared to Abram and made a covenant with him. On this occasion, his name was changed from Abram, which means "exalted father," to Abraham, which has been translated "father of a multitude." On the same occasion, the name of his wife Sarai, believed to signify "contention," was also changed to Sarah, or "princess." Some Biblical students have suspected that the name Abraham is derived from "A Brahman," indicating an importation of Oriental doctrines at some remote time in the history of the Jews. After the blessing of the Lord had come upon Abraham, his wife Sarah conceived, and a son was born. He was named Isaac, meaning "laughter" or "joy." In due time, Abraham rested with God, and was buried in the cave of Machpelah, near Hebron. When Isaac was full of years, his sight was dimmed, and as a result of the contrivance of Rebekah, his wife, be bestowed his blessing upon Jacob ("he supplants"), his younger son, instead of upon Esau, to whom the honor was properly due. It was this same Jacob who, sleeping with stones for a pillow, dreamed of the ladder connecting earth and heaven upon which the angels of God ascended and descended. This ladder is an ancient symbol for the orbits of the planets, and occurs in the sacred writings of several nations. It is also the ladder of the seven senses and the seven cardinal virtues by which man's salvation is assured. Ladders or flights of stairs, usually with seven rungs or steps, occur in the rituals of ancient Mystery Schools.

In Genesis 32 is described Jacob's wrestling with the angel, and the 28th verse reads: "Thy name shall be called no more Jacob, but Israel." This point is further emphasized in Genesis 50:2, the word *Israel* being used as a synonym for the name of Jacob. The verse reads: "And Joseph commanded his servants the physicians to embalm his father: and the physicians embalmed Israel." According to the Cabala, there are seven keys to the meaning of all the names, incidents, and circumstances set forth in the Holy Scriptures. Substantially, these keys are as follows: theological, cosmological anthropological, astronomical, mathematical, physiological, and theurgical. The so-called 8th key, corresponding to the eighth sphere, or the material world, was called historical, but was not considered of mystical importance.

According to the commentaries, the angel with whom Jacob combatted was the Archangel Michael, who was assisted by a host of other angelic beings. When Michael injured Jacob, God rebuked the Archangel, saying: "Thou art my priest in heaven, and he [Jacob] is my priest on earth." From the above quotation, it is obvious that the accepted translation of the word *Israel* is hopelessly inadequate. The secret meaning of *Israel* is "the objectified power of God;" that is, the Divine Nature as manifested through the universe of which the heavens with their stars are the highest visible part.

The astronomical key reveals that by Jacob we are to understand the sphere of the fixed stars; that same celestial world which Pythagoras called the parent of all celestial things. In the Greek mythology, the starry heavens are called *Argus,* a god with many eyes. These eyes are the archangels and the celestial hosts, for it is written that, "the eyes of the Lord run to and fro throughout the whole earth." The word *earth* in this sense means the world, or the solar system. Jacob (or Israel) being the whole of the starry heavens, his immediate progeny are the twelve constellations which form the zodiacal belt. In the Biblical allegory, these are figured as twelve suns. In the mystical teachings, the twelve zodiacal signs are the source of twelve great streams of life which, flowing through all parts of creation, fill the world with their progeny. The stars are the races of heaven, the population of the firmament, and they are ruled over by kings greater than any monarchs of the earth, and these are called the "Lords Over the Stars." When we think of Israel, therefore, we must consider not only a tribe of people or a nation, but the whole life of Nature originating among those heavenly spirits who at the dawn of time cast their shadows upon the deep.

Another key to the mystery of Israel interprets the fable anthropologically, or in terms of mankind. The twelve heavenly races of the sky are reflected upon the surface of the earth as the twelve tribes of Israel. This is the same as the statement by Pythagoras that souls come into birth through the bodies of the twelve holy animals. The popular belief that the twelve tribes of Israel make up only the Jewish nation is not in the spirit of the original meaning. Israel means all life. The tribes of Israel are the orders of living things. *Israel* is a generic term for humanity as a collective, regardless of race or nation. When this collective humanity is signified by a single term, it may be called Adam, or again Jacob. This is the same practice as that which we use when we apply the word *man* to signify either one man or all men.

THE EXODUS OF ISRAEL

The opening chapter of Exodus is devoted to an account of the oppression of the Jews in Egypt. Here again, history becomes the instrument of a secret mystical tradition. Egypt is not a country in this account, but a condition of obscured consciousness. The story of the wanderings of the twelve tribes escaping from Egypt is identical in meaning with the parable of the Prodigal Son, the wanderings of Ulysses, or the Adventures of Sinbad the Sailor. The same general meaning also may be discovered in the legends of the twelve labors of Hercules, who reappeared in Jewish tradition as Samson, whose name is also a thinly veiled reference to the sun.

The outpourings of universal light are measured by two vast cosmic motions. One of these is termed *involution,* or the descent of life principles into forms and bodies. By this process, units of divine energy take upon themselves vestments of obscurity fashioned from the material elements, until they are almost completely obscured by the forms with which they have surrounded themselves. This state is typified by the seed with its hard shell and the living germ concealed within it. A seed-pod may be called a calyx, which in turn is represented by a cup. Here is an important key to the cup of death presented to Christ in the Garden of Gethsemane. The second cosmic motion is called *evolution*. By this, life releases itself from form by the slow processes of growth. It may require aeons of time for the cosmic plan to unfold its internal mysteries through growth and to maturity, but by evolutionary processes, all things are ultimately released from bondage to form and restored to their divine state.

The bondage of the children of Israel in Egypt represents the nadir or lowest point in the involutionary process. The spiritual monads or germs have become completely enmeshed in the material elements. So it is said that the Israelites were strangers in the land of Egypt, even as man as a spiritual being is a stranger in the material world. Gradually, in due time, the forces of evolution assert themselves and the restoration, redemption, or ascension, of life begins. The wanderings of the twelve tribes symbolize the story of man's slow and painful course out of the state of darkness and ignorance and through the long struggle in the desert of hope and despair. Another key to this allegory is even more mystical. The human soul in a state of complete materiality is in bondage in a land of darkness. Man, searching for truth, is humanity collectively seeking for enlightenment, and the object of this search is well described as the Promised Land. Here, in beautiful and peaceful Canaan, the mortal quest ends in happiness, security, and the cessation of strife. This is in the spirit of the Buddhist nirvana, the internal peace which results from the restoration of man's inner life.

Thus, the Exodus of Israel is also part of an ancient initiation ritual depicting vividly the liberation of the human soul from bondage to its animal desires and aspects. With this perspective, the story of the forty years in the desert of waiting and the splendid leadership of Moses and Aaron becomes not only more meaningful, but has a direct bearing upon the present state of man. The wilderness is simply material life, where oases of rest and peace are few, and the hardships many. The search is always for that wonderful and abundant land, Canaan, the place of milk and honey. It is written in the 19th chapter of Exodus that it was in the third month after the children of Israel had gone out of Egypt that they came to the wilderness at Sinai, where the Tables of the Law were given unto Moses.

THE TABERNACLE IN THE WILDERNESS

The building of the Tabernacle is described in Exodus 25-27. According to this account, the design of the structure was revealed to Moses by the Lord upon the peak of Sinai. Moses assumed that he was to superintend the building, but the Lord said that this honor was reserved for Bezaleel, the son of Hur, for he was a man possessed of wisdom, insight, and understanding, and by these God himself had created the world. Bezaleel was of the noble tribe of Judah, and according to the divine will, another man was chosen, Aholiab, of the tribe of Dan, which was without reputation, in order that the great and lowly should be equal in the works of the Lord. This same allotment was made in later times when the great temple was built at Jerusalem. For Solomon was of the tribe of Judah, and Hiram was a Danite. In the construction of the Tabernacle, each man of the tribe was asked to contribute of his goods or his labor, but only according to the willingness of his heart. In the construction of a holy place for God, nothing could be demanded, for only that which was freely bestowed was acceptable in the sight of God.

In its form and arrangement, the Tabernacle appears to have been patterned after the great shrines of the Egyptians. This movable temple is a wonderfully appropriate symbol of an ideal spiritual institution. Truth does not abide in any one place, but moves about the earth and is entrusted in different times and under various situations to the noblest, wisest, and most virtuous of human beings. The Egyptians built their great temples, such as those at Karnak or Luxor, of everlasting stone, but nomadic shepherds and wanderers found a tent more practical than a permanent temple. Josephus, in his *History of the Jews,* gives an excellent description not only of the Tabernacle itself, but of its priests, its festivals, and its sacred implements. The mystical commentaries contribute a wealth of lore regarding every part of the Tabernacle and its equipment. They agree that the Tabernacle in the Wilderness is a figure or symbol of the universe, a microcosm, or miniature representation, of the whole vast sidereal order.

There were also learned rabbis of older days who insisted that the Tabernacle is made in the likeness of man himself —not only of his physical body, but of his complete compound constitution. As man is a miniature of the greater world, so the Tabernacle is an emblem or similitude of both the universe and man. The Greeks believed that creation itself was the first and most enduring symbol, and that man, when worshipping his God, should contemplate the mysteries of the heaven and of the earth. The universe is the living temple of that Universal Spirit who is the great architect of the world, and man's human body is the living temple of his own human spirit. The ancient commentaries declared that the great Tabernacle of the Lord is in the sun, and that in man the heart corresponds to the sun and is the proper dwelling-place of the Most High.

When the time came to build the Tabernacle, Bezaleel approached Moses and recommended that the Ark of the Covenant should be constructed first. In this way, the resting-place of the Torah was to be assured first, and afterwards the house in which it was to be enshrined. The tent of the Tabernacle and its environs were made of three parts. There was first an outer court consisting of a wall of curtains stretched between wooden uprights. Within this wall was the enclosure set aside for holiness, and in the midst of this enclosure, stood the Tabernacle itself—a tent-like structure divided into two rooms. The larger, or outer, room was of the proportion of a double cube, and the proportion of the inner room was of a single cube. The outer room was called the Holy Place, and the smaller inner room was named the Holy of Holies. These three parts of the Tabernacle were symbolic of the divisions of the universe as they were understood at that time. The outer courtyard represented the sphere of the elements, the symbols of material or mundane existence. The Holy Place, wherein stood the seven-branched candlestick, the tables of the shewbread, and the altar of burnt incense, signified the sidereal world, or astral sphere, containing the orbits of the seven planets. The small inner room corresponded to the sphere of the fixed stars, the upper heavens, or the constellational diffusion. The cherub figures woven upon the hangings of this inner room represented the star angels, whose shapes, filled with eyes, adorned the curtains of heaven.

The early writers emphasized that the separate parts of the Tabernacle revealed correspondencies between heaven and earth. They tell us, for example, that there are stars above, but also there are stars below, for "a star shall come out of Jacob." God has his dwelling in the empyrean, but his abode is also in the sanctuary of Israel. The creator stretched out the heavens like a curtain, and in the sanctuary there were curtains of goat's hair. The number of the vessels was seventy, like the names of God, of Israel, and of Jerusalem. Paracelsus, the Swiss Hermes, wrote that man's spirit comes from the stars, his soul from the planets, and his body from the elements. This is the arrangement followed in the structure of the Tabernacle, and is an important key to the interpretation of the architectural symbolism of countless shrines and temples.

The three divisions of the Tabernacle also bear witness to the three states of consciousness. The lowest is ignorance, the second is knowledge, and the third is wisdom or illumination. In the Tabernacle rites, these states of consciousness are personified as classes of human beings. Ignorance is assigned to the multitudes, who may bring their offerings but do not understand the sacred rites. Knowledge is represented by the priests, who serve within the Holy Place; and wisdom or illumination by the High Priest, for he alone could enter the Holy of Holies. Only perfect wisdom can gaze upon the face of the Infinite and live. There is also a tradition that the three parts of the Tabernacle correspond to the three revelations of the law given to Moses upon Sinai. The outer court is the Torah, or the written law; the Holy Place is the Mishnah, or the soul of the law; and the Holy of Holies is the Cabala, which is the soul of the soul (spirit) of the law.

The parts of the Tabernacle appear in nearly all ancient Mystery System rituals, and are still retained among groups perpetuating the old symbolism. There are three degrees in the Egyptian Mysteries of Osiris, three parts or dramatic episodes in the Eleusinian rites, and three degrees in the Blue Lodge of modern Freemasonry. One of the first great initiation temples of the world was the great Pyramid of Gizeh. This structure also contained three rooms, in order of ascent as follows: the subterranean chamber, the Queen's chamber, and the King's chamber. Neophytes entering this house of hidden places seeking the Master of the secret house, passed through elaborate rituals performed in these chambers and their connecting passageways.

All of the furnishings of the Tabernacle and its court-
yard are also significant. At the gateway or entrance of the
outer court stood .he altar of burnt offerings to which the
multitudes brought their sacrifices. This altar is symbolic
of the literal aspect of the Revelation. It is inevitable that
those not advanced in the science of religion should obey the
instructions of the priests, and fulfill the outer rites of worship by bringing offerings from their stores of possessions.
This altar was adorned on its four corners with the horns
of rams. These are called the *four horns of atonement*, and
are the horn of the Torah, the horn of the Shekinah, the
horn of priesthood, and the horn of the kingdom.

Within the court of the Tabernacle, stood the laver of
purification, its sides encrusted with the mirrors of the
women of the twelve tribes. Purification is probationship,
or preparation for acceptance into the higher mysteries of
the doctrine. The mirrors are symbols of human vanity,
egotism, or selfishness, which must be voluntarily relin-
quished by those who seek the life of holiness. Within the
Holy Place of the Tabernacle, stood three objects. The table
of shewbread, which signified the sustenance that was given
to Israel, for the people were sustained by manna which
came down from heaven while they wandered in the wilderness. There was also the seven-branched candlestick
fashioned by Bezaleel, which represented the light of the
Shekinah and the seven spirits of God, and this was so
precious that God concealed it when the temple was destroyed by Nebuchadrezzar, and will restore it when his
house is built again in the hearts and souls of men. In the
Holy Place was likewise the altar of burnt incense, which
was symbolically represented as fashioned of gold. Thus
there were two altars; one outside the Tabernacle, made of
brass, and one within, fashioned of fine gold. The brazen
altar corresponded to the body of man, and the one of

gold, to his soul. As the body is sustained by food, such offerings were made upon the brazen altar; but upon the golden altar only spices and sweet incense were offered, for the soul delights in the perfume of righteousness.

As the altar of burnt incense stood at the entrance of the Holy of Holies, and was therefore between the larger and smaller rooms, it was related to the breath of uprightness, and the arrangement of these various objects is most suggestive of the sacred centers of the human body familiar to students of Raja Yoga. By its location, this altar corresponds to the larynx, which is the altar of the sacred word in man because it is the center of speech; and the incense smoke rising therefrom is likened to the songs and chantings of the priests, and the words of righteousness forever ascending before the face of the inevitable. The tables of shewbread were placed at the north side of the Tabernacle, and the seven-branched candlestick at the south side. This may refer to the teachings found in many ancient systems of philosophy that the north was the abode of secret, remote, and hidden gods, the agents of high destiny not directly available to man. The candlestick was placed at the south, because in the astronomical procedure known to the ancients it was believed that the sun and its planets never ascended into the northern part of the world. Here is a further indication that the Menorah, or seven-branched candlestick, represented the planetary bodies; also, the seven days of creation, the seven great laws ruling life, the seven races, the seven continents of the earth, the seven directions of space, and the seven parts of the human soul.

Some Hindu schools teach that the five elements which together make up all material substances are symbolized by parts of the human body as follows: earth, from the feet to the knees; water, from the knees to the waist; fire, from the waist to the throat; air, from the throat to the forehead;

and *akasa,* or the fifth subtle element, called in alchemy the *quintessence* or *fifth essence,* from the crown of the head up-ward into the invisible magnetic field which surrounds the physical form. Actually, the Tabernacle presents the sym-bolism of the human body in approximately the same way. The altar of burnt offerings represents earth; the laver of purification, water; the candlestick and the shewbread are ascribed to fire because they represent the two extremes of the emotional nature; the altar of burnt incense is air; and the Ark of the Covenant, over which hovers the Shekinah's glory, is the *akasa* or subtle ether.

Beyond the Holy Place, curtained off even from the sight of the priests, was the Holy of Holies. In the midst of this stood the Ark of the Covenant. It is said that the Ark con-sisted of three caskets. The outer one was of gold, and this held one of wood, which in turn contained one more, also of gold. This Ark was a replica in miniature of the divine throne in heaven, and when it was carried about, it was overspread with a fine cloth of blue, the color of the sky. Upon the top of the Ark knelt two cherubs with the faces of boys. The face of each cherub measured a span, and their wings measured ten spans, so that together they made up twenty-two spans, which were equal to the letters of the Hebrew alphabet. The space between the kneeling cherubs was called the Mercy Seat, for God dwelt between his two sacred names, Adonai and Elohim. The Ark was fitted with rings through which rods could be passed, and the sacred chest was lifted by these poles onto the shoulders of men, so that it could be carried from place to place. Within the Ark itself, according to the Cabalists, were three sacred objects: the rod of Aaron that budded, the pot of manna that fell in the wilderness, and the Tables of the Law. When the migrations of Israel were finished, and the Ark finally came to rest in the Holy of Holies of King Solomon's temple, the pot of manna and the rod of Aaron had disappeared, and only the Tables of the Law remained.

The spiritual triad is repeated in the three sacred objects contained within the Ark. Thus manna represents spirit, truth, or wisdom. It is the food which comes down from heaven, for truly it is said that, "Man doth not live by bread only, but by every *word* that proceedeth out of the mouth of the LORD doth man live." (Deuteronomy 8:3) In the New Testament, Christ, the personification of the divine wisdom, is made to say, "I am the living bread which came down from heaven: if any man eat of this bread, he shall live for ever." (John 6:51). It should therefore be evident to the most conservative Bible student that manna is not a precipitated dew, as some have suggested, or merely some mysterious form of bread, but, as the Greeks said, it is the food of the inner man, who lives not upon the fruits of the earth, but upon the fruits of the spirit.

In the 17th chapter of Numbers is described the budding of Aaron's rod. Verse 8 reads: "And it came to pass, that on the morrow Moses went into the tabernacle of witness; and, behold, the rod of Aaron for the house of Levi was budded, and brought forth buds, and bloomed blossoms, and yielded almonds." The Orientalist will recognize the staff of Aaron to be the spinal column, and the blossoms upon it the ganglia and plexi that are animated or caused to blossom by the yogic disciplines of regeneration. On a moral level, the blossoming of the rod refers to the regeneration of the emotional nature, of which a flower is a peculiar symbol. The same allegory was used by Wagner in his opera-drama *Tannhauser*. The repentant hero was refused absolution by the Pope until the papal staff should blossom as evidence of divine forgiveness. It should also be remembered that in the New Testament story, Joseph was selected to be the husband of Mary because his rod had budded.

The manna, the budded staff, and the Tables of the Law, thus represent the spiritual, emotional-psychical, and physical natures of man, and the mysteries pertaining thereto. The loss of the manna and the disappearance of Aaron's rod imply that the keys to the spiritual and psychical mysteries were lost or hidden, and only the physical or bodily interpretation, represented by the stone tablets, remained in the Ark. This is another instance of the loss of a "word" or key to power by which the higher degrees of initiation could be substantially conferred.

In some of the older accounts, the faces of the cherubim upon the Mercy Seat of the Ark were simply those of young men. In the original construction, these faces were slightly turned back, as though taking a regretful parting, but later, by a miracle, the faces turned of themselves, so that the cherubs are sometimes shown with four faces, representing the four fixed signs of the zodiac, the four material elements, and the four bodily or material natures of man—the mental, emotional, vital, and physical. When represented with four heads, these are of four creatures—a man, a bull, a lion, and an eagle. In this arrangement, the human head represents the sign of Aquarius; the head of the bull, Taurus; the head of the lion, Leo; and the head of the eagle, Scorpio. These together are the rulers of the four corners of the world, for they form the boundaries of the great square in which the mystery of creation takes place. In the Christian rites, these four creatures are often shown accompanying the four Evangelists, and were carved upon the corners of sarcophagi. This usage conforms with the old nursery rhyme, "Matthew, Mark, Luke and John; bless the bed that I lie on." These same cherubs guard the throne of the Great One in the vision of St. John.

The fifth element, which is in the midst of the cherubs guarding the Mercy Seat of the Ark, is called the *Shekinah,* the mysterious light of splendors which hovers between the cherubim, who are the guardians of its glory. In the Cabalistic system, Shekinah is equivalent to the Virgin Sophia of the Gnosis, and it is also the Eternal Virgin, the mother of the Messiah. It is written that the mystery of the Shekinah may not be revealed. The allegorical statement that it is a column of smoke by day and a pillar of flame by night should not be taken literally. The Shekinah is the mystery of the presence, the contact between the higher and lower parts of the universe. It is called the "Mother of Mysteries," and it is even Diana, the Great Goddess of the Ephesians. It is intimated that in the body of man the Shekinah is a subtle essence, the medium through which the spirit acts upon the blood. This concept is involved in the old rites of blood brotherhood. In the macrocosm, or the larger universe, the Shekinah is that mysterious field of energy by means of which the solar light acts upon and is diffused throughout the creation. Its location in man is particularly the ventricular orifices of the brain. It is the nimbus around the head of the saint, the aureole of light, the witness of the Presence.

The 28th chapter of Exodus describes the vestments of the priests. As the Tabernacle itself was a symbol of universal law and revelation, so the robes of the priests confirmed the cosmic plan. It is said that God ordained eight garments for Aaron, who was the High Priest of Israel. For his two sons, there were four garments. Each garment had wonderful virtues, and atoned for one of the eight kinds of sin. The undergarment of the priest was of a fine linen, identical in meaning with the one-piece white robe of the Nazarenes. Over this was worn a colored garment that came to the knees, embroidered in various shades and designs, usually with depictions of pomegranates. Over this was worn a short jacket, called the *ephod*, which had a jewel on each shoulder. To this was attached a breastplate bearing the twelve jewels with the names of the twelve tribes preceded by those of the three patriarchs. The great onyx stones on the shoulders of the ephod were called the *Urim* and *Thummim,* and these, with the other jewels upon the robes, made altogether seven in addition to the twelve in the breastplate. Upon his head, the high priest wore a bonnet or helmet, divided by a strip going from back to front. Upon the visor or band of this bonnet were the words, "Holiness unto the Lord." The robe was hung with seventy-two pomegranates and bells of gold, which represented the seventy-two stars, six from each of the zodiacal signs, and also symbolized the seventy-two elders, six from each of the tribes of Israel.

The robes of the high priest, like the vestments of the hierophants of other ancient Mystery systems, represented the spiritual bodies of man—those auras or magnetic emanations which were regarded as the true garments of glory. The white linen garment signified the purified physical body, and the long colored garment the regenerated vital or etheric body. The ephod typified the emotional or psychic body; and the helmet, the intellectual or mental body. The jewels were the seven senses,* and the twelve stones of the breastplate were the twelve celestial principles which reside in and manifest through the purified human soul. The high priest, therefore, was adorned with the manifested glory of the perfect microcosm. He was the divine man, robed in the splendor of his redemption.

It was the high priest alone, whose garments revealed him to be the perfect initiate, who could enter the Holy of Holies and come face to face with the power of the Shekinah that hovered over the Mercy Seat. In simple words,

---

*The sixth and seventh senses are still in the extra-sensory band.

only the Master of the mysteries of life can stand in the presence of universal reality. For all other mortals, the divine power must be obscured by the veils of sanctity and secrecy. It should be noted, however, that even the high priest could not wear his robes of glory when he entered the Holy of Holies. He must put aside all adornment and symbols of temporal authority and approach his God only in the simple white robe of purity. It is not seemly that man should wear ornamentation of any kind in the presence of the Divine. Only virtue should adorn him, and his works be his ornaments.

Deuteronomy ends with the death of Moses. The tribes came to the broad plain "over against Jericho," and "all the land of Judah, unto the utmost sea." Here on the lonely hill of Moab, Moses, the good man, was hidden away in God, and the people of Israel wept for thirty days, and then the mournings for Moses were over. At this point, therefore, we must reluctantly turn from the great pageantry of the Pentateuch and consider another important cycle of Old Testament symbolism, the story of Solomon the King and the Temple which he built to the greater glory of the Most High.

THE ARK OF THE COVENANT SUPPORTED BY CHERUBS

CHAPTER VII

THE GLORY OF SOLOMON THE KING

When he was about twelve years old, Solomon became king over Israel. The given name of this prince was Jedidiah, "the Friend of God," but this was superseded by the name Solomon, "the Peaceful," because peace prevailed throughout the realm during his reign. Some said that the change was the result of the counseling of Nathan the Prophet, but most historians were of the opinion that it referred to the tranquillity of the times. Solomon was the youngest of the sons of David, and it seemed that Absalom was the destined successor. Absalom died, however, when Solomon was ten years old, and, inspired by Nathan, David passed over the claims of all his elder sons and selected Solomon as his heir. The feebleness of David's elder years caused Adonijah, the next in order of birth to Absalom, to cast his eyes hopefully upon the throne. Adonijah openly assumed the prerogatives of his birthright, and laid a strategy to have himself proclaimed as king. In this emergency, Nathan and Bathsheba reminded David that he was bound by an oath that Solomon should succeed him. As a result, David, accompanied by Nathan, Zadok the Priest, and the important officers of the court, went to Gihon, where David abdicated and Solomon was proclaimed and anointed King of Israel. This took place even while the conspirators were assembled at a banquet given by Adonijah to perfect his own plans. The assembly broke up, and the guests departed quietly to their own houses. The attempted coup had failed miserably.

It is also said that Solomon bore three other names: Ben, because he was the builder of the temple; Jakeh, because he was the ruler of the whole world; and Iphiel, because God was with him. Solomon married the daughter of the Pharaoh of Egypt, which was contrary to the law of Israel. He was also guilty of two other transgressions. He kept many horses, which was not proper for a Jewish king, and he amassed great quantities of gold and silver. For these sins, he was later to atone. If Solomon was remembered for his wealth and for the splendor of his court, these were as nothing when compared to the wisdom with which his name has long been associated. While he was still a young man, God appeared to him in a dream at Gideon, giving the king permission to ask any grace that he most desired. On this occasion, Solomon chose wisdom, for he was already wise enough to know that if he possessed this, all else would come as a natural consequence. God also gave Solomon power over spirits and the demons of the air, and even the animals likewise obeyed him.

The wit and wisdom of Solomon is also attested to by his relationship with Hiram, King of Tyre, who was a devoted friend of the house of David. There are many accounts of the intellectual fraternity that existed between these two kings. Hiram loved to send riddles and curious problems to Solomon. The wisest of kings answered them all, and made an arrangement with Hiram to exchange conundrums and catch-questions. In each case, the one who failed to answer correctly was to pay a fine. This added many an honest penny to Solomon's treasury. The Tyrians, to defend the honor of their nation, sought one from among themselves who had a great wit. They finally discovered Abdemom, who was able to fashion problems so remarkable that even Solomon was frequently baffled.

The old lore contains many accounts of Solomon's wonderful judgment and skill. When the time came for Solomon to build a temple in Jerusalem according to the will of his father, David, he sent messages to the various rulers of friendly provinces asking that they send artisans to his court. Among those to whom he wrote was the Pharaoh of Egypt. This cunning man evidently had no heart for the project. He called his astrologers together and examined the nativity of many workmen. The Egyptians then selected those who were destined by the stars to die within twelve months, and dispatched them to assist Solomon. But the king of Israel was not so easily deceived. He gave each of the artisans a grave-cloth and returned them to their own country with a letter to Pharaoh which said: "I suppose thou hast no shrouds for these people. Herewith I send thee the men, and what they were in need of."

Solomon must certainly be included among the solar heroes, and while it is quite possible that such a king once ruled in Israel, the historical facts became obscured by myths and confused by legends until the mortal man was transformed into the great Light of the World. It is indeed the sun that solves all riddles and finds answers for the most

perplexing doubts and questions. The name of Solomon
may be divided into three syllables: SOL-OM-ON. Each of
these syllables is a name for the Supreme Power, or the
Eternal Principle at the root of life. *Sol,* of course, means
the sun; *Om* is the sacred monosyllable of the *Vedas,* the
most magical of all sounds according to the religion of the
Hindus; and *On* is a name of the Supreme Being in the
secret rites of Persia.

THE EVERLASTING HOUSE

When the plans for the building of the Temple were
properly prepared, Solomon was uncertain as to where he
was to erect the Everlasting House. At last, a heavenly voice
instructed him to go to Mount Zion in the middle of the
night and find a field which was owned jointly by two
brothers. One of these brothers was unmarried and poor,
and the other had large wealth and a considerable family.
During the night, the poorer brother added part of his own
share of the harvest grain to the store of his richer brother
because he had many mouths to feed. Under the cover of
the same darkness, the rich brother also carried part of the
grain and placed it upon the stack of his poorer brother
because his need was greater. Neither knew of the gifts of
the other, and the benevolent conspiracy went on for a long
time. Solomon was so impressed by the brotherly love of
these two men that he considered the place to be sanctified
and bought it, that he might build thereon the Temple.

Before Solomon actually began the construction of his
Everlasting House, he communicated with his friend, Hiram,
King of Tyre, saying: "Thou knowest how that David my
father could not build an house unto the name of the LORD
his God for the wars which were about him on every side,
until the LORD put them under the soles of his feet. But
now the LORD my God hath given me rest on every side, so

that there is neither adversary nor evil occurrent. And, behold, I propose to build an house unto the name of the LORD my God, as the LORD spake unto David my father, saying, Thy son, whom I will set upon thy throne in thy room, he shall build an house unto my name." (I. Kings 5:3-5) Hiram, King of Tyre, rejoiced greatly and promised to send timbers of cedar and of fir and other materials essential to the completion of the structure.

Knowing the reputation of the Tyrians, Solomon also asked his friend Hiram to send to Jerusalem a skillful and clever workman who could superintend the casting of the various ornaments and vessels of the Temple. This workman was also named Hiram, and one must be careful not to confuse the Tyrian King with the master artisan. In I. Kings 7:13, it is stated: "And king Solomon sent and fetched Hiram out of Tyre." In verse 14 is found additional information about this Hiram: "He *was* a widow's son of the tribe of Naphtali, and his father *was* a man of Tyre, a worker in brass, and he was filled with wisdom, and understanding, and cunning to work all works in brass. And he came to king Solomon, and wrought all his work."

Da Costa, in his *Dionysian Artificers,* declares that this Hiram, the widow's son out of Tyre, was an initiate priest of the Mysteries of Dionysius. He was therefore a member of a secret order of architects that flourished in the ancient world. In legendry, this Hiram was an adept of the mysteries of fire, for this is the only element that will work metals. Hiram, the Dionysiac initiate, claimed descent from Tubal-cain, the master of all metals and the first to pound swords into ploughshares. There is an apocryphal story that this Tubal-cain appeared to his illustrious descendant among the seething vapors and fiery metals of the molten sea, the great vessel which was to be borne upon the shoulders of twelve oxen and which Hiram was casting to adorn the Temple of Solomon the King.

Hiram was the personification of the solar fire, and, according to the old tradition, the patron of those alchemists who, with the aid of fire, sought to perfect Nature through art. Heat is one of the attributes of the solar energy, and it is through this agent that light becomes generative. By warmth, all generations are made possible, and the light of truth kindles in the human soul the fire of aspiration. It is this fire, in turn, which, as Tubal-cain, tempers the spirit and establishes resolution in the human heart. The corona of the sun reveals the flame pouring out into space from the great luminary. The fires of Nature are reflections of celestial combustions. Over these lower and lesser fires, the Master Artisan asserts his authority in order that the Temple be adorned with splendid vessels and instruments.

Baron de Welling called attention to the fact that the word *Hiram* was originally *Chiram,* and that in the course of time confusion arose because of the similarity between the Hebrew H and CH. The word is therefore composed of the letters C R and M, which stand for *Chamah, Ruach,* and *Majim,* which in turn stand for fire, air, and water. These unite together to form the universal alchemical agent. *Chamah* is the light of the sun, the universal, invisible, cold fire of Nature gathered into a focus and manifested as light. *Ruach* is spirit, air, or wind, the vehicle which conveys and collects the light and, agitating it by a circular motion, causes it to manifest as heat and burning fire. *Majim* is water, or humidity. Philosophically, it is the mother of water, a radical humidity. These three constitute together the universal agent which must supply the materials for the building of the Everlasting House. The alchemical implication is that King Solomon was a master of the spiritual art, and by means of his knowledge was able to call upon the secret wisdom of fire, which in turn becomes the master of workmen, being the only element which can control metals.

The story of Hiram the Artificer, called *Hiram Abiff* (Our Father Hiram), is carefully preserved in Masonic symbolism. Modern Masonry traces its original descent from the Three Grand Masters of the Lodge of Jerusalem; namely, King Solomon, King Hiram of Tyre, and Hiram the Artificer. The building of the Temple, therefore, was supervised by these three Grand Masters, who symbolized the powers of the creative trinity, the divine agencies by which cosmos is brought out of chaos. Such a trinity or triad is present in most of the great theological systems of the world. The Trimuti, the three-faced Brahma in the caves of Elephanta in the harbor of Bombay, depicts the principal deity of the Hindus in its three-fold manifestation. The three faces stand for the creative, preservative, and regenerative powers resident in the divine energy. Thus the ultimate perfection toward which all life is inevitably moving was said to be accomplished through the skill of three Master Builders.

The account of the building of Solomon's Temple is set forth in the First Book of the Kings, beginning with chapter 5 and continuing through chapter 9. It is generally believed that the account is historically true and describes the actual building of the Temple, fashioned from rock and wood and ornamented with gold and precious stones. If subjected to analysis, however, it becomes apparent, as in the case of Noah's ark, that much more is intended. There is no reason to doubt that Solomon built the Temple, but the description has certainly been enlarged and altered by interpretation, and caused to conform with the symbolical teachings of the ancient religious Mysteries. The architecture generally associated with the Temple is Babylonian and Chaldean. The story is substantially as follows.

It came to pass that the building of the Temple was commenced in the 480th year after the children of Israel had come out of the land of Egypt. From the dimensions given in I. Kings, chapter 6, it is evident that the Temple was of no great size, for it was not much larger than many modern homes. It is difficult to imagine, therefore, that seventy thousand men bore burdens and eighty thousand hewed wood in the mountains and thirty-three hundred overseers directed the work for seven years to build this comparatively modest structure.

If a cubit is the distance from the end of the index finger to the elbow (about 18 inches), then the length of Solomon's Temple was approximately 90 feet, the breadth was 30 feet, and the height, 45 feet. Various methods of determining the Jewish cubit have been attempted, but in all probability, the dimensions as given are approximately correct. Of course, there were the approaches to the Temple, the massive foundation upon which it stood, houses for the priests, chambers for storing sacred utensils, and other works, but still there is a wide discrepancy between the available facts and popular opinion. The Temple was built on Mount Zion, (traditionally also called Mount Moriah), one of the low hills in the cluster upon which the city of Jerusalem stands. There is still a flat rock, called the Rock Moriah, jutting from the top of this hill. Today, a Mohammedan mosque occupies the site of Solomon's Temple, and of the building itself nothing remains except a few mutilated stone carvings and fragments of uncertain origin. Of course, the great foundations of Herod's Temple, which later occupied the same site, are also to be seen.

The commentaries explain that Solomon was so assiduous in the erection of the Temple that it required but seven years, approximately half the time that had been taken for the building of King David's palace. For this reason, the work of Solomon was more meritorious than the work of David, who had first built a house for himself and had then given thought to a house for his God. It was the great merit of Solomon's work in the building of the Everlasting House that saved him from being reckoned by the wise as one of the impious kings.

According to the measure of the zeal displayed by Solomon, so were the help and favors bestowed upon him by the Lord. During the seven years it took to build the Temple, not a single workman died, nor did one even fall sick. As they were strong and of abounding health from the first to the last, so the tools and instruments of their work did not wear out, nor did they ever become dull. There is a legend, however, that after the Temple was dedicated, many of the workmen did not live much longer, but departed to receive their wages in another and better world. Thus it was that they built no other structures to foreign gods. The master of the workmen, Hiram the Artisan of Tyre, was especially favored by the Lord, and it was given to him that he should reach paradise without knowing death. This is contrary to some other accounts, but it is certainly one of the older legends. During the building of the Temple, there were also many other evidences and indications that the spirit of God was present and blessed the undertaking.

The reference to seven years helps us to understand one of the keys to the story of the Temple. Seven is the old sacred number associated with creative processes, both cosmogenic and psychogenic. In the 7th verse of the 6th chapter of I. Kings, it is written: " . . . there was neither hammer nor axe *nor* any tool of iron heard in the house, while it was in the building." This was indeed the Temple "built without the sound of hammer or the voice of workmen." It was the Everlasting Temple, eternal in the heavens. Josephus, the Jewish historian, was aware that the Tabernacle in the Wilderness was a symbol of the universe, and this was also true of King Solomon's Temple, in even more perfect measure.

The building of Solomon's Temple takes place on several planes of symbolism simultaneously. The solar system is a product of creative energies; each of the planets is a house built in space. All the races and orders of living things evolving upon the planets are likewise structures, or lesser temples, built to manifest the glory of the creating gods. All forms are houses for the soul. One spiritual principle, as three persons or powers, builds all these houses, functions through them, and finally discards them for better dwellings. As the poet writes, "Build thee more stately mansions, O my soul."

Man, too, is a master builder. Each human being is erecting a temple of his own character, even as he is building a body through which he must function. He is casting beautiful ornaments for his father's house when he ennobles his emotions, refines his appetites, and improves his mind. Those initiates of ancient rites who achieved outstanding proficiency in these endeavors of regeneration were called *master builders*. They were building not houses of wood and stone, but invisible temples fashioned without the sound of hammer or the voice of workmen.

The sciences, philosophies, and religions of the world are dedicated to the enrichment of man's internal resources. They supply him with the material from which to built the living temple of his soul. This house is made strong and suitable by science, sufficient to its various purposes by philosophy, beautiful by art, and purposeful by religion. When it has been completed insofar as man is capable of fulfilling his own destiny, it is consecrated to the service of the God for whom it was built. If the work is well done, the sanctuary becomes the abode of that God, according to the promise which was given in the beginning of time. The soul, or psyche, however, is not an inanimate thing, but is the source of living processes which must be subdued, transmuted, regenerated, enlarged, and perfected. Furthermore, the soul has rights and prerogatives of its own, so that it is actually the immortal-mortal. It is a being which has a beginning but no end. It begins as an essence distilled, and in the course of time becomes an over-self, a knowing essence with all the complex and involved processes occurring within it which are familiar to the psychologist. In fact, for those without sufficient discernment, the soul appears to be the self, but actually it is the handmaiden of the self, which is made immortal when it is united in the Hermetic marriage with consciousness itself.

The whole motion of the universe is toward truth. Truth is growing up in everything, manifesting through all forms and natures. Truth, therefore, may be called the hidden god, or the secret god who dwells in the temples that are built according to the eternal laws as places suitable for the worship of the Divine. In the account of Solomon's Temple, the principal structure was patterned after the symbolism of the Tabernacle. The sanctuary was divided into two parts—the Holy Place, and the Most Holy of Holy Places, the latter reserved to receive the Ark of the Covenant. These Holy Places were sanctified to the service of the living God. The Holy Place of man is his mind, and the Most Holy of Holy Places is his heart. It is in the sanctum sanctorum that the finger of God traces the designs for the work of the day. It is also in the heart that the sacrament of consecration must take place, for the heart is the small room in the deepest part of the temple for which all the rest is protection and adornment

The Dionysian Artificers concealed under the symbolism of architecture the secret and spiritual mysteries of the regeneration of man. It is said in I. Kings that the Cedars of

Lebanon were cut down and were floated to Joppa to become the beams and uprights of the Everlasting House. The commentaries tell us that the Cedars of Lebanon were not actually trees. There was a holy temple of the old wisdom upon Mount Lebanon. As in the case of the British Druids, who were known as the "men of the oak trees," the initiates of Mount Lebanon were called trees, or cedars. It was the living wisdom of these men that supported the temple. Their sacred knowledge was the beam, and their wisdom was the upright. Houses that endure forever are not built by men from the substances of the mortal world, but of the secret substances of wisdom that shall endure through all the vicissitudes of physical existence. It is therefore said that the Cedars from Lebanon which Hiram, King of Tyre, sent to King Solomon, came to life and bore fruit after they had been made into the pillars of the Temple. This was possible because they were wonderfully nourished by the incense smoke which clouded the sanctuary. The fruit that came upon them nourished and sustained the priests, and this subtly reveals the true meaning of the account.

The Temple was finished in the month of Bul, but it stood closed for nearly a year because it was the will and favor of God that the dedication of his house should take place in the month of the birth of Abraham. In great measure, likewise, Solomon's Temple reflected honor upon King David, who had departed to his fathers. When the time came for the Ark of the Covenant to be brought into the Holy of Holies of the Temple, the door of the sacred chamber locked of itself and it was not possible for anyone to open this door. Solomon prayed fervently to God, but his entreaties produced no effect until he said, "Remember the good deeds of David thy servant." The door of the Holy of Holies then opened without human aid, and those who had made comments about David's impiety were forced to acknowledge that God had forgiven him. David had been adverse to the idea that any gold which he had taken in war from unbelievers should be used for the sanctuary at Jerusalem. He feared that those of other faiths might boast, if the Temple should ever be destroyed, that strange gods had taken vengeance. Fortunately, Solomon was so rich that there was no need to resort to any of the wealth inherited from his father, so David's wish was exactly fulfilled.

Second only in beauty and wonder to the Temple was the throne of Solomon, fashioned as a microcosm of the universe. It was covered with fine gold from Ophir, inlaid with marble, and jeweled with the most precious gems of all the world. On each of the six steps that approached the throne were two golden lions and two golden eagles, a lion and an eagle on each side. There were many other wonderful decorations, including animals of gold, birds, and chains of pomegranates and lilies. There were likenesses of seven patriarchs and of other great prophets and teachers. On the upper part of the throne were the seventy golden chairs for the members of the Sanhedrin. There was strange machinery within the throne which caused the various creatures that adorned it to be put into motion. But this throne did not remain long in Jerusalem, for during the time of Solomon's son it was taken away into Egypt. From there it passed to one kingdom and then another, until at last it was carried to Rome.

SOLOMON AND SHEBA

Solomon, king of the world, was not only the ruler over men, but also governed animals and plants and controlled demons and spirits. The Archangel Michael gave to the King a small ring consisting of an engraved stone, so that with this seal he could force the invisible beings of the heavenly and infernal regions to do his bidding. Solomon understood the language of the beasts and birds, and they would gather and form a court to amuse and entertain the King. One day, a bird called the *hoopoe* was absent from his usual place in the strange gathering. Solomon was offended, and ordered the hoopoe to be punished for his tardiness. In due time, the bird appeared with an extraordinary story. (See, Ginzberg, *Legends of the Jews*). In substance, the hoopoe explained that he had decided to fly into all parts of the world to see if there were a domain anywhere that did not acknowledge Solomon to be the king of kings. He had gone to the east to a place called Kitor, where he had found a fantastic city where the men wore flowers upon their heads and knew nothing of war. The ruler of this remote kingdom was a woman, and she was called the Queen of Sheba. The hoopoe then recommended that it be permitted to lead an expedition to capture the ruler of Kitor and bring her in chains to do homage before the throne of Solomon.

The King was both pleased and amused. He summoned the clerks of the court, and they prepared a letter which they bound to the bird's wings, and bade it serve as their messenger to the Queen of the land of Sheba. When the Queen received the letter, she was greatly disturbed, for the message was most arrogant. It required that she come and pay homage to the King of all the world. She would be royally received and all honors would be bestowed upon her, but if she refused, an army of soldiers, accompanied by legions of birds and animals and a vast array of demons and ghosts, would march against her, destroy her, and devastate her land.

Balkis the Queen decided that the wiser course would be to make the journey and at least learn the strength of King Solomon and keep his friendship. She therefore loaded her ships with treasures and, accompanied by six thousand of the youths and maidens of her court, traveled to Jerusalem.

Solomon received her in a house composed of glass, so that the Queen thought he was seated in the midst of water. After she had been presented, Balkis explained that she had heard that Solomon was the wisest of men. Therefore, she would ask him several questions to test his knowledge. Each of the twenty-two questions which she propounded, he answered immediately. And the Queen was convinced that he had received the blessing of God.

There are numerous legends associated with the visit of the Queen of Sheba to the court of Solomon. She is said to have brought the King the same gifts which the Magi afterwards placed before the manger of Christ. There is an old Jewish Cabalistic account which states that the soul of Solomon was reborn as Jesus, thus uniting two parallel stories. The Queen appeared under three different names: Nicaule, Balkis, and Makeda. In the Arabic tradition, she is said to have come from Yemen, while the Ethiopians said she was of Meroe. In each account, the Queen of Sheba bore a son from Solomon, and the Ethiopians claim that their royal house is descended from this union. Twelve thousand Jews returned with her to her own country, and from the descendants of the Jews of Ethiopia came the mysterious Prester John, the Emperor of the East.*

The *Book of the Glory of Kings*, the *Kebra Nagast,* translated from the Ethiopic by Sir E. Wallis Budge, contains the traditional history of the Queen of Sheba and her only son, Menelik I. In the Ethiopic version, it was a merchant by the name of Tamrin, returning to his own country, who conveyed to the Queen of Sheba an account of the wisdom of Solomon and the glory of his court. The Queen, who respected wisdom and understanding above all other virtues, then resolved to visit the court of the distant ruler whose fame had reached

---

*For an account of this fabulous monarch, see *The Land of Prester John,* by Elaine Sanceau.

to the most remote parts of the world. She arrived in
Jerusalem while Solomon was supervising the building of
the Temple, and she was deeply impressed by the perfection
of his words and thoughts. He went each day and mingled
with the workmen and instructed them and supervised all
their constructions.

In the Ethiopic version, the Queen is called Makeda, and
the admiration she felt for the King of Israel may be gathered from her words to him: "I look upon thee and I see
that thy wisdom is immeasurable and thine understanding
inexhaustible and that it is like unto a lamp in the darkness,
and like unto a pomegranate in the garden, and like unto a
pearl in the sea, and like unto the Morning Star among the
stars, and like unto the light of the moon in the mist, and
like unto a glorious dawn and sunrise in the heaven. And
I give thanks unto Him that brought me hither and showed
thee to me, and made me tread upon the threshold of thy
gate, and made me to hear thy voice."

According to the *Kebra Nagast,* Makeda remained for several months as a guest in King Solomon's court and, after
a splendid banquet, he made her his wife. When the Queen
knew that she was to bear a child, she returned to her own
country, carrying a signet ring from Solomon. She gave birth
to a son, Menelik, who was called "the son of the wise man."
When this lad grew up, he desired to visit his father in Jerusalem, and the Queen gave him the ring and sent him to
Solomon with the caravan of the merchant Tamrin. The boy
so nearly resembled his father that there could be no question
as to his paternity. Solomon embraced Menelik with great
tenderness, proclaimed the young man's parentage, and recognized him as a royal prince. After a considerable visit,
Menelik desired to go back to his mother, for it was his destiny that he should rule in his own land, and not over the
kingdom of Israel.

It was then that Menelik resolved to take back with him the Ark of the Covenant, which had been patterned according to the Spirit-Tabernacle in heaven. With the aid of the merchant Tamrin and the sons of prominent Jewish families who were dedicated to assist in the founding of a Jewish Empire in Ethiopia, the Ark was removed from the Most Holy Place on the Temple and carried away. Solomon made every effort to regain the sacred relic, but it was taken to the court of Queen Makeda. So great was her rejoicing at the arrival of this sacred treasure that she abdicated in favor of her son Menelik, and he established in Ethiopia a kingdom modeled after that of Israel. The Negus of Ethiopia is still referred to as the "Conquering Lion of Judah." This title was carried by Haile Selassie even through the tribulations of the disastrous Italian invasion. The royal insignia of Ethiopia is the crowned lion.

In the introduction to his translation of the *Book of the Glory of Kings,* Budge writes: "The object of the author, or compiler and the later editors of the KEBRA NAGAST (no matter what its original form may have been) was to glorify ETHIOPIA by narrating the history of the coming of the 'spiritual and heavenly ZION,' the Tabernacle of the Law of the God of ISRAEL, of her own free will from JERUSALEM TO ETHIOPIA, and to make it quite clear that the King of ETHIOPIA was descended from SOLOMON, the son of DAVID, King of ISRAEL, and through him from ABRAHAM and the early Patriarchs. But CHRIST also was descended from SOLOMON and the early Patriarchs, and he was the Son of God, so the King of ETHIOPIA being a kinsman of CHRIST was also a son of God, and he was therefore both God and king to his people. The KEBRA NAGAST was intended to make the people of ETHIOPIA believe that their country was specially chosen by God to be the new home of the spiritual and heavenly ZION, of which His chosen people the JEWS had become unworthy."

The legends which have sprung up around the meeting of Solomon and Sheba do not obscure the rational circumstances involved. The story is surprisingly simple in its substance; in fact, one hardly expects to find so few embellishments to an Oriental account. The Queen is made to come from a distant region where women enjoyed unusual temporal and spiritual privileges. She discoursed with Solomon and, having convinced herself of his wisdom, accepted his favors, received his talismanic ring, and departed to her own land. The Arabs like to believe that Sheba was the daughter of a jinn, or supernatural spirit, and there are parallels between her career and that of the Persian queen, Hutaosa, who was converted by Zoroaster. In passing, it should be noted that Balkis is the Moslem name for the Queen of Sheba and suggests that she was from the great Zoroastrian city of Balkh, which stood near the confluence of the seven rivers where they mingled to form the Oxus.

The word *sheba* means *seven* in Hebrew. Balkis was therefore queen of the seven, a possible reference to the seven rivers which watered her kingdom. This, however, is the lesser of the possible meanings. The cosmos of the ancients consisted of seven spheres, and their entire universal scheme was made up of septenaries, of which the most important were the seven heavens which surrounded the earth and which were the abodes of planetary deities and their legions of invisible spirits. In the astral theology of that remote time, the term *Queen of Sheba* was almost equivalent to *Queen of Heaven*. The old symbolists frequently referred to the moon as the "queen of the seven heavenly lights," and even in Christianity, the Virgin Mary, as Queen of Heaven, is usually depicted with the lunar crescent beneath her feet. Dimly, through the myths and legends, Balkis, Queen of

Sheba, reveals the attributes of the lunar divinity. It is perfectly consistent with the religious symbolism of the Near East and Northern Africa to regard Balkis as a form of the great Mother of Mysteries, like Diana, the multimammia, or mother-goddess, of the Ephesians.

Josephus, for reasons not entirely obvious to the average Bible student, referred to Sheba as a *Queen of Egypt*. The kingdom of Pharaoh was a land of dark people, and the mythologies used this to imply darkness in the sense of ignorance, magic, or sorcery. Egypt was a land of mystery, and Balkis is believed by some to be the dark maiden of Solomon's Song. The Ephesian Diana was originally represented as black, for she was queen of the night, and it was a proverbial saying that there was no darkness as deep as Egypt's night.

What light is to the physical world of men, wisdom is to the soul. The light of reason transforms all darkness, and the illumined, or internally enlightened, form the royal house from which descend all the initiate-kings of the world. How else shall we explain reasonably that Solomon was king not only over Israel, but also over all nations, and all creatures, and all living things? The whole world pays homage to the radiant orb of day. It is the sun that is rich beyond all calculation. Its rays are its golden treasure, and the planets and stars and all the mysterious lights of the firmament are its wives and concubines. Its court is so splendid that no other mortal kingdom shall ever arise that shall equal the glory thereof. By reducing the two characters, Solomon and Sheba, to the basic elements of astrolatry, we have the two great orbs—the sun and the moon—which were regarded as the male and female principles of life by the wise star-gazers of long ago.

The old symbolists frequently employed the sun as an appropriate emblem through which to unfold the concept of wisdom. What light is to the body, knowledge and understanding are to the soul. They not only bestow a luminous internal life, but also radiate as a garment of glory. Paracelsus said that there was a sun in the intellectual world that warmed and lighted human thoughts and emotions. We refer to "benighted" individuals as those abiding in a state of mental darkness. The term *enlightened* we reserve for those who have attained a rational state of consciousness. The crowns and coronets of princes are themselves solar emblems, indicating that the ruler of the nation or state is a political luminary bestowing the light of his skill and erudition upon his people. The vestments of clergy, often decorated with sunburst designs, have a similar meaning. In Christian mysticism, Christ was early referred to as the "invincible sun," and there are numerous references to sun worship subtly included in the story unfolded by the Four Gospels.

It must be remembered that early symbolism implies certain analogies, but the devices used are not perfect and should not be subjected to critical analysis. It is the large idea which is important, and not the fragile form of picture or device which contains it, but not completely. The moon was the Lady of the Night, and there are many wonderful doctrines concerning the place of the lunar orb in the story of cosmic unfoldment. The old religious teachers seem to have realized that the moon shone with the reflected light of the sun. It was therefore a magic mirror, a silvery disc of enchantment which captured the sun's power and held it by strange and occult means. Nearly always where the moon is used, it represents first and foremost those religious institutions called the Mysteries, which were the first earthly custodians of the solar wisdom.

The sacred religious institutions were mirrors of wisdom established in the dark world of human struggle. They rose, like the Pyramid, from the earth and stood as altars to the Light of the World. Over them ruled the hierophants and initiate-priests who served as focal points for the reception and transmission of the invisible light of truth. As the temple of the hidden god was suspended midway between God and Nature, it became, in turn, the peculiar symbol of humanity. Man himself was suspended twixt heaven and earth, participating in the mysteries of both by the powers of his own soul. In him, all Nature epitomized its works, and he was and is the living temple of the living God. In the composition of man are mingled the powers of the sun and moon, which, by their union, generate the heroic creature of the future.

In his book *Solomon and Solomonic Literature,* Moncure Conway devotes considerable space to the probable Persian origin of certain references which occur in the books of the Old Testament. He concludes that the title *Queen of Sheba,* or *Queen of Seven,* had come to mean a wise woman, whether of Jewish of Persian origin; a woman instructed among the Magi and thus enjoying the intellectual freedom which was the traditional heritage of women among these people. He writes "There is no geographical difficulty in supposing that a Persian queen like Hutaosa, a devotee of Armaiti (Queen of the Seven, genius of Peace and Agriculture), might not have heard of Salem, the City of Peace, of its king whose title was The Peaceful (Solomon), and visited that city,—though of course the location of the meeting may have been only a later tradition."

The same writer points out that in the Book of the Wisdom of Solomon* the Queen of Sheba is transfigured as personified wisdom, and the gifts which she brings take on mystical significance. The King is made to write: "Now all good

---

*Apocryphal work, probably composed in Alexandria in the 1st or 2nd century B.C., and included in the Douay (Catholic) Bible.

things came to me together with her, and innumerable riches through her hands." (7:11). Thus our position in assuming that the Queen of Sheba represents the great structure of the Esoteric Schools is not an unreasonable interpretation of the available records. These institutions were together personified by the woman clothed with the sun. She is always Sophia, the soul-wisdom, who gives birth to the Savior-god by an immaculate conception and is not defiled. She is the Egyptian Isis, crowned with the lunar crescent and bearing the heroic man-child, Horus, who is to become the generalissimo of the army of the enlightened. The creating power of the universe was represented by the sun, and the redeeming power by the moon. Thus Solomon stands for the principle of creation, and Sheba for the principle of redemption. The whole concept of redemption is associated with the esoteric doctrine concerning the world-soul and its embodiment as the human soul. In alchemical mysticism the sun is spirit, the moon is soul, and Mercury is the catalyst or agent—the first-born of the Mystery. The formula is expressed in the production of the Philosopher's Stone through the union of sulphur (sun), salt (moon), and the catalyst (Mercury). The balance of these forces in the consummation of the Magnum Opus is revealed through the forty-seventh proposition of Pythagoras, falsely attributed to Euclid.

Solomon was the Prince of Peace, and it is interesting that this title should also have been bestowed upon Jesus, although it is nowhere justified by the Gospels. Peace in this case contains the implications of rest or repose, and the peace of God is peace *in* God, the wonderful Sabbath which follows the days of labor. According to the Old Testament, Solomon ceased from the works usual to the kings of his time in order that he might build the Eternal Temple. In this way, his reign came to be associated with quiet and industrious activities dedicated to the service of the Most High.

It was during this period of repose from the aggressive professions of kingship that the Queen of Sheba was inspired to visit the King of Glory.

In the esoteric writings, a pilgrimage or journey always has the same meaning. Those who travel in search of the eternal light are experiencing the adventure of becoming. Growth is an ascent into the secret place of the Most High. The pilgrimage is a qualitative departure from worldliness and toward the source of life itself. The devout Moslem making his pilgrimage to Mecca, the Hindu mendicant journeying toward the remote shrines of his faith, and the pious Shintoist climbing Fujiyama, are all performing a ritualistic journey in search of spiritual consolation. The endless journey in Nature is called evolution. It is the inevitable unfoldment of living creatures through the eternal mystery of growth. Man, having become at least partly conscious of his appointed destiny, is permitted to dedicate himself to a purposeful journey toward truth. Initiates of the ancient Mysteries were led about the temples and through the crypts and arcades of the sanctuaries as a symbol of the quest for enlightenment. At the end of their circumambulations, they approached the throne of the Master of the Secret House. Here they received the insignias of their ranks and offices, which were, in substance, the wages of the faithful servant.

If we accept Solomon in this beautiful legend as symbolizing human consciousness, then Sheba becomes the psyche; that is, the complex of faculties, instincts, impulses, and functions, which constitute the personality. The chemistry of life results in enlightenment through experience. The individual becomes aware of certain aspects of universal laws because these operate upon him and indicate their proper purposes and intentions. Gradually, a psychic organism is built which contains within it the essence of growth and the elixir extracted from experience by reason and intuition. In time to come, this vehicle of proved knowing will be as serviceable to the inner purposes of the person as is his physical body on the plane of objective activity. This soul-body, the wedding garment of St. Paul and the splendid robes of the high priest of ancient religion, is the essence of form transmuted from a mortal to an immortal state through the intercession of consciousness. It is the growth of the soul which intensifies the demands for wisdom and understanding.

The Ethiopian account includes the founding of their royal house by Menelik, the son of Solomon and Sheba, who thus establishes a theocratic dynasty. Although the incident is made to refer only to the descent of the Ethiopian kings, the symbolism has much larger implications. Menelik personifies the union of spiritual and temporal authority by divine right. He is the Hermetic child of the sun and moon, whose union represents the principle of equilibrium in Nature. Like the Egyptian Horus, Menelik becomes the embodiment of his own father in the dark land. Esoterically, Menelik introduces a new world-order justified and sustained by the fulfillment of alchemical processes on the psycho-political level. It is intimated that he carried the esoteric tradition to his own country and established there the true worship. From the Ethiopian point of view, Menelik was the Messiah, one of the House of David upon whom the Lord looked with favor.

The fulfillment of the marriage of spirit and soul is made possible by the birth of the heroic son. This is always the veiled account of the advent of the Adept-King. We have so long considered these Adepts as persons that we overlook the deeper meaning as it is applied to the individual. Adeptship stands for a condition of human consciousness, and when conferred upon a person, it implies that the initiate has accomplished the Hermetic Marriage within himself. The great restorations, reformations, and reorganizations of society originate within man himself. The spiritual purpose is released or brought into incarnation when the soul, impregnated by the spirit, gives birth to the heroic enlightenment. This, in turn, establishes world policy which unfolds as rapidly as the internal resources will permit. From Menelik, therefore, descends an order of rulers, by which is to be understood convictions and concepts which come to dominate and direct the progress of the race.

The soul, which is the living sanctuary, receives to itself the objective faculties which are candidates seeking initiation. It elevates these until they are able to experience the divine power which is already held within the soul, and which is, therefore, also the Chalice or Grail—the cup of sacrament. In the Egyptian rites, Isis (the moon) works an enchantment upon Ra (the sun) and forces him to reveal his secret name (the Word which is later to become flesh). The magical Isis is the mystic power of the soul, which requires the hidden truth to make itself known through the triple wand of science, philosophy, and religion. When these branches of learning have become ensouled, and the human being approaches the riddle of his own origin, proficient in the divine magic, he compels the sun-god to communicate his secret name, which is Truth.

Sheba cast a spell over Solomon, and by her ingenious devices penetrated his wisdom and received into herself his son. She immediately took the boy to her own country, like the woman clothed with the sun who gave birth to her child in the wilderness. When spiritual power is captured within the structure of the soul-body, it is present as a ray or extension of the divine glory. Sheba could not hold Solomon (truth), but she caused truth to become fruitful and she captured the fruit. In old mythology, the moon was the mistress of enchantment and mysterious works, so the symbolism is consistent. In the Egyptian story, Horus, the hero child, becomes the avenger of his own father, who had been killed through the conspiracy of evil men. This conspiracy was worldliness, which, as a principle or force, had gained control of the universal kingdom by violence and was perverting or frustrating the laws of Nature. Materialism, whether used to indicate the physical body of man or the physical-economic civilization which he has fashioned, has worked a strategy against the light of truth and sought to take the empire by violence. It is the wonderful child, secretly born and hidden from its enemies, that must restore the genuine descent of the royal house of heaven.

Art perfects Nature, because the very term *art* means *soul*. Even as worldliness perfects its house, unconquerable ideals come to birth within man himself. These are not immediately strong enough to restore the Golden Age. They must first work in darkness and in silence, but in time all that has been concealed will be revealed, and all that is hidden will be made known. Herod, although he slaughtered the innocents, could not capture or destroy the Word that had been made flesh. The infant Jesus was taken into Egypt, and this journey has the same meaning as Sheba's return to Ethiopia. The soul builds a wonderful protection around the internal apperception of truth, which has been made possible through the secret art. This truth, in turn, comes in the end to its maturity and is proclaimed the King of Kings, the ultimate ruler of all things that live and before whom every knee must bend. Only when we keep this symbolism on its large foundation can we understand the meaning of the legend.

It is almost certain that the entire Solomonic cycle was originally derived from one of the old Mystery rituals, and cannot be clearly interpreted except with the aid of the keys of the ancient wisdom. The student of comparative religion and the esoteric doctrines is in a fortunate position because he already knows the metaphysical structure of ancient learning. Symbolism then simply extends a general knowledge along new lines of application and reveals particulars previously obscured. As light spreads, it contributes to the ultimate enlightenment of all that lives.

THE SONG OF SONGS

The *Shir Hashirin,* or Song of Songs, is the first of the Five Scrolls. It is divided into eight chapters, and is attributed to King Solomon, though the actual authorship is uncertain. It has been traditional to date the work in the 10th century B. C., but in its present form it may be more correctly assigned to the 4th century B. C. Many early rabbis doubted the propriety of accepting this work into the Holy Scriptures, as it appeared rather a collection of secular love songs. On the other hand, the popular belief that it was written by Solomon, together with its wide popularity, gravitated toward its final acceptance in the Jewish collection of sacred writings.

Two distinct schools of interpretation have developed around the Song of Songs. According to the first, and older, the poem was actually composed by Solomon and referred to a peasant girl who was brought to his court and whose favors he sought to win. The words are therefore those of the King, and the poem is a literary work with religious or mystical overtones. Complications of meaning are simply due to the license of the poet, who wrote according to his fancy and ardor. The second school holds that at least sections of the work should be attributed to the Shulamite maiden, and that several voices speak in the poem. Some verses certainly seem to belong to Solomon, but whether they are authentic cannot be known. The literary integration may have resulted from the gathering of popular tradi-

tions by a skillful poet at a later date. It has also been suggested that the elements of the Song of Songs were derived
from early Syrian marriage rites. There was an old custom
that for the eight days directly following their nuptial, a
young couple was referred to as "king and queen," and was
treated with appropriate honors and distinctions.

As most of the earlier elucidations of the poem assume
that it was an inspired work composed by Solomon, containing profound spiritual implications, it seems best first to
approach the subject in this light. The alternative explanation will be considered later. Whatever may have been the
original intent, the theme and its development certainly invited philosophical speculation. It parallels so closely in
wording and content the vast mystical literature of the
world, and seems to have inspired so many later mystics,
both Eastern and Western, that it is natural to assume that
it was included in the Sacred Writings because it was more
than a romantic poem. Rabbi Aben-Ezra, representing an
early Jewish school of opinion, believed that the Song
should be accepted both literally and mystically. It was both
a secular love-poem and an inspired spiritual work. Under
the influence of Arab philosophy, the poem was approached
psychologically, and the Shulamite maiden became the active
intellect of Nature, which Solomon sought to possess. Dominated by the concept of a polarized universe, what could be
more natural than to assume that the radiant King and the
dusky maiden symbolized light and darkness, God and
Nature, spirit and matter, or soul and body?

If we acknowledge that the Zohar unfolds a valid ex-
position of Jewish metaphysics long preserved secretly by
scholarly mystics, references in this work to the Song of
Songs should be indicative of the veneration in which the
poem was held. In the Zohar (Section *Terumah*), Rabbi
Jose is made to say: "This Song King Solomon called forth

when the Temple was erected and all the worlds, above and below, had reached their perfect consummation . . . we may be certain that it was not sung until that time of absolute completion, when the Moon—the Shekinah—came to her fullness and was revealed in the full perfection of her radiance, and when the Temple had been erected in the likeness of the Temple that is above." The Zohar continues and explains why the work is called the Song of Songs. The first word, *Song,* stands for King David, who was the mover of song, and the latter word, *Songs,* stands for the Fathers, who possessed the true doctrine. Because the Song is the everlasting mystery of the divine voice, the title also means "from eternity to eternity" and it contains the secret wisdom of the whole faith.

The word *Shekinah* is derived from *Shachan,* which means "to dwell," and is usually translated "the presence of God." As it was used by Cabalists and mystics in a special sense, it should be clearly defined when associated with the Shulamite maiden. According to the Zohar, the Holy King is beauty, and the Queen, the Shekinah, is the perpetual activity of the divine emanations permeating all existence. A trinity is set up, consisting of God, the Father of All; Shekinah, the Great Mother; and Israel, the Beloved Son. On another level of interpretation, the Community of Israel is itself the Shekinah, the mystic rose, and, by further extension, the Assembly of the Fathers, the illumined ones. This led to the conviction that in the Song of Songs, God, as Solomon, is the lover, singing to Israel, his beloved. After the Diaspora, the concept was further extended. Israel became the lover, and raised his song to the Princess Sabbath—the peace of God, resplendent as a bride. Thus the sacred dreams of a lonely wandering people found their expression in the hope for a better future.

The commentary in the Zohar thus explains that the dark bride is the glory of the Shekinah, and that Solomon is to be understood not as an earthly ruler, but the universal bridegroom, or divine consciousness itself, which, united with the soul, reigns forever in glory because it contains the secret method by which "the King to whom peace belongs" may be restored to sovereignty over all universal powers and energies. It was written that without the King's union with Shekinah, there could be no remedy for the sorrow of the Moon. The Holy Assembly of the Fathers also explains that the Song of Songs was a microcosm, or miniature, of the whole of Israel's existence. It contained in condensed form the story of all of the works of creation, the mystery of the patriarchs, the exile of Israel in Egypt, Israel's deliverance from the Egyptians and their song at the passage of the Red Sea, the Decalogue, Israel's wandering in the desert, Israel's entry into the Holy Land, and the construction of the Temple, the dispersion of Israel among the nations, and its final salvation, the mystery of the holy name, and lastly, the resurrection of the dead and the wonders which would occur upon that day which is the Sabbath of the Lord.

Although available versions of the Zohar do not unfold the complete pattern of these analogies, it is evident that, by careful reading, sections of the poem reveal what can well be a double meaning. For example, chapter 3:6: "Who is this that cometh out of the wilderness like pillars of smoke, perfumed with myrrh and frankincense, with all powders of the merchant?" This could well refer to the wandering of Israel in the wilderness accompanied by the glory of the Shekinah, which appeared as a column of smoke by day and a pillar of flame by night. Verses 7-10 of the same chapter describe the bed palanquin, or chariot, of Solomon. It is guarded by the valiant men of Israel. The chariot was made of the wood of Lebanon, and the description given in verse 10 is strongly reminiscent of the description of Solomon's Temple. It would be far more reasonable to assume that it was the Temple that was "paved with love" than merely a ceremonial chariot. The old explanations were based upon mystical reverie seeking to strengthen the conviction that the poem was truly a love song in which God sang to Israel, his beloved.

The alchemists of the Middle Ages declared that the Song of Songs contained the whole secret of the transformation of base metals into the true gold of the philosophers. Its eight chapters set forth the secret formula and the steps necessary to the working chemist who sought the purification of natural elements. We know that the alchemists were really mystics who concealed their metaphysical speculations under the strange and complicated terms of chemistry. To them, gold meant the redeemed and regenerated powers of the soul, and the philosopher's stone was enlightened wisdom. It is believed that the first verse of the second chapter of the Song, "I am the rose of Sharon, *and* the lily of the valleys," is the source of the old Rosicrucian symbolism which often combines the rose and the lily. The verse also appears upon alchemical diagrams and symbols, but is never interpreted for the profane. The rose and the lily were said by the Cabalists to represent the community of Israel, but primarily they stand for love and wisdom, and according to the Hermetic philosophers, these must be united within the chemist's own consciousness before he can attain adeptship in his art. They represented this union through the Hermetic Marriage, the wedding of the sun and moon. The King symbolizes the sovereign intelligence of the world. He is the wisest of all rulers, and his wisdom endures forever. The dark maiden is reminiscent of the Black Ishtar, the Black Diana of Ephesus, the Black Melitta, and the Black Virgin of early European Christianity. She is the "hidden mother," the Black Isis, the Dark Mother of Mysteries. In substance, she is the mother of the gods, to whom the Emperor Julian addressed his hymn of praise. Thus, the Song which is Solomon's contains a mystical description of the union of heaven and earth, of God and Nature.

According to the Assembly of Rabbinical Fathers, every verse, chapter, fable, and parable, contained in the Sacred Scriptures has seventy-two meanings. These venerable men, therefore, would have been the first to admit that the Song of Songs could be variously interpreted, according to the subject under consideration or the level of the inquiry. It would be well to remember, however, that allegories and similes can be overtaxed. The parable cannot be exact in every detail, nor can it exhaust the total content of the facts or reality for which it stands. Interpretations arise within the student or reader. He understands according to his own capacity, and finds what he seeks or expects. In centuries dominated by mystical concepts, it was right and proper to study the Scriptures in this light. Attitudes have changed, and the reverse is evident today, for a subtle materialism pervades modern man's attitude toward Biblical writings.

It is not difficult to understand why modern Biblical interpreters with little or no time or patience for the mystical speculations of the ancients consider such works as the Zohar to be completely incomprehensible, and seek more obvious, if less inspiring, solutions for the symbolism of sacred writings. Ariel Bension devotes considerable space and thought to the Song of Songs and similar allegorical writings by Christian and Moslem mystics. He concludes: "Under the Oriental ornamentation describing the love of Solomon for Shulamite, they found a deeper meaning. It represented to all of them the heavenly love which is free from sensuality and in which the lovers are humanity and God. Or the mystical union between God and the soul." (See, *The Zohar in Moslem and Christian Spain*).

When the Shulamite maiden took the Christian veil, to borrow a phrase from one commentator, it was inevitable that the new sect should base its interpretation upon the foundations of the old religion. The Gnostics, both Syrian and Egyptian, venerated the Virgin Sophia, who symbolized to them the pure love-wisdom of God. It was among the troubadours, or wandering minstrels, of the Middle Ages, who were the philosophical heirs of Gnosticism, that the old mystical concepts were revived. These troubadours were sweet singers of songs, and they always dedicated their ballads to a beautiful, virtuous, and mysterious woman, the Virgin of the World. These songs came finally to be regarded as merely amorous expressions of human passion, but they were actually mystical hymns of adoration to Sophia, the Virgin Mother of the mysteries of the soul. The elusive and ethereal Beatrice of Dante, and the Dark Woman of the Shakespeare Sonnets, like the Shulamite maiden of Solomon's Song, certainly originated on the same level of mysticism. They may seem to have certain historical orientations, but their significance transcends history.

The alternative explanation of the poem considerably complicates the story. While it is assumed that this will prove devastating to the older mystical symbolism, such is not actually the case. In terms of recent criticism, it is taken for granted that the Song of Songs, called the *Canticles* in the Douay Bible, is simply a romantic poem possibly originally prepared for dramatic presentation. These critics acknowledge, of course, that very little is known of the ancient Jewish theater or early plays. The principal characters in the Song are King Solomon, a Shulamite maiden, and a young shepherd, her lover. The village girl is brought into the seraglio of the great Israelite king, who woos her with great ardor. Her thoughts and emotions, however, are completely centered upon her rustic lover. She finally leaves, or escapes from, the palace, and returns to the house of her mother, where she is reunited with the shepherd. The moral of the story is expressed in chapter 8:7: "Many waters cannot quench love, neither can the floods drown it: if a man would give all the substance of his house for love, it would utterly be condemned."

Because of the curious structure of the Song, it is entirely possible to either accept or reject the character of the shepherd. If the work is read bearing his existence in mind, he can be sustained in chapter 1:7, where the Shulamite maiden is musing about her beloved: "Tell me, O thou whom my soul loveth, where thou feedest, where thou makest *thy flock* to rest at noon: for why should I be as one that turneth aside by the flock of thy companions?" A woman of the harem answers her question: "If thou know not, O thou fairest among women, go thy way forth by the footsteps of the flock, and feed thy kids beside the shepherds' tents." (1:8) The burden of these verses can easily be interpreted as the Shulamite's statement of devotion to some person who is a shepherd, and with whom she longs to be reunited. It would seem more reasonable to assume this than to assign these verses to King Solomon or to consider that he is the shepherd. Continuing this reflection, it is quite conceivable that Solomon can have spoken the line: "I have compared thee, O my love, to a company of horses in Pharaoh's chariots." (1:9). We know that the King of Egypt sent gifts of horses to Solomon's court. Chapter 4:8 is the principal quotation attributed to the shepherd: "Come with me from Lebanon, *my* spouse, with me from Lebanon: look from the top of Amana, from the top of Shenir and Hermon, from the lions' dens, from the mountains of the leopards." These lines would be most unlikely if attributed to Solomon. Much depends, therefore, upon the attitude of the reader and the school of interpretation to which he belongs.

It is obvious that most of the earlier interpreters of the Song have ignored the shepherd, and have assumed that the verses concerned only Solomon and the Shulamite. Even Origen, the first Christian Father to extol the Song, held it to be allegorical of the union of Christ (the bridegroom) and the Church (the Shulamite girl). In light of his general attitude on theological matters, Origen also affirmed that the dark maiden could represent the soul of the individual believer seeking mystical union with Christ. The introduction of the shepherd, and there are certainly traces of him in the poem, provides a triangulating complication, but does not necessarily destroy the symbolical integrity of the drama.

It would seem remarkable that Christian scholars have not recognized the importance of the shepherd. If the Shulamite returns to her true love, it is the shepherd lad, and not Solomon, who actually becomes the bridegroom. Christ, as the good shepherd guarding his flock, is a familiar figure in early Christian art. The longing of the human soul for peace and release from worldliness would scarcely be satisfied in the harem of Solomon. Would not the mystical overtones be more clear and satisfying if the Shulamite turned from the pomp and glory of the fabulous king, renounced profane love, and chose a humble life with the "Good Shepherd?"

There seems to be no real justification for the somewhat prevalent attitude that the wording of certain verses of the Song of Songs is objectionable to the sensitivities of refined persons. Even those modern authors and commentators who are inclined to regard the poem as secular have been quick to defend the essential sincerity and morality of its sentiments. Ernest Renan notes: "The traits of detail, though they may seem to shock our modesty (too often carried to a ridiculous extent), are those which are to be found in all antique poetry." Later he adds, "The sentiment of the book, like that of all Hebrew books, is pure." Renan, who devoted many years to the study of the poem, pays tribute to the Shulamite maiden in the following words: "None of her contemporaries in the heathen world, although more civilized —the Chamite and Couschite races—has accomplished what she has done; no daughter of Memphis or of Babylon, a thousand years before Jesus Christ, has resisted a king, or preferred a hut to a seraglio. The Shulamite was a saint of her time. She signalized the first appearance of the virtue of love the moment when, sensual though it yet was, the profound instinct which God has concealed in the bosom of human nature attained, in the free and proud conscience of a young Israelite maiden, the highest sphere of morality. Do not criticize, according to the rules of our modern proprieties, each sentence of the ingenious peasant girl; do not require of her the extreme refinements of a Saint Teresa. She was a simple daughter of *naive* antiquity. Though her heart was not touched with the flame of seraphic fire, she knew 'that love was stronger than death,' she felt 'the glow of the fire of Jehovah.'" (See, *A Study of the Song of Songs*).

From the above it will be obvious that the attitude of most modern critics is highly respectful, if not reverent. Perhaps many of them are closer to the mystical overtones of the Song than they realize. When asked why he believed that the Song of Songs was entitled to a place in the Bible, the critic Neibuhr replied very simply, "For me, I should think that the Bible was lacking in something if one could not find in it expression of the deepest and strongest sentiments of humanity." Here we are confronted with the levels of interpretation, but we also understand why the Song of Songs, though always a controversial book, was retained among the sacred writings. Its message on either a religious or secular level is clear and deep. It rewards the contemplative heart with a rich treasure of courageous insight. The casual reader should remember the motto on the ribbon of the Order of the Garter "Honi soit qui mal y pense."

CHAPTER VIII
FAMOUS BIBLE STORIES

By including in the present work a group of Bible stories selected from various sections of the Old Testament, it will be possible to provide further insight into the manner in which ancient fables and legends came to be incorporated into Scriptural writings. Referring to those processes by which intelligible accounts gradually lost their clarity of definition and became comparatively unintelligible, at least to the average reader, Professor Max Mueller, the celebrated orientalist, writes: " . . . there was a tendency to change the original conception of divine powers, to misunderstand the many names given to these powers, and to misinterpret the praises addressed to them. In this manner some of the divine names were changed into half-divine, half-human heroes, and at last the myths which were true and intelligible

205

as told originally of the sun, or the dawn, or the storms, were turned into legends or fables too marvelous to be believed of common mortals . . . . This process can be watched in India, in Greece, in Germany. The same story, or nearly the same, is told of gods, of heroes, and of men. The divine myth becomes an heroic legend, and the heroic legend fades away into a nursery tale. Our nursery tales have well been called the modern patois of the ancient sacred mythology of the Aryan race." (See, *Chips From a German Workshop,* V. 2).

THE STORY OF SAMSON

The account relating to Samson occurs in the 13th to 16th chapters of The Book of Judges. His name in Hebrew was *Shimshon,* meaning the "sun-man," but the Greek form *Samson* was retained in the Latin Vulgate and has come to general acceptance. According to the Book of Judges, there was a certain man named Manoah, of the family of the Danites, whose wife was barren. And the angel of the Lord appeared to her, saying: "For, lo, thou shalt conceive, and bear a son; and no razor shall come on his head: for the child shall be a Nazarite unto God from the womb: and he shall begin to deliver Israel out of the hand of the Philistines." (13:5). After Samson was born, in fulfillment of this prophecy, he grew rapidly in stature and his strength became so prodigious that he killed a lion with his bare hands, slew many of his enemies, and even carried away the gates of a great city.

It was finally Delilah who discovered the secret of his strength, which lay in his long hair. After she had cut off his seven gleaming locks, he was easily taken by the Philistines, who blinded him, bound him with fetters of brass, and caused him to turn a grindstone. But after a time, Samson's hair grew again, and he realized that his strength was returning. When the lords over the Philistines gathered to offer sacrifices to their god, Dagon, they had Samson brought to the temple to entertain the people. He then took hold of the two middle pillars which supported the house, and brought down the roof upon the assembly, and so died with his enemies.

Samson is listed as the last of the Judges of Israel, and it is written in Judges 16:31 that he judged Israel for twenty years. The propriety of the inclusion of Samson among the venerable Judges has been seriously questioned, however, for he was not actually a leader over his people, nor was he truly their deliverer. Although it is quite possible that Samson actually lived and was a person of phenomenal physical strength, the account of him as it has descended to us has certainly become involved in a cycle of solar legends. In fact, there is no part of the Old Testament in which the story of the sun-hero is more clearly set forth. Some may doubt that the early Jewish people made use of the astro-theological myths of other nations in their sacred writings. It is obvious to the serious student, however, that they did, and no better example can be advanced than the arrangement of the twelve tribes around the Tabernacle in the wilderness. Such symbolism also abounds in the New Testament, and it is reported that Leonardo da Vinci, who understood this practice, so grouped the figures in his painting "The Last Supper" that they correctly represented the sun surrounded by the twelve zodiacal signs.

It has frequently been noted that there are many parallels between the Jewish legend of Samson and the Greek myth of Hercules. The name Hercules is from the Greek *heracles* and probably means the "glorious gift of Hera (the queen of heaven)." Hercules, as a solar personification, performed certain labors consistent with his role. It has been pointed out that Hercules also was in all likelihood a real man, a chieftain of the Tyrians in Mycenaean times, as it was not the habit of the Greeks to call a god by a name compounded with the name of another deity.

We cannot doubt the solar significance of the myth of Hercules. As he lies dying, he is comforted by Iole (the fair-haired dawn). While the dark mists gather, he speaks to her. "Ah, Iole, brightest of maidens, thy voice shall cheer me as I sink down in the sleep of death. I saw and loved thee in the bright *morning time,* and now again thou hast come, *in the evening,* fair as the soft clouds which gather around the dying Sun." Hercules then comforts the sorrowing Iole with the words, "I shall see thee again in the bright land which is never trodden by the feet of night." (See, *Bible Myths,* by T. W. Doane).

The first of the labors of Hercules was the slaying of the Nemean lion, which he slew with his bare hands. The first exploit of Samson was the killing of a lion, also without the aid of any weapon. According to the ancients, the sun, entering its essential dignity in the sign of Leo, was said to overcome the celestial lion and clothe itself in the skin thereof. In classical symbolism, the strength of solar divinities is always associated with their hair. For this reason, the infant sun-god, born at the winter solstice, is usually represented with one lock of hair—the child-lock of the ancient Egyptians. The hairs—that is, the powers or rays—of the sun-god increase as the sun moves from the winter solstice to the summer solstice. Under these conditions, he will reach his throne in Leo, with seven locks of hair. The great Alexandrian Serapis, who also represented a solar deity, was called Theon Heptagrammaton, or "the god with the name of seven letters." Serapis is sometimes depicted with a coronet of seven rays, signifying the seven divine intelligences manifesting through the solar light, a kind of spectrum of attributes. Frequently, also, a sun deity is shown crowned with a circle of rays, each of which bears the sign or name of one of the seven sacred planets recognized by the ancients. The solar lion of the Gnosis is often surrounded by seven, twelve, or fourteen rays, all these numbers having astronomical and magical significance.

It is therefore evident that the astro-theological myths of the adventures of the sun in its annual journey through the twelve signs of the zodiac provided the framework for many hero cycles. In the ancient temple system of religious education now known as the Mysteries, the prevailing astronomical concepts also supplied the symbolical elements of the initiation rituals, including "the perilous journey" of the neophyte or truthseeker, who personified the human soul seeking union with its own spiritual source. Porphyry, the Neoplatonist, in his description of the Cave of the Nymphs, states that this grotto signifies the mortal world, and that those who enter this lower region come in through the Gate of Cancer, and those who are victorious over the illusions of the flesh depart in triumph through the Gate of Capricorn. As these rites and ceremonies were established at the time when the sun actually passed over the vernal equinox in the sign of Aries, it means that the summer solstice occurred in Cancer, the sign governing birth, and the winter solstice in Capricorn, the sign associated with physical death.

According to the ancients, the two solstices divided the circle of the zodiac into two hemispheres, which they called *oriental* and *occidental*. The western hemisphere, with its six zodiacal signs, constituted the region of the perilous journey. The sun, having passed the summer solstice in Cancer, was said to enter the underworld. At the autumnal equinox, its benevolent powers are markedly reduced and continue to decline until its annual death at the winter solstice. In the Greek myth of Hercules, twelve labors are described, for the travel of the sun through all the signs of the zodiac is explained. In the story of Samson, only six exploits are specifically mentioned, and these cover the second half of the sun-god's annual life. The works of Samson are associated with the solar myths in the following order as they occur in the Bible:

> Sun in Cancer: Samson is born of the ancient mother, who is barren until she bears him.
>
> Sun in Leo: He slays the lion in the vineyards of Timnath.
>
> Sun in Virgo: He takes the garments of the 30 men of Ashkelon. (Each sign of the zodiac has thirty degrees.)
>
> Sun in Libra: He ties the firebrands to the tails of the foxes and burns the fields of the Philistines.
>
> Sun in Scorpio: He avenges the murder of his wife.
>
> Sun in Sagittarius: He slays one thousand men with the jawbone of an ass.
>
> Sun in Capricorn: He carries off the gates of Gaza, his last exploit before the circumstances associated with his death.

Among the labors of Hercules was the separation of the great rocks that blocked the entrance to the Mediterranean Sea. These rocks now guard the Straits of Gibraltar. Montfaucon reproduces an ancient work of art which depicts Hercules carrying the gates of the Mediterranean in the form of two Greek columns, one of which he sets up on the European side, and the other on the African side of the narrow straits. Sometimes Hercules is depicted carrying what appears to be an actual gate, and this seems to parallel Samson and the gates of Gaza. The word *Gaza* means *strong,* but Sir William Drummond in his *Oedipus Judaicus* writes: "*Gaza* signifies a Goat, and was the type of the Sun in Capricorn. The *Gates of the Sun* were feigned by the ancient Astronomers to be in Capricorn and Cancer (that is, in Gaza), from which signs the tropics were named."

It is Delilah, whose name means *weak,* who learns that the strength of Samson lies in his seven locks of hair (rays). Of this, Professor Steinthal writes: "His hair is a figure of increase and luxuriant fulness. In Winter, when nature appears to have lost all strength, the god of growing young life has lost his hair. In the Spring the hair grows again, and nature returns to life again. Of this original conception the Bible story still preserves a trace. Samson's hair, after being cut off, grows again, and his strength comes back with it." (See, *The Legend of Samson*). Like other solar deities Samson is also blinded, for his light is obscured by the darkness of winter.

The temple of the Philistines, which is principally supported by two great columns, is symbolic of the material or mortal sphere, the "cave" of Plato. In the Egyptian mythology, the vast subterranean Judgment Hall of the god Osiris was ornamented with two huge columns. Having secretly regained his strength through the growth of his hair, Samson is led to the Temple of Dagon, where he casts down the two supporting pillars and perishes with his enemies. Thus the forces of good and evil, or light and darkness, die together, and the old sun-god sacrifices himself to prepare the way for the birthday of the new sun.

Another version of this myth is found in the Nordic mythology where the armies of life and death meet in mortal combat on the field of Vigrid. In this last great war, the Armageddon of Christian theology, Odin, the one-eyed solar hero, is slain by the monster-wolf Fenris, which in turn is killed by Odin's son, Vidar. Thor, the mighty thunderer, slays the Midgard serpent, but is himself drowned in its venom. Good and evil perish together, the worlds fall into the ocean of chaos, and only the measureless sea of oblivion remains. In due course, however, Alfadur, the Eternal Power, brings forth a new heaven and a new earth where peace and happiness are universal, and where sin and death are unknown.

Even the astronomical symbolism contains a deeper meaning, however, for the solar cycle always has a Messianic significance. All sun-gods are in some ways prototypes of the Messiah or Savior. Old theological writings declare that Christ, by his death, destroyed or overcame death, and thus brought to an end the reign of the Adversary. This is partly prefigured by Samson, who gave his own life to destroy the temple of the Philistines. As Samson's seven locks of hair were the source of his power, so, later, the Lamb of God (the Sun exalted in Aries) bled from seven wounds,* and this blood was for the cleansing of the nations.

The sun-god myths are indicative not only of the radiant orb in the sky, but also of that mortal sun, or spirit of light in man, which achieves redemption by the performance of the twelve labors which make up the moral zodiac of experience. The trials reported of Ulysses in the Odyssey, and the marvelous adventures of Sinbad the Sailor in the Arabian Nights Entertainment should be interpreted by the same key. The solar heroes are personifications of humanity's struggle for truth and light, and the final accomplishment of man's liberation from igno ʾnce and fear. This perilous journey is the long road home which the Neoplatonists describe as "the alone seeking for the Alone."

THE BOOK OF RUTH

The Book of Ruth is one of the five Scrolls, and the events took place "in the days when the judges ruled." (1:1) Ruth, whose name means "friend," is the Moabite heroine of this book. The story has a place in the legendry that sprang up around King David, and Ruth is mentioned in

---

*Two wounds in the head were caused by the wreath of thorns.

the genealogy of Christ (Matthew 1:5). Although intensive research has been devoted to the interpretation of this book, it has not usually been considered a philosophical work. The prevailing attitude has been to consider it a simple story of early Jewish society in an agrarian period, with references to old rites and observances and the customs of ancient days.

A certain man of Bethlehem in Judea, by the name of Elimelech (God is king) with his wife Naomi (lovable) and his two sons, departed from his home and settled himself in the country of Moab. Elimelech died soon after and Naomi was left widowed. Her sons took wives from among the women of Moab, and they dwelt in the land for about ten years. Both the sons of Naomi then also died, and she resolved to return to the place of her husband's birth. Ruth, a Moabite woman who had been married to one of Naomi's sons, resolved to return with her mother-in-law to Bethlehem. She united herself with Israel and took its God as her God, and later married a wealthy man of Bethlehem named Boaz, a kinsman of Elimelech. In chapter 4:13, it is implied that Ruth bore a son for Boaz by the grace of God, and in verse 17, this son, Obed (worshipping), is stated to be the father of Jesse, who in turn was the father of David.

The ethical burden of the Book of Ruth involves two subtle points, neither of which is strongly emphasized in the writings. One deals with inter-marriage, which was strictly forbidden by Ezra and Nehemiah. The second point is that David was descended from a Moabite woman, a stranger and not one of the chosen people. Yet Ruth, who was born an alien, through the integrity of her own life, her abiding faith, and her great loyalty, was deservedly chosen to become an ancestress of David, the greatest of the Israelitish culture-heroes. At the time the book was written, these considerations were certainly more real and vital than in our day.

They contributed toward the elevation of the state of woman in general and also broadened and liberalized the Jewish tradition. These circumstances are in themselves sufficient to justify the incorporation of the work into the body of the Sacred Scriptures.

The legends relating to Ruth add something to the picture. When she journeyed to Palestine with her mother-in-law, Naomi, she was warned by the older woman of the strictness of the Jewish law. Naomi said to her; "We have one Torah, one law, one command; the Eternal our God is one, and there is none beside Him." To which Ruth replied, "Thy people *shall be* my people, thy God my God." They reached Bethlehem on the very day that the wife of Boaz, a man high-born and of good substance, was being taken out for burial. Ruth supported herself and Naomi by gleaning in the fields of Boaz, but she was most careful not to exceed the privileges of the gleaners as set by law. Boaz watched her from afar, and was deeply impressed with her gentle and modest ways. The legends tell us that Boaz was of great age when he married Ruth, and he did not live long thereafter. But Ruth was privileged to see the glory of Solomon. Before his death, Boaz told Ruth of a vision he had seen. Because of the good she had done for Naomi, and because she had been virtuous and gracious in all things, kings and prophets would spring from her womb.

It sometimes happens that the deepest mysteries are revealed through simple and apparently meaningless stories and fables, and such is the case in the Book of Ruth, which is the veiled account of the journey of the truth-seeker in quest of light. Elements of old initiation rituals can be discovered if the text is carefully examined. There is a legend that when Solomon the King caused the great Temple to be built in Jerusalem, he placed on the porch of the Everlasting House two great columns, intricately ornamented, which had been fashioned for him by Hiram, the master craftsman. The names of these columns were Jachin and Boaz, and they are still represented in certain symbolisms by the letters *J* and *B*. In the Cabala, these columns are referred to as *strength* and *wisdom,* which are the great supports of the House of God. They are also sometimes called *knowledge* and *understanding,* which ornament the entrance to the universal temple. The Cabalists further said that the pillar named Boaz was placed at the left side of the great door, and that this is the pillar of Hokhmah (wisdom).

In the story of Ruth, Boaz (wisdom) is the master of a great field and has many harvesters who reap his grain. It requires no stretch of the imagination to understand this subtle reference. All the world belongs to wisdom, and all the harvests are gathered by understanding. Boaz is old, and wisdom is traditionally represented as an ancient person. His wife is dead, which implies that ancient systems of instruction which he had founded had perished away. Ruth comes to glean in his field; that is, to learn the ways of wisdom, and, with proper sincerity, she takes only that which is her lawful share. It would be quite fitting that the Moabite woman who took upon herself the faith of Israel and possessed true greatness of spirit should have been placed under the guardianship and guidance of the masters of Israel, personified by Boaz.

Running through the Book of Ruth are a series of intimations and implications which seem to relate the book to that level of philosophy generally associated with the initiation rites of ancient nations. There is no reason to assume that fragments of old ritual should not be found in Biblical writings. In fact, we know that they frequently occur. Broadly speaking, all candidates seeking admission into the sanctuaries of secret learning were said to personify or impersonate the human soul and the long and perilous journey by which the redemption of the soul was accomplished. When the neophyte applied for admission into a college of the Mysteries, he was asked by the priests whence he had come and why he was seeking knowledge. A literal answer was not expected or acceptable, for he had already been instructed that he was to say that he was a stranger, a wanderer, a traveler from a far place who had journeyed out of the land of darkness in search for truth. Frequently, the material world of illusions and ambitions was also symbolically associated with some remote place or a nation notable for its physical and soulless splendour; thus the children of Israel left Egypt in search of the Promised Land, and when Israel sinned, it was led into captivity by the Babylonians. In the story of the Prodigal Son, the young man left his father's house and descended into the flesh-pots of Egypt, where he wasted his substance in riotous living. The enemies of a tribe or race became the embodiment of evil. They were the unbelievers, or those who worshipped false gods, and therefore stood for spiritual ignorance.

Moses was versed in the wisdom of the Egyptians. Among these people, Isis, whose husband-brother, Osiris, was foully murdered, represented the school of the Mysteries. Osiris was the esoteric wisdom, the secret science of regeneration, and as a result of his death, the "word of power" was lost. Isis was thereafter represented as invested with the weeds of the widow, and is said to have covered her head with ashes and to have mourned for her lost lord. This means that the State religion was deprived of the living presence of God, who thereafter was represented by a symbol—the empty throne-chair of the hierophant. The initiates of the rites were referred to as the "sons of the widow," for they were bound by obligations to restore the lost doctrine. When they had accomplished this end, Osiris would return to them in the form of his only begotten son, Horus, and would rule over them forever. For many peoples, therefore, the State religion, or the theological institutions, were referred to arcanely as the "widow," who would bear a son for the salvation of the world. This son would be the Messiah.

The entire story, of course, is not set forth in the Book of Ruth, but there is a reference to a widow—in this case, Naomi—who lost not only her husband, but her sons. The text could well signify a religious system or institution belonging to the old cycle of the Mysteries. After the death of Elimelech, Naomi takes the name Mara, which means "bitter," (in this sense, sorrowing), because of the loss of her lord. Ruth becomes the handmaiden of Naomi, and we know from the open text that she associates herself with the wisdom religion of Israel. It seems probable, therefore, that Naomi signifies the Torah, or the body of the law. Deprived of its inner spiritual meaning, this law becomes bitter, demanding vengeance and judgment, which is not its spirit, but its letter. Because Ruth serves Naomi faithfully, with love and humility of spirit, she is said to find favor in the eyes of Boaz. He is her kinsman because he is related to the family of Elimelech—that is, the priesthood of the temple. But Boaz is also a great column in the house of the Lord; that is, he belongs to the assembly of initiates, the custodians of the spiritual mysteries. Ruth, as the human soul, the faithful servant of truth, first represented by the Torah, is united in marriage or a sacrament of union to Boaz, and he restores to her and her family their proper portions of goods and properties—that is, their spiritual heritage—for her sake and because of her goodness.

Thus the soul, or the truth-seeker, departed out of the land of Moab, the house of the strangers, and sought communion with the true God—the spirit and its divine attributes. To those who seek first, and with their whole hearts,

the kingdom of righteousness, all other things are added in
due time, according to the workings of the law of wisdom.
As the symbol of the soul brought into spiritual union with
the divine power, Ruth becomes the mother of sages and of
scholars, and it is proper that the great kings, David and
Solomon, should be descended from her. After the union
of Ruth and Boaz, it is said that the older man did not live
long, but the name of their son, Obed (worshipping), is
consistent with the tone of the story. Wisdom, having fulfilled its work by restoring Ruth's estates (her spiritual understanding), completed its purpose and, like Moses, was
taken to its father. Thus, Ruth, the soul-power in man, is
born in the land of the stranger, is brought to life by faithful service, receives her proper portion through philosophical
discipline(the gleaning in the fields of Boaz), and becomes
the mother of heroes.

DAVID AND GOLIATH

The account of David slaying the giant Goliath is contained in I. Samuel, beginning 17:4, but it is written that the
Scriptures contain only a small part of what could be told
about Goliath, for there were many legends telling of his
impiety and evil. It is said that he even challenged the God
of Israel to do battle against him, and that at one time, he
had gone so far as to seize the Holy Tables of the Law, but
King Saul took them away from him. As a consequence
of this incident, Goliath was resolved to destroy Saul. When
the time appointed by the Lord had come, David put on
Saul's armour, but it fitted him so ill that he would not
wear it. Thus he went forth against the giant dressed as a
simple shepherd. When the pebble from David's slingshot
struck Goliath in the forehead, he fell on his face, so that
the mouth that had blasphemed God was filled with earth.
The huge Philistine also wore the image of Dagon on his

breast, and this, too, was humbled upon the ground. Goliath wore many suits of armor, and had not the Angel of the Lord descended, David's victory would have been uncertain.

The name Goliath means "shining," but some authorities say that it is derived from an Arabic word meaning "stout" or "huge." According to the Bible, his height is said to have been six cubits and a span, which would have made him stand above ten feet. Josephus, more conservative, says four cubits and a span, which might be nearer to the fact. From the description of his arms and armament, Goliath may have increased his appearance of size in order to frighten the armies of his enemies. Although the story was included in the First Book of Samuel, it is generally believed that it is a comparatively late narrative arising after David had been elevated to the estate of a national hero. By degrees, Goliath came to personify the numerous enemies who perturbed the years of David's reign.

King David has been called the Israelitish King Arthur. Around him many legends gathered, and accounts of his exploits were perpetuated, with numerous embellishments, from one generation to another. Even the Scriptural writers had difficulty in distinguishing between fact and fable, and the story of his life exhibits a number of inconsistencies. As founder of the Judean dynasty in Jerusalem, David has been remembered both as warrior and statesman, and as the moving spirit of the kingdom which he established. His personal life, exemplifying both his frailties and his strength, is so essentially human that it appealed to every class of his people. He thus became the central figure in the Jewish age of chivalry, and can be compared with the Frankish King Charlemagne, or the figure of Gessar Khan in Tibetan lore.

Among the accomplishments of these semi-legendary, semi-historical personalities, there are always giants, ogres, dragons, and other hideous monsters which must be overcome in mortal combat. The meaning is always the same, for these are the adversaries, personifications of evil, and the negative forces operating in human society. Goliath embodies the whole concept of materiality, worldliness, and the power of might over right. This is the more obvious when we remember that Goliath of Gath was also a great warrior of the Philistines, a people held in violent contempt by the Jews. The very word has come to carry this meaning, for the third definition of Philistine in the dictionary reads: "an active or passive opponent of progress or progressive ideas." Obviously David, in the establishment of a dynasty, was forced to strive against reactionary groups and the gigantic force of inertia which opposes the ways of progressive leadership.

On the Cabalistic level of interpretation, Goliath signifies arrogance, pride, or the will to power, which each human being must combat within himself, and whose excesses he must overcome if he is to keep faith with his God and his fellow men. Goliath corresponds to what Boehme, the German mystic, calls "self-will," which dares to assail the divine will. He is the rebel angel, Satan, who also was stoned. Goliath, as self-will, even dared to challenge the God of Israel to mortal combat, and it is in the proper spirit of folk-lore that David, the sweet singer, the culture-hero, should be the one to destroy this giant. David thus also becomes a prototype of the Messiah, who shall overcome the prince of this world and his legions. There also appears a parallel between Goliath and the Great Image of Nebuchadrezzar's dream, which was also dissolved by a stone.

In Greek mythology, giants are frequently introduced as symbolical of primordial forces and elements. The Titans

belonged to this class. They were destroyed by the thunder-
bolts of Zeus, and from their ashes, mixed with the blood
of Dionysius, primitive humanity was fashioned. It was assumed, therefore, that within man himself a perpetual struggle resulted from the mixture of divine and Titanic principles. In the Zohar, the giants are those unbalanced forces
which must perish in the void. They were the kings of
Edom—original chaos, which preceded the dawn of cosmos.
Like the huge pre-historic animals that once roamed the
earth, they vanished away in the dawn of time as man
(David) began his systematic conquest of the primitive
world (Goliath).

In Neoplatonic psychology, the Cyclops, or one-eyed giant,
was regarded as the personification of the vast, subjective, un-
differentiated human potential. Man, the rational being,
must struggle with titanic forces, not only around him, but
also within him. The unknown always appears gigantic and
menacing, and there are times when it seems that the powers
of the soul are not equal to the challenge. The ultimate
victory of mind over matter, of cosmos over chaos, of civilization over savages, was the burden of the Arthurian cycle
and the legends of Charlemagne. It is not difficult to trace
the same concept in the story of David and Goliath. It is
ever the symbolic account of the final victory of soul-power
over brute force on every level of creation. This old lore is
also preserved to us in the countless nursery tales centering
around the theme of Jack the giant-killer. Each child instinctively associates himself with Jack, although he may
not yet be able to estimate the proportions of the giant which
he must face. In all encounters, however, the hero-self must
be victorious. The giant must either be slain, as in Western
versions, or redeemed, as in the Tibetan hero-myths. Life
as mystery must be solved, and the solution is usually entrusted to a young and inexperienced person whose sim-

plicity and directness of action confounds the machinations of the shrewd and deceitful. Youth has always been the hero of the world, for it must solve the riddles which age bestows upon it as an inevitable heritage.

THE BOOK OF ESTHER

Esther, originally Hadassah, was one of the seven prophetesses of Israel, and a woman of great beauty. The name *Esther* means "star," and in the Hebrew Bible, the Book of Esther is the last of the Scrolls, and is placed between Ecclesiastes and Daniel. It is one of the books involved in controversy, various authorities placing its composition between the 5th and 2nd centuries B. C. There was early opposition to its inclusion in the Bible because it does not mention the name of God, and because it is concerned particularly with secular matters. It deals with the origin of the Feast of Purim. This festival occurs on the 14th of Adar, generally falling in February or March. It celebrates the deliverance of the Jewish people from grave danger in some early time. According to the Book of Esther, the 13th of Adar was the day on which the Jews of Persia were to have been destroyed during the reign of King Ahasuerus. It was due to the efforts of Esther and her cousin Mordecai that this calamity was averted. It is by no means certain, however, that the account given in Esther correctly explains the Feast of Purim, which has also been traced to Persian and Babylonian sources. The Book of Esther was first read only on the morning of Purim, but later its popularity so increased that it became a general favorite. It is especially significant to women because it presents Esther as one of the great heroines of the Jewish people.

In substance, the book relates that Ahasuerus (Xerxes), having become displeased with his queen, Vashti, orders the most beautiful maidens of the kingdom to be brought to him so that he may select a queen. He chooses Esther, who was descended from the tribe of Benjamin. She is made queen, but tells no one that she is a Jewess. At this time also, Mordecai, her cousin and guardian and a most learned and noble man, learns that there is a conspiracy against the King, and conveys the news to him through Esther. Haman becomes prime minister of Persia, and when Mordecai refuses to bow before him, Haman resolves to destroy the Jews. He casts lots (Pur) to determine the day most favorable for his conspiracy. He then goes to the King, declaring that there is a people within the empire who is disobedient and rebellious and constantly plotting against the King's life and possessions. Haman does not say that these people are Jewish, but he gains the consent of the King to exterminate the rebellious subjects. Learning of the decree, Mordecai pleads with Esther to appeal to her King and husband. Esther reminds Mordecai that if she enters the King's presence without his command, and contrary to his wishes, she can be put to death unless the King holds out to her his golden scepter.

At last, realizing the desperateness of the situation, Esther risks her life, but is wonderfully preserved because the King extends his scepter. She contrives to have the King and Haman attend a banquet which she prepares for the following night. In due course, the King learns that Mordecai has discovered another conspiracy against him. Esther finally tells the King the truth about the destruction that threatens her and her people. Haman is denounced and is himself hanged upon the gallows which he had prepared for Mordecai.

As the historical circumstances are in serious conflict, it is now generally assumed that the story was derived from older sources, probably Babylonian, and was gradually adapted into the literature, and finally the Scriptures, of the

Jewish people. One group suggests that Mordecai and Esther are the Babylonian gods Marduk and Ishtar, who triumphed over the Elamite deities Humman (Haman) and Mashti (Vashti). It is quite probable that Esther, as her star-name implies, was a symbol of the human soul achieving victory over the conspiracy of the material world. This book is said to have been written by the Great Assembly.

Mordecai plays the part of a Merlin, and there are many things remembered of him that are not recorded in the Scriptures. His name is said to mean, strangely enough, "consecrated to Merodach" (one of the hero-deities of Babylon). On his mother's side, he was of the tribe of Judah, and he refused to touch food that was forbidden, even at the banquet of the Persian King. His name has also been derived from *mor,* meaning "myrrh," and *decai,* meaning "pure." He was called "the one who illumined the eyes of Israel," and among his epithets was *Bilshan,* meaning "master of languages." He was a member of the great Sanhedrin, and understood the seventy languages of the world, and also the language of mutes. He later established an academy, and became teacher over the mind of Israel. After Esther became the wife of the Persian King, she was no longer able to mingle with her own people, but Mordecai was permitted to visit her, and he tended to her welfare in all things. Mordecai discovered the plot because the conspirators spoke in a foreign language, which they did not know he understood. It is also said that when Haman was resolved to destroy the Jews, he consulted the twelve signs of the zodiac to find which was most unfavorable to Israel. He decided upon the sign of the fishes because there was an ancient saying that the Jews would be swallowed like fishes. God, however, decreed it otherwise, for he said: "O thou villain! Fishes are sometimes swallowed, but sometimes they swallow, and thou shalt be swallowed by the swallowers."

The structure of the story of Esther seems to imply a hidden meaning. Conway, in his *Solomon and Solomonic Literature,* points out parallels with the mystical speculations of the Persians. He mentions specifically the recurrences of the number seven, which nearly always intimates the introduction of astro-mythological elements. Conway writes: "That the sanctity of 'seven' was impressed on all usages of life in Persia is shown in the story of Esther. King Ahasuerus feasts on the seventh day, has seven chamberlains, and consults the seven princes of Media and Persia ('wise men which knew the times'). When Esther finds favor of the King above all other maidens, as successor to deposed Vashti, she is at once given 'the seven maidens, which were meet to be given her, out of the king's house; and he removed her and her maidens to the best place of the house of the women.' Esther was thus a Queen of the Seven,—of Sheba, in Hebrew,—and although this was some centuries after Solomon's time, there is every reason to suppose that the Zoroastrian social usages in Persia prevailed in Solomon's time." Through the association with the sacred number seven, therefore, Esther must be included among the personifications of the principle of wisdom.

Very little commentary material on the Book of Esther is available among the productions of early scholarship. There is, however, an intimation in the Zohar, for the Great Holy Assembly declares that the Matrona is the Heavenly Esther, who fights against the evil designs of the demon, even as Esther fought against those of Haman. Here is another instance in which the understanding of Jewish metaphysics is essential to the interpretation of a Scriptural text. The symbol of the Matrona is especially difficult and obscure. She is described as the daughter of God who becomes the mother of man. It is said of her that she is myrionymous in her aspects and attributes. She is Shekinah and

Elohim, because to her are entrusted all the works of God. Matrona is the betrothed, the bride, the mother, and the sister. As the divine principle of womanhood, she unites with the King, for his perfection is in her and through her. It is said that The Holy One gave Matrona in marriage to Moses and that she stands as mediatrix between God and humanity. It is possible that certain doctrines of Latin Christianity relating to the intercessory powers of the Blessed Virgin have been derived from the concept of the Matrona.

The love and mercy of God, personified as Matrona, accompany the children of Israel in the wilderness as the Shekinah's glory, and she is said to depart from those who disobey the Lord. She is the divine presence filling the temple with holiness. She sits with the elders when they gather for mystic contemplation, and she abides in the hearts of the righteous. It is said that when the law was given to Israel, it was also bestowed as a vestment upon Matrona, and when men broke the law, the garments of Matrona were rent. It is also written that at a certain time, the oral law—that is, the Mishnah—was bestowed upon Matrona as a servant, but it destroyed this natural bond by attempting to usurp her powers. Gradually, the picture becomes clearer. Matrona shines forth as the secret doctrine in Israel. She is the spirit of the Great Assembly, the custodian of those powers of the soul by which man may inwardly experience the life and presence of his Creator. She is the spirit of the law and the prophets, for she is the living truth that walks before the Lord in glory.

If Esther personifies the Matrona, she stands for the soul of Israel; that is, the soul of the people set apart or chosen for the service of God. As the soul of the law, she is given the body of the Torah as her servant, but men, living by the letter of the code, have forgotten that the letter of the law kills, but the spirit of the law gives life. Without Matrona, which is therefore also inner understanding or the perceptive powers of the soul, the mind cannot experience spiritual union. As the soul of Israel, Matrona, through Esther, her handmaiden, rescues her people and becomes the inspiring symbol of ideal Jewish womanhood. The powers of evil, representing ignorance and perversion, attempt to exterminate the human race (Israel), but the Matrona, full of compassion for her people, intercedes for them before the heavenly King. On the moral level, as on the psychological, the story now becomes comprehensible. The human spirit (Xerxes), dissolves its union with worldliness and vanity (Vashti), and makes divine love (Esther) its queen. Ambition and greed (Haman), representing the attributes of the mortal mind, then attempt to take the kingdom by treachery, but are prevented by wisdom (Mordecai), who is the cousin of divine love. The destruction of the Jews in Persia which Haman attempted, symbolizes that the soul-power of Israel with its laws, rules, statutes, and convictions, had to be exterminated before the tyranny of ignorance and selfishness could accomplish its evil ends. Esther reaches the King, who graciously receives her, and reveals to him the evil strategy. Xerxes then punishes the traitor, Haman, who comes to the tragic end which he had prepared for Mordecai and the Persian Jews.

Like the Indian story of the *Ramayana,* the Book of Esther established a model for womanhood. The gracious Queen, risking her own happiness and even her life for the preservation of her people, set a standard for conduct which strongly appealed to the Jewish mind and heart. As a result, the book has exercised a wide sphere of influence, and has helped to bind the spirits of a wandering people, fortifying their souls and uniting them through their long centuries of misfortune. It is useful to the student of comparative religion because it invites research into the elements upon which powerful and surviving legends have been built.

NEBUCHADREZZAR'S DREAM

In the Hebrew Bible, the Book of Daniel is inserted between Esther and Ezra, and belongs to that section called the *Hagiographa,* which includes those works not forming parts of the Law or the Prophets. The name *Daniel* means "God is my judge." In general the book attributed to him comes under the heading of apocalyptical writing, emphasizing dreams, visions, and highly symbolical occurrences. It is in that class of writing which, while presumably of an early date, probably belonged to the 2nd century B. C., as it is definitely concerned with incidents which occurred during the persecution of the Jews by Antiochus Epiphanes. The Book of Daniel has one outstanding peculiarity. Chapters 2-7 are written in Aramaic, and the rest of the work in Hebrew. This has been attributed to the fact that part of the manuscript was lost, and only an Aramaic version was available. Historically, the book is most confusing, and students are invited to consult the *Jewish Encyclopedia* for further details relating to the historical controversy. Suffice it to say that most of the incidents are not supported by the history of the time.

The first six chapters are the most interesting from a philosophical point of view. They include Daniel's interpretation of Nebuchadrezzar's dream, Belshazzar's feast, and the account of Daniel's deliverance from the den of lions. The second part of the book, chapters 7 to 12, is concerned largely with the visions of Daniel. The prophetic section is climaxed by a description of the effort of Antiochus Epiphanes to uproot the Jewish religion, the wars of the Maccabees and their final victory over the adversary.

In chapter 2 of the Book of Daniel, beginning with verse 1 and continuing through verse 45, is the account of a strange dream of the King of Babylon, and the interpretation thereof by Daniel. The King beheld in his sleep a great image, the head of which was of fine gold, its breast and arms of silver, its body of brass, its legs of iron, and its feet a mixture of iron and clay. As the great figure stood in all its glory, a cubic stone was mysteriously cut from a quarry and cast by invisible hands at the feet of the great image. As the stone struck the feet, the image was destroyed, changing into fine dust. The cube afterwards grew greater in size until it became as vast as a mountain.

The explanation given by Daniel certainly does not exhaust the meaning of the strange dream. The prophet explains to Nebuchadrezzar that the golden head, the silver arms and breast, the brazen body, the iron legs, and the feet of iron and clay symbolize empires which shall fall one after another. From this account has arisen much confusion in modern theology. Many nations of the ancient and modern world have been associated with the parts of Nebuchadrezzar's image. Various adventist sects have justified their beliefs by reference to Daniel, and several Bible societies have announced the millenium as a result of calculations based upon the parts of this symbolic figure. These milleniumites have been fixing dates of the "second coming" for nearly a thousand years, "but the end is not yet." This practice is a notable example of the general lack of research and scholarship evident among most groups of religious enthusiasts.

The figure of Nebuchadrezzar's dream is definitely a macrocosmic man; the grand Cabalistic man of the Zohar; the Adam Kadmon; the mundane world symbol which appeared in Alexandria under the name of Serapis. The Alexandrian Serapis is described by the early Church Fathers as a figure composed of many metals and substances, including even plants. It was venerated as an epitome of Nature, both divine and human. Therefore, its upper parts were of more precious substances, and its lower parts of baser materials. Although the description given in Daniel is somewhat mutilated, the symbolism is apparent. Compare the metals and materials described in the giant figure of the dream with the four ages of the Greeks. Thus, the golden head of the image is the golden age; the breast and arms of silver are the silver age; the lower body of bronze is the bronze age; and the legs and feet composed of a mingling of iron and clay correspond to the iron age. In the four Yugas of the Hindus, the same arrangement prevails, and the fourth or lowest part of these time cycles, the Kali Yuga, corresponds also with the feet of iron and clay.

According to the teachings of the Zohar, the four worlds were represented by four Adams, or the four parts of one colossal figure, "whose body nature is, and God the soul." This great figure is always described by the Cabalists with its face in profile, without eyelids, and ornamented with a long beard ending in thirteen points. The head of this being is of gold, symbolizing the pure nature of divinity, which is the head and cause of all life. The silver arms and shoulders correspond to the active parts, the hierarchies which emanate from the golden head. They are the builders, the angels, arch-angels, seraphim, cherubim, thrones, dominions, and principalities. The bronze body is the zodiac, the planets, the material cosmos, and the extensions or emanations of these hierarchies into the world of form. Lastly, the fourth world, of iron and clay, represents the earth and the subterranean regions, which, according to these ancient philosophers, were girdled by a wall of iron. Here, the iron is the firmament, and the clay, the planet earth itself.

Nor do the analogies end here, for the great figure represents the cycles of generation. The head is birth, the shoulders growth, the body maturity, the legs old age, and the feet death. Here also is represented the compound constitution of man as it was understood in early times. The mental nature corresponds to gold, the emotional to silver, the vital principle to bronze, and the two-fold division of the physical body—magnetic and material—to iron and clay. The figure is therefore a kind of *Sephiroth,* a tree in the form of a man; the great tree that bears the world and the heavens upon its branches and symbolizes by its various parts the divisions of both the macrocosm and the microcosm. Here, also, are signified the five races and the four world periods—the fourth being divided into two parts, the Mars-Mercury halves of the earth's cycle, according to the Astronomical Cabala.

Christian Cabalists have considered the cubic stone as a prophecy of the mystery of Christ. This is the stone which the builders rejected, but which was to become the head of the corner. Early theologians believed and taught that the age of the Laws and the Prophets, the great structure of ancient philosophy, and the machinery of the sacred Mystery institutions, were to be dissolved and destroyed by the Messianic Dispensation. But consider the symbolism of the cube. It is the most perfect of the geometric solids, being equal in all its parts. It consists of 6 faces, which represent the days of creation, and is bordered by 12 lines, which symbolize the zodiac. If each of the faces be opened to the core, the result will be a cruciform design consisting of 6 pyramids. Each of the separate pyramids will have 4 faces (not including the base), and the total of these faces is 24, the number of the elders before the throne in Revelation, and also the number of the hours of the day. If the 24 be added to the 6 faces of the cube, the result will be 30, the number of degrees in the zodiacal signs and a twelfth part of a circle. It is written, therefore, that the perfect cube was symbolic of the New Jerusalem, the "City Four-square."

According to the Pythagoreans, the cube is a symbol of both matter and man, and the unfolding of the cube represents the opening of human consciousness and the releasing of the geometric mysteries therein contained. To the Christian, Christ is the perfect man; therefore, he becomes the embodiment of the perfect measure of a man—a cube. In Freemasonry, the perfect ashlar, or trued stone, is the proper figure of the righteous human being, for he is square, upright, and true, which are the moral qualities anciently represented by the cube. The trued and perfected cube represents the personality that has had all the unevenness, roughness, and inequality polished away by experience and discipline. Such a stone is ready to become a living ashlar in the Everlasting House not built by hands, but eternal in the heavens.

If, then, Nebuchadrezzar's man symbolizes the universe and the world, and the stone symbolizes the Adept, the perfect man, then we can understand how worldliness is dissipated by divine wisdom; how the material universe is overcome by the perfect self which is square and true, and, being overcome, is entirely dissipated, leaving "not a rack behind." We can then also understand why this cubic stone becomes larger and larger until it appears as a mountain. Wisdom itself is frequently symbolized by a mountain or hill. Truth, having overcome error, fills the whole world with itself. It also becomes the cube foundation upon which a new order of life can be sustained and brought to fulfillment. Nebuchadrezzar's dream warns that materiality and the pomp and circumstance of worldly grandeur have no adequate foundation and are vulnerable. They fall before the symbol of greater reality. It is another statement of man overcoming all external things by the perfection of his own inner life.

The concept of the world-tree is further unfolded in the 4th chapter of Daniel. There can be no doubt that Nebuchadrezzar is advanced as a personification of worldliness. Daniel proclaims this in 4:22 when he declares that the tree of the king's vision refers to the mighty monarch and the dominions of his empire. The cutting down of the tree is therefore a prophecy of the tragic termination of material ambitions. Madness descends upon Nebuchadrezzar, and he becomes like a beast of the field. This madness afflicts all who depart from righteousness and who become the victims of their own selfish ambitions.

BELSHAZZAR'S FEAST

It is written that when the Most High had resolved to humble Babylon because it had afflicted Israel, he selected Cyrus, the King of Persia, and Darius, the King of Media, to be the instruments of his judgment, and these Kings went against Belshazzar, the ruler over all Chaldea. In the midst of this war, which remained for some time uncertain, the Chaldeans attained a decisive victory. In celebration of this event, Belshazzar the King prepared a great banquet which he caused to be served from the vessels and sacred plates which had been taken from the Temple of Jerusalem by his father. At this banquet, the princes and their wives and concubines praised the Babylonian gods of gold and of silver, of brass and of iron, of wood and of stone. (See, Daniel 5:4).

While this impious king and his court were feasting together, an angel sent by the Lord came and was among them, and this angel traced in letters of red pigment certain words in Aramaic written in Hebrew characters, upon the plaster of the wall of the King's palace, over against a candlestick that was standing there. Belshazzar did not see the angel, but only the hand that wrote the characters upon the wall, while the others who were present saw only the writing. He was sorely troubled and cried aloud that the astrologers and Chaldeans and soothsayers should be brought to him, and promised that any man who could read the writing and divine the interpretation thereof, should be advanced to great honor and share in the rulership of the kingdom. But all those who came were unable to explain the mystery which had been wrought for God by the angel.

It was then that the Queen reminded Belshazzar that his father had called upon Daniel the Prophet, who was wise in all mysteries, could interpret dreams, and possessed the wisdom of the gods. This Queen, according to some writers, was Belshazzar's mother, but Josephus says she was his grandmother. The writing that was written upon the wall was MENE, MENE, TEKEL, UPHARSIN. Daniel interpreted the mysterious inscription thus: "MENE; God hath numbered thy kingdom and finished it. TEKEL; Thou art weighed in the balances, and art found wanting. PERES; Thy kingdom is divided, and given to the Medes and Persians." (Daniel 5:26-28)

This inscription has been most troublesome to Biblical students. If the words were Aramaic or Hebrew, certainly the wise men of the kingdom could have read them. It has been suspected, therefore, that the strange message was actually in some form of hieroglyphics or picture writing, and that Daniel had the insight to discern the true meaning. It has been customary also to translate these words as ancient weights thus: "A mina, a mina, a shekel and hath minas." This would suggest the idea: "He has counted, counted, weighed, and they assess." The original Biblical wording has been used in this sense by several writers. Perhaps the concept which has found favor with Cabalistic scholars meets best the requirements of this case. Belshazzar is included in the list of cosmocreators or kings of the world. If so, his palace could well symbolize the mundane creation contained within the sphere of the fixed stars. The handwriting on the wall would refer to the positions of stars and constellations.

James Gaffarel, who was astrologer to Cardinal Richelieu, in his book *Unheard of Curiosities, Etc.,* explains that the ancient Jewish philosophers represented the stars of heaven by the letters of their alphabet, and he appends to his work two large charts showing the constellations figured as what he calls "the celestial Hebrew alphabet." Gaffarel also makes reference to a number of celebrated Jewish scholars to the effect that the prophets and patriarchs called the heavens a sacred book. This is supported in the Zohar, Section *Terumah,* where there is a commentary on the first three verses of the 19th Psalm. This Psalm opens with the line: "The heavens declare the glory of God; and the firmament sheweth his handywork. Day unto day uttereth speech, and night unto night sheweth knowledge. *There* is no speech nor language, *where* their voice is not heard." The commentary in the Zohar referring to the stars reads: "They flash and lighten of themselves through the lightning and flashing of the Supernal Book; they lighten and flash towards all the sides which are attached to them, and each sphere retains unto itself a little of this light, for from that sapphirelike radiance every ring in the chain derives its light and radiance."

It would therefore be well within the mind of these early peoples to consider that Daniel was able to read the secret meaning of the star groups. The celestial wording changed continuously because the planets, moving through the constellations, supplied the vowel points and other markings by which the words were formed. Daniel was ac-

knowledged to be an astrologer of rare genius, and he may
have seen in the stars the impending doom of the Babylonians. He could also have read correctly that which the
other soothsayers were unable or unwilling to interpret. In
any event, according to the Book of Daniel, Belshazzar died
in the same night and Darius, the Median, took the kingdom.
Thus was fulfilled also the prophecy of Jeremiah, that the
Jews should return to Palestine after the Babylonians had
ruled over them for seventy years.

JONAH AND THE WHALE

The Book of Jonah, although dealing with ancient times,
was probably compiled or written in the 3rd or 4th century
B. C., and it is included among the Minor Prophets. The
name Jonah means *dove,* and his story, though spectacular,
is essentially simple. The Lord commanded Jonah to go to
Nineveh, the great city, and cry out against the wickedness
of the people. But Jonah was afraid and took a ship to
depart from the region. Then the Lord sent a storm, and
the sailors discovered by the drawing of lots that Jonah was
responsible for the tempest. Jonah then said to them: "Take
me up, and cast me forth into the sea; so shall the sea be calm
unto you: for I know that for my sake this great tempest *is*
upon you." (1:12) The seamen did not want to injure
Jonah, and they tried desperately to weather the storm, but
at last they cast him into the water and he was swallowed
by a huge fish which the Lord had prepared for him.

Jonah remained for three days and three nights in the
belly of the great fish, and his prayers were answered, and
the prophet was cast up upon the dry land. He then obeyed
the command of God and went to Nineveh, and the people
of Nineveh listened to his words, repented of their evil deeds,
and were spared. Jonah, who seems to have had an unfor-
giving spirit, was disgruntled because the Ninevites were not

appropriately punished for their sins. But the Lord caused another miracle to occur to Jonah, so that his folly was revealed to him. It was only then that the prophet realized in his heart the infinite love of God for all his children, and was warned against a narrow and intolerant attitude.

There have been many interpretations of the legend of Jonah, some of which should be mentioned briefly. Several early and important locality myths are associated with the scene of Jonah's travels. He went down to Joppa and took a ship to Tarshish. In Greek mythology, Neptune sent a monstrous serpent to ravage the seacoast in the neighborhood of Joppa, the port from which Jonah sailed. Here also Andromeda was chained to the rock as a sacrifice to a sea monster, and was rescued by the hero Perseus. According to Jerome, the very rock where Andromeda awaited her doom, was outside the port of Joppa and was duly pointed out to all travelers. It was also on this Mediterranean coast that Hesione was rescued by Hercules. This last account in particular requires amplification.

Godfrey Higgins, whose researches were prodigious, has this to say concerning the parallel between Jonah and Hercules: "The story of Jonah swallowed up by a whale, is nothing but part of the fiction of Hercules, described in the Heracleid or Labors of Hercules, of whom the same story was told, and who was swallowed up at the very same place, Joppa, and for the same period of time, three days. Lycophron says that Hercules was three nights in the belly of a fish." (See, *Anacalypsis.* V. I.). The learned Bernard de Montfaucon, describing a piece of Grecian sculpture, writes: "Some ancients relate to the effect that Hercules was also swallowed by the whale that was watching Hesione, that he remained three days in his belly, and that he came out bald-pated after his sojourn there." (See, *L'Antique Expliquee*). It would seem, therefore, that more than a semi-historical account is intended. The reference to Hercules losing his hair suggests the ever-recurring solar myth. It should also be noted that it was in this same general locality that St. George had his celebrated battle with the dragon.

Nor should we forget Oannes, or Dagon, the fish-man, who was divinely sent to the region of the Tigris and Euphrates rivers to instruct the people of this land in arts, sciences and religions. Oannes came out of the sea and returned to it each night, and figures of him have been found in the ruins of Nineveh. He is represented as a noble-looking person, his human form partly covered by the body of a fish. In some cases he is made to appear as though rising out of the fish. It has been suspected that the names Jonah and Oannes are of common origin. Some of the old Jewish rabbis considered Jonah to be a Messiah, and an entire chapter of the Koran bears his name.

In India, the deity Vishnu, in his first incarnation, appeared as a human being with the body of a fish, or rising from such a body. He holds in his hand the Veda, the Great Book of the Law. In the Talmud, the Messiah is called *Dag,* or "the fish," and one of the old astronomers declared that the Messiah would come when there was a conjunction of Jupiter and Saturn in the sign of the fish (Pisces). Joshua, the son of Nun, led the children of Israel into the Promised Land, where Moses could not go. The word *Nun* means either *a fish* or, by extension, *a ship.* The Christian Messiah was called by his disciples "fisher of men." He fed the multitude with two small fishes. He brought about the miraculous draught of fishes, and his sign, long before the cross was introduced, was that of a fish.

For some reason, Jonah, "the dove," was afraid to go to Nineveh, where, strangely enough, the dove was sacred. He chose rather to go first to Joppa (Jaffa) which was sacred to Dagon, the man-fish. The people of that region ornamented their ships with likenesses of Der-Keto, a form of Astarte. Keto is the great fish Cetus. Figureheads were long used on the bows of ships as symbols of protection. According to one rather prosaic interpretation of the adventure of Jonah, he was rescued from the sea by a vessel decorated with the symbolism of the great fish, and under such circumstances he could well have been held prisoner in the belly of this ship until it reached port. The quest for deeper meaning, however, impels us to seek a more valid and significant explanation.

The Zohar contains the following stimulating thoughts: "In the story of Jonah, we find an allegory of that which happens to the soul when it enters the body . . . When a man sins, he is like Jonah, who imagines that he can flee from the wrath of his master. Then does God send a great tempest, for the Angel of the Rigour demands the chastisement of the sinner. The fish that swallowed Jonah is like the tomb . . . and even as the fish, after keeping him three days in her belly, threw up Jonah, so will the earth throw up her dead." (See, *The Small Holy Assembly*). This would certainly imply that the learned elders regarded the great fish as a symbol of mortality or materiality. Here is a version of the fall of man. The sinning human soul, (the disobedient Jonah), is cast into physical existence, which the Lord has "prepared" to receive it, and where it remains until, through repentance and prayer, it is delivered safely upon the shore of the higher region. This may also be a veiled allusion to initiation into those sacred Mysteries and Rites which were held in caves and grottos—that is, in the belly of the earth—and from which the neophyte was released after three symbolic degrees or days.

This approach to the legend is sustained by the reference in Matthew 12:40, where it is written: "For as Jonas was three days and three nights in the whale's belly; so shall the Son of man be three days and three nights in the heart of the earth." Thus it is Jesus himself who first calls the great fish a whale. With this statement available it is difficult to understand why St. Augustine believed the whale to signify God, who received Jonah back into himself after he had been cast overboard. In John 2:19, Jesus says: "Destroy this temple, and in three days I will raise it up." This is generally accepted as a prediction of his own resurrection, and is so explained in the text.

In medieval Christian religious art it was customary to picture the gate of hell as the open mouth of a horrible marine monster, and the abode of lost souls was in its belly. Sometimes a wild boar with dripping tusks takes the place of the whale. This refers to the fate of the solar spirit-hero Adonis, who was killed by a wild boar. In Scandinavia, the wolf Fenris plays the evil role. As E. B. Tylor points out, the story of Little Red Riding Hood has been badly mutilated in the English version. In the original form, the little maid in her shining red cloak was actually swallowed by the great black wolf, and she came forth uninjured when the hunters cut open the sleeping beast. (See, *Primitive Culture*. Vol. I.)

Here, then, we have the primordial story of the struggle between light and darkness, not only on the physical plane, but in the region of spiritual mystery. The earth devours the bodies of the living. As written in Ecclesiastes 12:7: "Then shall the dust return to the earth as it was: and the spirit shall return unto God who gave it." In the Greek legends, the human soul, considered either individually or collectively, is the helpless maiden chained to the rock as a sacrifice to the monster of materiality. She is saved by the radiant truth-hero, who personifies the Messianic power sent by God.

Jonah, the self-will in man, departs from the task which God has assigned to him. He is swallowed up by the illusion of mortality, but because he repents and accepts the leadership of the divine will, he is restored and fulfills his mission.

CHAPTER IX
THE SOUL OF THE WISDOM LITERATURE

It was said by the ancient scholars that when Solomon was young, he wrote a book of Songs which expressed the longings of his youth. When he attained to maturity, he wrote the Proverbs, which are the ripe fruit of a man who has known life. But when he had come to age, he composed Ecclesiastes in which is set forth the vanity of human pleasures and desires. Many other works are attributed to the great King, and some of these are mentioned in the Zohar. During the period of the Second Temple, a type of religious-moral writings known as the *Wisdom Literature* attained lasting popularity. In the Jewish classification, the principal books of the Bible belonging to the class of Wisdom Literature are the Psalms, Proverbs, Job, and Ecclesiastes. The Book of Psalms is not always included in this list, but is said to share in the spirit of this type of writing.

The works are of various dates between the 7th and 2nd centuries B. C., although in some cases tradition suggests a greater antiquity. The burden of the writings is practical instruction. Through the long centuries of uncertain fortune, the Jewish people had developed a psychology of life with a rich patina of lore, fable, legend, and proverb. This became an integral part of their racial heritage, and was augmented by learned rabbis and the findings of the Councils of the Elders. The Wisdom Books, therefore, do not necessarily reflect the opinions of a single author, or even of a group. They set forth a way of life, enriched and deepened by tribulation, and strengthened by spiritual conviction.

Christian writers have accepted the Psalms and Proverbs almost without reservation. The lofty spirit which pervades these books, the contrition which they exemplify, and the common sense which runs through them, leave little ground for criticism. Attributed to David and Solomon, the Psalms and Proverbs bear the highest seal of Jewish approval. These great Kings had found favor with God, had communed with him, had been his servants, and had dwelt under the shadow of his wing. They were thus sanctified and set apart, and their words rang with the strength of the Most High. These writings are so familiar and, for the most part, their meanings are so obvious, that the thoughtful person can interpret them for himself according to his own need and with his own understanding. He may not reach into the depths of the rabbinical lore, but he will be profoundly moved and inspired to a constructive way of life.

It is customary to divide the Wisdom Literature into two broad divisions: secular and religious. Under the secular heading are treated such concerns as inducements to industriousness, temperance, honesty, friendship, and utilitarian morality in general. Though beautifully expressed, it is the homely kind of advice which has gradually come to broad

acceptance in human nature. It was addressed mainly to
the farmer, the herdsman, and the small merchant. They
were taught that the pleasures of life, if moderately practiced, were right and proper, but that all immoderation led
to disaster. Wealth accumulated through intelligence and
industry was a proper reward for labor, but if gained dis-
honestly, was an abomination. The importance of the home
was given due attention, and those faults of human nature
which disrupted private life were criticized and condemned.
There was no place for the lazy man or the nagging wife.
The rights of children and the privileges of the stranger were
unfolded and clarified. Although secular, this wisdom was
rooted in the Mosaic code, and was the natural extension of
the Ten Commandments on the level of common and familiar
practices.

The religious part, together with the ethical recommen-
dations, was also based upon Deuteronomy. It goes beyond
those obvious virtues affecting human relationships to more
subtle considerations arising from the contemplation of the
will of God and the moral duties of the God-loving man.
There is emphasis upon a personal nobility, including piety,
the service of the poor, courtesy to the enemy, and the cultivation in general of such practices as were acceptable in
the sight of God. The weight of security is shifted, and
wealth and happiness are made to depend upon the righteousness of the individual. The love of God must come
first, and the search for truth is above all worldly pursuits.
Man does not keep the law merely because it is profitable,
but because obedience is God's will for his creatures. The
rich and the poor are alike in the presence of God, and
righteousness is before all worldly honor. Those who choose
ways of wickedness are punished by sorrow and must be
redeemed through repentance. Punishment is for the sins
of the heart, and thoughts have power even though they are

held secretly. True religion invites men to wisdom, and through wisdom to understanding, and through understanding to God. The Supreme Being sees into the heart of every man and is the unseen guest at every table.

ECCLESIASTES

Although Ecclesiastes is included among the Wisdom Books of the Old Testament, it has always been recognized as inconsistent with the spirit of Jewish sacred writing. The Greek word *ecclesiastes* literally means "a person who is a member of an assembly (ecclesia)" or who takes part in discussions of a learned group. The Hebrew name for the book, *Koheleth,* is usually translated *preacher,* or more generally, a *sage* or *learned person.* It has been assumed that the author was not a priest or a prophet, but an instructor whose opinions were founded in personal experience or in observation of the conditions of the time in which he lived. Although the book is attributed to Solomon, it was certainly compiled at a later date, not earlier than the 3rd century B. C. It is possible, of course, that earlier beliefs and attitudes, perhaps traceable to the Solomonic time, are included in the work. It has been suspected from the internal evidence that Ecclesiastes was a production of the Jewish community in Alexandria. It certainly includes Greek and Egyptian influence, and is permeated with a kind of pessimism familiar to us in the *Rubaiyat* of Omar Khayyam. There are also strong indications that the work is fragmentary, and it cannot be said to present any dominant constructive theme. The Jewish sages, in deciding which books were to be included in the Biblical Canon, were moved to reject Ecclesiastes because of its internal inconsistencies, because it was tinged with heresy, and because it originated on the level of human thinking and did not reveal divine inspiration. It was finally accepted, however, because of chapter 12, with special emphasis upon verses 8 and 13.

The authors or compilers were certainly acquainted with Greek philosophy, including Stoicism, Skepticism, and Epicurianism, but it is assumed that such learning was available to a scholar whose mind had been exposed to comparative thinking. Wisdom is presented as essentially material and gloomy. Disillusionment and melancholy have pervaded the mind, and there are grave doubts. Man lives within a strange inflexible pattern of laws, and the world is revealed as a vast machine against whose fatalistic processes there is no appeal. The heart of man is wearied and saddened. There seems to be no way whereby the human mind can discover the mysterious workings of the divine will. Bodily pleasures fall away; the search for wealth and power brings no contentment; even wisdom ends in argument and uncertainty. Only one thing is certain: naked, man comes into the world, and naked, he departs therefrom. The living at least know that they shall die, but it is not certain that the dead know anything. Like Job, this old sage has struggled with his faith, but he has not had the patience of Job. It may follow that Ecclesiastes, by its very spirit of frustration, has strengthened faith among those who have read it. It has revealed the uselessness of a materialistic attitude in the solution of man's search for inspiration and spiritual guidance.

There is another school of thought which should not be overlooked. In Ecclesiastes, we find strong traces of a kind of mysticism which permeated the thinking of the Dervishes and the Sufis, who also sang of the vanity of all things. The wisdom which the sage rejects may not be the true wisdom which clings to God in all things, but the wisdom of men, which comes to nothing. It has been traditional for mystical writers to denounce the involvements of material living, and this seems to be an underlying motive of the book. The emphasis is upon the complete acceptance of the mysterious unknown, for by this acceptance man becomes reconciled with the vicissitudes of mortal existence. Ecclesiastes concludes with a summation of its entire intent in these words: "Let us hear the conclusion of the whole matter: Fear God, and keep his commandments: for this *is* the whole *duty* of man. For God shall bring every work into judgment, with every secret thing, whether it be good, or whether it be evil." (12:13-14) This may well be the cry of a burdened people in those critical years of the later Greek and Maccabean rulers.

THE BOOK OF PROVERBS

The Book of Proverbs has gradually formed around a nucleus of material which may originally have been compiled by Solomon. It is now generally believed that several collections of aphorismic sayings which had long found favor were brought together between 400 and 200 B. C. to form the present text. The Book was not included in the Jewish Bible until approximately the beginning of the Christian era. While most of the text is clear, there are certain sections which indicate confusion and probably early misunderstanding. For example, Proverbs 1:7 reads in the Vulgate: "Timor Domini principium sapientiae." This is translated in the Septuagint: "The fear of the Lord is the beginning of wisdom," and in the King James Version: "The fear of the LORD *is* the beginning of knowledge." It is difficult to reconcile such statements with the religious admonition to love God with all our heart, for love and fear cannot abide together.

There is another statement of this concept in Psalms 25:14, which reads: "The secret of the LORD *is* with them

that fear him." Obviously both verses have a similar meaning. S. F. Dunlap renders the quotation from the Psalms
thus: "SOD Ihoh (the Mysteries of Iahoh) are for those
who fear him." The same author renders Proverbs 3, last part
of verse 32, as follows: "And his SOD (Mysteries) are for
the Isarim (the good, initiated)." (See, *Sod, the Mysteries of
Adoni*). The burden of this interpretation conforms with the
ancient wisdom-religion of Israel that affirmed that the
Sod was reserved for the *Chasidim*. This means that such
terms as "the secret of the Lord," or "the wisdom of God"
refer directly to the arcanum or secret doctrine of Israel,
and signify a kind of Cabalistic system of knowledge such
as was usually communicated in a school of the Mysteries.
This is St. Paul's "wisdom of God in a mystery, even the hidden *wisdom*." (I. Corinthians 2:7 and 15:51). The true meaning is completed through a study of the words "those who
fear him." Obviously, this implies those who are obedient,
who have accepted God and will not depart from his ways.
These are the *Kedeshim,* the *Isarim,* the Priests, the Holy
Initiated Ones, the Shining Ones, and those who walk in the
house of Elohim. It would seem, therefore, that the spirit
of the original tells us that the wisdom of the Secret Assembly is the beginning of true knowledge or understanding,
and that this secret teaching is for those who have been
accepted into the sacred rites. We are invited to such reflection, and to seek for hidden and deeper meaning, by
references in Proverbs 1:6 and Psalms 78:2, where mention
is made of certain "dark sayings;" that is, the hidden teachings of the Elders or Initiates of the *Sod*.

It does not necessarily follow, however, that all the translations are incorrect. A considerable part of the Proverbs
is devoted to moral teachings, with special emphasis upon
the desirability of wisdom. Solomon, the son of David,

exhorts those who would be close to God to achieve wisdom. In his day, great schools and libraries were not available to the people. To him, wisdom was the accumulated knowledge of his tribe, the law and tradition handed down from father to son. (See, Proverbs 1:8). Thus, the Book of Proverbs seems often in strange contradiction to the more familiar teachings of modern Christianity. Solomon cries out that a man must be wise. He invites those who love truth to incline their ears unto wisdom, and apply their hearts to understanding. Solomon says of wisdom that: "She *is* more precious than rubies: and all the things thou canst desire are not to be compared unto her." (3:15). Solomon also teaches that wisdom is found in ways of Godliness. Only the man who seeks God can partake of wisdom. It requires some thought to reconcile the words of Solomon with the teachings of the New Testament, where the emphasis is almost entirely upon faith.

There are many in the modern world who have rejected or ignored the inferences of religious instruction. Men have come to believe they can be truly wise without being truly good, but this can never happen, for wisdom and virtue are inseparably related. If modern thinkers could realize that true depth of understanding requires a positive spiritual perspective, we would have less of war, struggle, and conflict, and more of peace, security, and friendship, as these are described in the Book of Proverbs. What is true wisdom? Wisdom comes not out of books; nor does truth always result from study and research. Wisdom is knowledge perfected through inward realization. Understanding comes from within man. It sanctifies knowledge; it transmutes and perfects education; it spiritualizes thought and culture.

Why do we regard Plato as a wise man, and at the same time realize that most modern thinkers are only well edu-

cated? Contemporary man may possess far more actual
technical knowledge than his predecessors; he may not suffer from Plato's inability to number correctly the teeth in
the human head. Yet the very man who can number these
teeth and split the atom, may still be an essentially ignorant
human being. Conversely, some old Indian sage seated
under a Banyan tree, with none of this world's goods and
no share in Western schooling, may be a truly learned and
enlightened person. If education could bestow wisdom,
most of us would be wise. But instead of this we are foolish,
burdened with prejudices and conceits, and almost incapable
of real friendliness and honesty.

It is therefore appropriate for modern man to meditate
upon wisdom even as did Solomon the King. Perfect wisdom is the most precious thing in the world. It bestows
absolute security, and makes man one with that Sovereign
Truth which sustains the universe. Plato was wise because
he transmuted knowledge into soul-power. This great man,
gentle and patient, too wise to be angry and too learned to
be unjust, is a magnificent example of that breadth and
depth bestowed by true wisdom. A comparison between the
present-day intellectual and Plato is most humiliating to
modern conceit. The materialist may know more, but he
understands so little of what he knows. He may have convinced himself that there is neither God nor reason in the
universe, and therefore that there is no truth or wisdom
within himself. Plato saw God in everything and found
truth in all the workings of the universal plan.

Solomon also tells us something else in the Proverbs. He
tells us that it is impossible to be wise without living in harmony with the divine plan. Only the soul that is gentle
and filled with the love of truth is capable of great learning,
and no man can learn more than his own consciousness
permits. Increase of real knowledge implies increase of spir-

itual stature. We become capable of wisdom as we grow in integrity and build everlasting foundations within ourselves. In Proverbs 9:1 Solomon writes: "Wisdom hath builded her house, she hath hewn out her seven pillars." What are the seven pillars of wisdom? They are the seven great laws which sustain the universe. They are the seven colors of truth. Wisdom indeed hath built her house, and her house is the universe. The power that has built, has also the wisdom to sustain. Man, immersed in wisdom, is still foolish. Surrounded everywhere by the evidences of a majestic plan, he is still ignorant and perverse. Ever in the presence of the mystery of life, he lives only a fragment of his divine potential.

It is most interesting that in this work wisdom is personified as a woman. She is indeed Sophia, the Mother of Mysteries and the Virgin of the World. It is said that she dwelt with God in heaven before the creation, and in the Cabalistic writings, as we have already noted, the Torah, or the Law, is also referred to as a veiled woman with whom God counseled before he fashioned anything. There is certainly here an allusion to the secret teachings. In the Nordic myths, when Odin, the All-Father, desired to come up to consult the oracle of mysteries, he invoked Erda, the Great Mother, who alone knew the secrets of all living.

Proverbs also tells us that the wicked man cannot flourish: "The righteousness of the perfect shall direct his way: but the wicked shall fall by his own wickedness." (11:5). The whole world desires to be happy, but happiness must be earned. The stupid, the foolish, and the selfish, can never be happy. Any man who departs from wisdom, departs from peace. If we cling to the evils in us, we must suffer for our decision. It appears in this world that the evil flourish, but if we examine closely into their lives, we shall see sorrow, misery, sickness, and death. The universal law forbids that any man who is not intrinsically good shall enjoy either wisdom or peace.

The author of Proverbs, whether it was Solomon or some other illumined person, was indeed a man of rich inner life and understanding. He was a master of the mysteries of living, an Adept in the secret school of God. In 12:28 he says: "In the way of righteousness *is* life; and in the pathway *thereof there is* no death." This is the same teaching that was revealed in the Mysteries taught in the sacred temples of Eleusis and Sais. The Egyptians taught that immortality is the reward of wisdom; not immortality in the sense of the perpetuation of the physical body with its infirmities, but rather a conscious participation in eternal life. The wise man perceives the law, obeys it, and his inner life is perfected.

Modern dictators might profit by the verse, "Better *it is to be* of an humble spirit with the lowly, than to divide the spoil with the proud." (16:19). Man lives a little time in this world, and departs into the unknown from whence he came. Mortal life is indeed a brief span in the ante-chamber of eternity. How little we appreciate the impermanence of our physical existence; how seldom we look beyond this life. Perceiving only a physical existence, we live wholly for the day, ignoring and refusing to consider our eternal citizenship in the larger universe. But time brings to all things the rewards of their own actions. Each person, in the end, comes to that which is his own. We may regret the seeming injustice of mortal living, but there is a mighty honesty in space, and all men and their deeds come finally to their just desserts.

At this point, it may be helpful to remind the student of the Christian Bible that he will do well to consider also the sacred books of other nations. It is important for the Bible student to have the religious literature of the world always available to him. He soon realizes from the study of comparative religion that the scriptures of various peoples have a common origin and a common purpose. Not one of these sacred books is entirely complete in itself. Each is derived from the writings and customs of several racial doctrines. Religious intolerance must be overcome by all sincere truth seekers. The age of bigotry has passed. Evolving humanity demands and deserves a more tolerant religious perspective. We like to feel that sincere students have outgrown unreasonable addiction to sects and creeds, and have attained a concept of total religion. This is important in connection with the Proverbs, because this book clearly reveals indebtedness to several streams of sacred tradition.

It is impossible for a man to function normally without spiritual guidance. The present world chaos is due largely to the failure of idealism in the affairs of men. This failure is due at least in part to religion itself; that is, what we have come to call religion. It results from the intolerance of sects and the innumerable superstitions that have been foisted upon a gullible humanity. The commercialism of religion, greatly to be deplored, is inevitable under existing world conditions.

From the beautiful verses of the Proverbs, we pass to a testing of man's faith. If he believes good things, he must find in this believing an ever present help in time of trouble. There are long hours when only faith can sustain him, and lacking this inner strength, he is truly destitute. The Wisdom Literature of the Jews came from the heart of an afflicted people. In their infirmity, they sought peace, and their story is that of every sincere person who must decide for himself the concepts which are to guide his conduct. He must pass through his dark night, and watch and pray for the coming of the dawn. The burden of this experience is revealed through the Book of Job.

THE BOOK OF JOB

Of all the books of the Old Testament, there is none that more completely unfolds the Hebrew Wisdom Literature than the Book of Job. There is no certainty as to the date, but it is believed that the prose sections are the earliest. The present tendency is to assume that the book was compiled not later than the 5th century B.C. At least two authors can be recognized: one is associated with the prose, and the other, with the poetic sections. There is indication of dependency upon older tradition, as Job is mentioned in Ezekiel 14:14 and 20. The theme of the Book of Job unfolds the conflict between the deeply religious instincts of the human soul and those doubts or uncertainties which result from what appears to be undeserved pain and suffering. The question includes the effort of the good man to understand the misfortunes which come to him in spite of, or even because of, his piety.

The root of the argument is the mystery of evil itself. Why does a benign Deity permit human suffering? Job, as the virtuous person, comes upon evil times. He is unable to find in himself any fault or failing sufficiently reprehensible to justify the disaster, or chain of disasters, which befall him. It is not the intent of the story to indicate that Job was without fault, but rather that his punishment was unreasonably excessive. He had not committed any of the sins or misdemeanors which, according to his own understanding, deserved such retribution. Sustained by the promise that a virtuous life was acceptable unto the Lord, he had walked in ways of uprightness, and yet he was punished as though he had been a corrupt and dissolute man.

The story of Job unfolds as follows. There was in the land of Uz a perfect and upright man, and his name was Job. He had a very great household, and there were born to him seven sons and three daughters. He had many sheep and camels, so that this man was honored as one of the greatest of all the men of the East. In these days, it came to pass that the sons of God presented themselves before their Lord in heaven, and Satan came also and was among them. The Lord asked Satan whence he had come, and Satan replied: "From going to and fro in the earth, and from walking up and down in it." (1:7). It is the Lord himself who brings Job to the attention of Satan. It almost seems that the Lord laid a wager with Satan for the soul of Job, in order to prove that the good man in adversity will still cling to truth.*

Job, looking back upon his own years, was satisfied that he had lived uprightly. His friends, who could not share the actual experience of Job's integrity, insisted that he must have earned the calamity which descended upon him. Their reasoning and persuasions, however, had slight effect. Job refused to admit faults which, according to the dictates of his own conscience, he had not committed. This led to the long and persuasive efforts of Eliphaz, Bildad, and Zophar to prove to Job that he was suffering for his own sins. But Job stoutly refused to ask forgiveness for crimes of which he was not guilty, and he vehemently declined to consider himself in the position of a repentant sinner.

The only alternative was the patient acceptance of adversity as the will of God, which surpasseth all understanding. Job found no consolation in such an escape from an imminent dilemma, and slight comfort from the opinions of his friends. The God he worshipped was either good and just, or else unworthy of the admiration of mortals. All concepts, hypotheses, and opinions must take second place to obvious facts, and to preserve his own faith and his

---

*From the opening sections of the Book of Job, it is evident that it supplied the material for Goethe's prologue to the story of Faust. There are many parallels between the Book of Job and Goethe's treatment of the legend of Faust.

own center of spiritual conviction, it was necessary for Job to solve the mystery of adversity. The adventures of the old patriarch have become the classic example of steadfastness of spirit.

The explanation given in the story still leaves the subject of good and evil essentially untouched. Satan was introduced as a spirit of negation who attempted to explain the piety of Job as resulting from his prosperity and happiness. If this were true, then virtue would be not a matter of character, but of circumstances. The problem returns in different words in the New Testament, where virtuous conduct is defined as a procedure of doing good to those who despitefully use us. In The Book of Job, God was made to debate with Satan over the essential substance and nature of virtue. Substantially, Job was subjected to a series of tests to discover the quality of his own integrity. The sufferer naturally is unaware of the cause of his troubles. If he were aware, then the tests would be meaningless. It was only when left completely to his own resources that Job could make the heroic decision which revealed the firm ground of his own faith.

The apparent relentlessness of Nature in the distribution of its benefits and afflictions has always troubled the minds of mortals. The rain falls upon the just and the unjust, and the prayers of our enemies are as effective as our own. We often develop the conviction that the just are sorely burdened and troubled, while the unjust prosper and flourish. The law of compensation, as taught in Asia, is probably the most reasonable available explanation for the seeming contradiction that disturbs our ethical persuasions. The present state of man is founded upon the past and is bound to preceding events lawfully and honorably. We can realize this even within the narrow framework of personal experience. If, according to the limited vision of the moment, man appears to be unjustly persecuted, a larger and more inclusive estimation of his career may reveal that he is really being justly punished. On the other hand, the apparently fortunate mortal may be enjoying the well-earned profits of long and enlightened industry. It is therefore impossible to arrive at an adequate estimation of the workings of universal law by the observational faculties alone. All appearances are suspended from invisible causes, and until these are understood, both judgment and criticism are meaningless and unsound.

In this complicated situation, we must have a clearer insight into the nature of good and evil. The more we explore into the subject of the substance of evil, the more rapidly this substance dissolves. There is no actual, factual evidence in Nature to support the belief in the existence of a principle of evil. Nor is there any solid ground for assuming that there is a principle of evil within man or operating through his mental or emotional nature. Evil can be sustained only as an explanation for certain conditions that arise with those who limit their judgment to some fragment of a larger pattern. Increasing knowledge of causes, and broader contemplation of the phenomena of living, disprove the validity of the doctrine of evil. This may not lessen the intensity of an existing tragedy, but it supplies us with the incentive to search within ourselves for those causes which we have a tendency to assign to an infernal agency. Actually, the anthropomorphic concept of a god and a devil struggling for supremacy of the universe, and contending for ultimate control of the human soul, is not even intimated in the Book of Job. In this work, Satan acted only under the authority of Deity. He was permitted to afflict the patriarch, and until this permission was granted, he was, at least by intimation, powerless to trouble the virtuous man.

The afflictions that came upon Job were of three kinds and degrees of intimacy. First, he was deprived of his worldly goods; second, the lives of his children were taken; third, he was afflicted in his own flesh. The order of these infirmities indicates a definite pattern. Satan had insisted that Job was good merely because he had no incentive to be otherwise. A man with ample means, a congenial home, and good health, should instinctively give thanks for his blessings and be strong in his faith. The degree of Job's sincerity was tested much in the same way that the integrity of disciples was tried in the religious Mysteries.

The greater part of the trial was the direct attack upon faith itself. Had Job been an average man, he might well have taken refuge in the conviction that his previous sins were being punished. As things were, he had to go beyond this and, renouncing even the conviction of divine justice, maintain his love of God and faith in God's integrity. In the story, no effort was made to philosophize upon the merits or demerits of suffering. Job was God's good man, and to meet the test he must remain good, regardless of the apparent incentives to doubt and deny. To disprove the accusations of Satan, Job was required to make the internal statement of absolute and unconditioned faith. The story itself implies that the situation was exceptional, a kind of test case, and therefore not applicable in detail to the problems of average living. But, again, Job was not an average man, and an average decision was not sufficient to protect him.

The subject then moved subtly into the sphere of faith. To what degree must a man accept that which he cannot understand and cannot justify with his own reasoning power? This, again, depends upon the man and the level of his own consciousness. There can be no such thing as temptation unless a decision is involved which exceeds the immediate capacity of the one tempted. We cannot actually accept a standard less than our natural growth has revealed to our hearts and minds. The question then becomes concerned with the ability of the person to extend his faith to meet a larger and more complicated emergency. The strength of a faith is experienced by the testing of that faith. We can define faith itself as the inner conviction that the unknown is an extension of the known. In this case it was the extension of the divine power and the divine grace beyond the contemplation of the human mind. The goodness of God remained goodness, even though it surpassed human understanding. Faith supports consciousness when understanding can no longer explain or justify conditions or occurrences.

Job, bereft of all those good things which are the natural harvest of virtue, was required to take his position firmly on the evidence of faith. He could no longer recognize any relationship between a good life and the misfortunes which afflicted him. In the story he was not asked to explain, interpret, or rationalize. All that was required of Job was one simple decision: the unquestioning acceptance of the will of God. To a degree, his misfortunes were complicated by his three friends, who impersonated the departments of learning which seek to explain the inner meaning of physical evidence. In his disaster Job was "comforted" by religion, philosophy, and science, or their equivalents in the culture of olden times. The comforters had ready explanations for everything, but they solved nothing, because Job himself realized that their interpretations did not fit his case. When he objected, they insisted that he was wrong, and went to some detail to enlarge upon the possible or probable disobediences of Job which might have led to such dismal results. In the formula it was not for his sins or his father's sins that Job was being afflicted; rather it was that the glory of God be manifested as an experience in his own heart. Job was not immediately able to accept this remarkable fact, but he was more and more certainly driven toward it by the well-intentioned ministration of his comforters.

The historical descent of human beliefs helps us to orient the poem of Job. In the earliest forms of religious doctrines there was no consideration of the problem of divine justice. Deity was an absolute autocrat, distributing his favors and bestowing his anger according to his own pleasure. Probably, the political tyranny served as an appropriate pattern to explain and justify spiritual tyranny. The leader might be strong, but not necessarily good. He might rule by divine right and still be burdened with mortal weaknesses and intemperances. As the God-concept could be understood only in the terms of human experience, it was the obvious duty of the believer to accept that which came, and be as patient as his disposition would permit.

The belief that the individual was responsible for his own actions and that retribution was individual rather than collective was late in appearing in the descent of religions. The concept of God was racial, national, or tribal. The fate of the foreigner was of no importance. It was only necessary to understand those occurrences which related to the particular people over which a god governed or ruled. If a nation sinned, all the citizens suffered, and an evil merited by a community descended upon both the just and the unjust if they belonged to the involved group. The doctrine that the sins of the fathers descended upon their children also offered a solution to the obvious fact of seeming injustice. A man might burden his descendants with numerous afflictions because of his own intemperances. This consideration had ethical utility, but presented an unhappy conclusion. The children and the children's children were required to suffer for sins that were not their own, and the essential concept of justice was still frustrated.

In his discussions with his friends, Job admitted that affliction descended directly from God, and also that God punished those who had sinned against his laws or his majesty. By such a statement of faith, the patriarch attempted no more than a general statement of God's will. The nature and degree of the sin was determined by the Deity, and from this decision there could be no escape or redress. Job also realized that the blessings which he had previously enjoyed must also be attributed to the goodness and mercy of God. Deity had been mindful unto the needs of Job and had blessed him and had revealed his favors unto his servant. Why, then, was the face of God suddenly turned away from Job? By what action or cause was Job deprived of the good things which God had given him? Had God blessed Job in order that in the end his afflictions might be greater? Was the apparent kindness of Deity a strange and perverse deceit? If so, what was the cause? Was the God that Job loved unworthy of this devotion? Even the thought was so terrible that the miserable man could not entertain it long. Apparently the patriarch considered the possibility that in some future state he might be compensated for his suffering. This solved nothing, however, as the real problem remained as to why unmerited affliction should be necessary in the case of a good man.

In his extremity, Job appealed to God for some sign, some indication by which the integrity of the divine power could be known. The intensity of Job's spiritual dilemma unfolded through a series of psychological conflicts. Even as the patriarch voiced his doubts and proclaimed his bitterness, his own doubts came into violent conflict with his spiritual convictions. Perhaps he sensed that he stood perilously close to an internal tragedy. He met his own emergency from within himself. His very doubts gave new strength and definition to his faith. In the struggle which ensued, faith triumphed. Through the urgency of his need, Job so intensified the psychic functions of his own consciousness that he accomplished a mystical experience. Even this experience is difficult to interpret due to the corruptions of the texts. It is not stated that Job understood what occurred to him, but he was permitted to see God. Thus in the presence of a sublime majesty, his doubts were resolved. Job's acceptance of the divine explanation has been variously interpreted as a fuller trust in God's will or as a mere submission to an acceptance of God's power. Actually, Deity never did answer directly the doubts of the patriarch. Nothing was finally explained or completely clarified.

In chapter 32 of Job, there is introduced Elihu, the son of Barachel the Buzite, of the kindred of Ram. The name Elihu means "my God is He." Barachel suggests two meanings: "Barach Al, the worshipper of God," or "Bar Rachel, the son of Rachel," or "the son of the ewe." "Of the kindred of the ram" can be interpreted, "of the kindred of the High." Altogether, these seem to suggest that Elihu was a very special person, and as he speaks, he assumes the dignity of an initiate or a hierophant of ancient Mysteries. It is believed that the speeches of Elihu were added at a later date and were not a part of the original book.

First the wrath of Elihu was kindled against Job because he had justified himself rather than God. Then his wrath was kindled against the three friends of Job because they had found no answer and yet had condemned Job. Addressing first the three friends, Elihu said: "But *there is* a spirit in man: and the inspiration of the Almighty giveth them understanding. Great men are not *always* wise: neither do the aged understand judgment." (32:8-9). After listening to Job's lament, Elihu said: "Behold, *in* this thou art not just: I will answer thee, that God is greater than man. Why dost thou strive against him? for he giveth not account of any of his matters." (33:12-13). Elihu then continued, admonishing Job to heed his words so that he might learn wisdom: "For God speaketh once, yea twice, *yet man* perceiveth it not. In a dream, in a vision of the night, when deep sleep falleth upon men, in slumberings upon the bed; Then he openeth the ears of men, and sealeth their instruction . . . Mark well, O Job, hearken unto me: hold thy peace, and I will speak. If thou hast any thing to say, answer me: speak, for I desire to justify thee. If not, hearken unto me: hold thy peace, and I shall teach thee wisdom." (33:14-33). Only after Job has learned to hearken to the words of wisdom does the Lord answer him out of the whirlwind. The presentation of this material is very subtle, but in complete harmony with the old method of instruction.

It has been especially noted that the unknown author of Job refrained entirely from introducing any explanation or justification for the incidents involved. This is most unusual, as it is customary for the writer to reveal himself through an attitude or a pattern of explanation or interpretation. The most likely place for such an insertion would have been when God himself was made to speak. The philosophy of the situation would then have been advanced to bring the poem to its proper moral and ethical conclusion. As interpolations were made after the book had passed into circulation, it is also likely that there were deletions, especially where the story conflicted with dominant theological convictions.

The 38th chapter of Job describes the eminence of God, introduced by the words: "Then the LORD answered Job out of the whirlwind . . . " In a strange way, God placed himself upon the defensive and justified his will by his works. He challenged Job to explain the wonders of creation: "Canst thou bind the sweet influences of Pleiades, or loose the bands of Orion? Canst thou bring forth Mazzaroth in his season? or canst thou guide Arcturus with his sons? Knowest thou the ordinances of heaven? canst thou set the dominion thereof in the earth?" (38:31-33) Although the poetry is majestic, it is substantially little more than a rhetorical argument. If we care to assume that a mystical experience occurred to Job, we must also recognize that the patriarch received only certain admonitions. He knew God as Supreme Sovereignty, against whose will and pleasure there was no recourse. Deity demanded submission, and Job submitted himself utterly and completely, saying: "I have heard of thee by the hearing of the ear: but now mine eye seeth thee. Wherefore I abhor *myself,* and repent in dust and ashes." (42:5-6).

This solution leaves the original premise also unsettled. Satan, in the original wager, had said of Job: "But put forth thine hand now, and touch all that he hath, and he will curse thee to thy face." (1:11). In order to restore Job, it was necessary for the Lord to appear to him in majesty, which certainly did not testify to the clarity of the patriarch's conviction. Job, the good man, was unable to extricate his own consciousness from doubt and fear without a miraculous intervention. Thus it seems that the story fails to sustain its own point, unless the very failure itself was the point involved. In any event, the Lord was satisfied by the complete submission of Job, but the wrath of God was turned against the four men who had actually been attempting to prove the omnipotence of the Creator. Apparently, God would have been satisfied had Job accepted calamity without question and at the same time maintained his own innocence of sin.

The 42nd chapter of Job concludes the story. God then required Eliphaz, Bildad, and Zophar to bring offerings to Job and render a burnt offering, to indicate that they likewise repented their follies. If the Lord would permit no accusations against himself, neither would he allow his ways to be defended by mortal men. He required acceptance in a mystery of the spirit and not through reason or debate. It is then written that "the LORD also accepted Job." And when Job prayed that his friends might be forgiven, God "turned the captivity of Job" and released him from the evil times which had come upon him. "So the LORD blessed the latter end of Job more than his beginning: for he had fourteen thousand sheep, and six thousand camels, and a thousand yoke of oxen, and a thousand she asses. He had also seven sons and three daughters . . . After this lived Job an hundred and forty years, and saw his sons, and his sons' sons, *even* four generations."

Once more the story presents structural difficulties. The sons and daughters of Job were miraculously restored, and there was no mention that the tragedy in the life of the patriarch overshadowed the peace of his future years. One explanation suggests itself: Was the entire poem intended to describe a vision, so that all parts of the drama were internal experiences rather than occurrences in the physical life of the patriarch? An alternative solution to the riddle could be that the poem in its original form was based upon an initiation ritual dramatically presented at the time of admission into one of the sacred institutions. Under such conditions, the drama would be self-contained and would require no historical or biological consistency. These initiation rites usually unfolded through three steps or degrees, and it should be remembered that Job's trials progressed in the same way. In the initiation rites, the disciple could depend only upon an abstract integrity for his security. He could not question and he did not presume to understand; he must obey or perish, until he had reached that degree of enlightenment which made possible those inner resources which could solve the riddle.

It is difficult to explain why God should pick out the most perfect of his prophets and turn him over to the tender mercies of Satan, to say nothing of Eliphaz the Temanite, Bildad the Shuhite, and Zophar the Naamathite. When understood as an esoteric fable setting forth acceptance into one of the schools of the old Mysteries, the confusion is immediately cleared away. Job is a personification of a neophyte seeking enlightenment. The Lord in this case is not God, but the hierophant of the Mysteries, the master of the Secret House. Satan then assumes his correct place as the tester, or trier. There was always such a tempter seeking to lure the candidate from the path of righteousness. He was frequently called the "Adversary" or the "Devil's Advocate."

In daily living, this fragment of the Wisdom Literature seems to teach the single purpose of the consecrated heart. In any and all emergencies there must be, first of all, the instinctive acceptance of the divine power. If for one moment we fall into complaint, there may be no end to our lamentation. Once we doubt the universal integrity in which we live and move and have our being, we are cast into the darkness of fear and are deprived of peace of mind. If we keep the faith, even the most difficult situation will ultimately clarify itself. We may not agree today that the wisdom of the Lord is beyond human comprehension, but we are constantly confronted with situations and problems which challenge patience and kindliness of spirit. The story of Job refrains from all effort to examine the merits or demerits of any case or crisis that may arise. If religion brings any consolation, if the love of God has any meaning in the human heart, these inner resources must sustain us in the presence of the unknown or what to us is the unreasonable. To blame ourselves may be as faulty as to blame others, for only a wisdom greater than our own can measure the debits and the credits. We must not escape through the mechanism of blaming or shifting responsibility. We must experience through the problem by a positive acknowledgment of the divine plan. If we can free our minds from debate over the jots and tittles and say, "This is necessary; therefore, this I will do," and support our mental decision with a prompt and decisive action, it is quite possible that the law of life will also bless our "latter end" more than the beginning.

CHAPTER X
THE MESSAGE OF THE PROPHETIC BOOKS

It is usual to group together those Prophetic Books of the Old Testament which originated in what is called the Golden Age of Jewish Prophecy. The earliest of these writings date from the 8th century B. C., or shortly thereafter, and include Amos, Hosea, parts of Isaiah, and Micah. The last of these Prophetic Books, Joel and Zechariah, are tentatively placed between the 4th and 2nd centuries B. C. In addition to the Prophetic Books now incorporated in the Old Testament, there are many others considered apocryphal, such as the Maccabees, the Book of Jashar, and the Book of Enoch. Most of these writings have been subjected to numerous levels and cycles of criticism and interpretation, both Jewish and Christian, and it might be useful to clarify the general pattern followed by the Biblical prophets rather than to indulge in a detailed analysis of such writings as are relatively familiar to the Bible student.

It should be borne in mind that true meaning implies an adequate knowledge of context. Verses, chapters, or even books, approached out of context or without reference to their proper places in the historical and cultural descent of a tradition, lose much of their significance. Fragments are also more easily misinterpreted and caused to substantiate points of view entirely foreign to the original. For this reason, we must pause for a moment and examine the interpretive instinct as this is found in relation to sacred and inspired writings. Most interpreters are not contemporary with their original authors. They live in different times and are dominated by different culture-patterns. Often they do not have an adequate understanding of the older languages, especially the idioms. In some cases, commentaries have originated among followers of a different religious conviction who have been strongly predisposed to impose their own beliefs upon older authorities. This has been especially true in the case of the Old Testament, which has been a subject of deep concern to many Christian theologians whose spiritual sympathy for the Jewish writers was neither complete nor profound.

The Prophetic Books of the Jews are primarily concerned with the tribulations of Israel. Clear examples of Biblical prophecy are overshadowed both quantitatively and qualitatively by the intense quest for consolation of soul. The inspired prophets were seeking in themselves for a strength of understanding which would satisfy their own hearts, and at the same time inspire and strengthen their people. The keynote of these writings, therefore, is not prophetic or predictional in the conventional sense of these words. Prophecies, as they exist, emphasize the ultimate salvation of Israel through the restoration of the Davidic House and the return of Israel to its homeland after the captivity, the Diaspora, and the centuries of exile in foreign countries.

The Jewish prophets revealed through their lives and works a singular characteristic of their national and racial structure. These prophets were men set apart by their own piety and by the popular belief that they were the instruments of divine revelation. They lived in remote places, fasted and prayed, and, like John the Baptist, they cried in the wilderness. These prophets considered it their natural right to rebuke kings and princes and to determine the political futures of their people. They often possessed a peculiar authority which they exercised by the common consent of their fellow men. They warned, admonished, promised, and threatened, usually with a degree of personal immunity, although in some cases they preached and taught at the peril of their lives. They were the anointed ones, under the care and protection of God, with whom they communed in their raptures and meditations.

The principal trends revealed through the Prophetic Books can be rather clearly classified. The writers were moved by certain pressures within themselves and assumed that these doubts, misgivings, and conflicts were present also in the hearts and minds of their fellow men. Certain obvious confusions arising on a religious level and due in part to the historical insecurity of ancient living, required constant clarification. The God of Israel was the Father of his children, and they were his chosen people. They worshipped him and depended upon him for their individual and collective survival. Yet this God permitted his children to come under great trials and adversity. For sins real or imaginary, the Jewish people had been enslaved, and their lands pillaged. They had come under the power of false gods, and with each passing century, their condition had become more desperate. It is inevitable that under such misfortune men should seek an explanation which would preserve their faith, help them to understand their tribulations, and give them some hope or promise of ultimate liberation. This is the three-fold theme of the Prophetic writings, and it is embellished with wonderful symbols, magnificent poems, and gentle words spoken from tired and lonely hearts.

The Book of Job is a poetic version of the patience and resignation of the good man under adversity. This book seeks to explain why sorrow falls heavily upon the just and the unjust. There appeared to be only one explanation—God was testing his children. He was testing them in their love for him and their willingness to obey his laws regardless of the cost to themselves. This theme reaches its grand and complete statement in the writings of Jeremiah. The prophet emerges as a mystic; he finds no other solution but complete resignation to the divine will. In his moments of rapture, he experiences the presence of God, as the perfect and complete justification of faith. He resigns himself unreservedly to the workings of the law, and in this exaltation of spiritual union attains the immediate and immanent proof of God's eternal plan. To a degree, then, the Prophetic Books prophesied this state, this becoming God-like, this solution to all things, by an unconditioned acceptance of the impact of God-realization.

Faith moved from the temple to its ultimate sanctuary in the heart of man. This made possible the perpetuation of a religion which had lost its formal, historical, and political landmarks. We hear of nations without religion, but in Judaism we become aware of a religion without a nation, surviving largely because of the early works of the Jewish prophet-mystics. They bound the souls of their people with the ties of an indissolvable unity which transcended all material doubts and vicissitudes. Gradually, monolatry gave place to monotheism. Monolatry implies the worship of one

God, although other gods, particularly those of other nations, may be recognized as existing. In monotheism, the
emphasis is either upon one God, peculiar and unique, or
the belief that various deities are only names or symbolical
representations of one supreme, indivisible, spiritual being.
The mystic, experiencing the impact of an omnipresent
divine power, almost inevitably drifts toward monotheism,
and this drifting had occurred in Egypt prior to the Exodus.
It certainly influenced many of the early Jewish mystics.

It is the natural instinct of man to defend the integrity
of his God-concept. It is almost equally natural for him,
therefore, to seek in himself the causes of his own infirmities. On the level of a national or racial religion, those who
suffer from what at first appear to be the shafts and arrows
of unrighteous destiny, take refuge in the theological mechanism of disobedience. Man must suffer because he has
sinned, because he has disobeyed the laws of his God, or has
departed from paths of righteousness. The historical books
of the Bible are filled with episodical fragments which would
sustain this conviction. The leaders and the people were
guilty of various sins and delinquencies. They broke the
stern Levitical code as revealed to Moses upon Sinai. They
followed in the ways of the flesh and, in their prosperities
and victories, turned their faces from the Lord. It was then
that the prophets arose with their warnings of impending
doom, crying out to the people to repent their errors and
return to the way of salvation.

Then followed the warnings and admonitions, and the
prophecies of doom. In the beautiful language of the Near
East, the teachings of the prophets found strange and wonderful vestments of words. The burden, however, is the
simple call back to the voice of conscience, and a vivid pic-
turing of the consequences of sin. Although the primary
implication related to the emergencies of the moment, there

was certainly a larger meaning which extends down through time. The Mosaic code still stands as one of the world's great moral and legal documents. We no longer have a descent of anointed prophets to cry in the wilderness, and to face fearlessly the corrupt leaders of states and nations, but the old sins go on, and the old crimes continue, and we should not be surprised if in due time they are punished by heaven as the prophets warned.

This suggests another dimension of an ancient truth continuously experienced through the ages. For the prophets, the way of divine favor was one of unselfishness and consecration. Man must resign his own will to the divine will. He must depart from worldliness and cultivate spiritual graces. If he dedicates himself totally to the will of God, that will is made known to him in the desert or in some distant mountain place where he kneels in prayer. His help comes from the Lord, who made heaven and earth. The prophet did not find God; God found him and consecrated him and blessed him for his labor, and sent him to preach the way of the Lord among men. In this sense, the prophet himself is Israel, for that which happens to the individual must ultimately happen to the whole nation, which then becomes the vessel of God, receiving into itself the waters of everlasting life.

In the beginning of the prophetic period, there does not seem to have been any clear indication as to how the ultimate salvation of Israel was to be attained. The general tone of the Prophetic Books indicates that the will of God was to be made known in due time through the law and the prophets. There would be good men rise up in Israel, and the hand of God would be upon them, as it had been upon Moses and Aaron. These men would be oracles of God to their people. Slowly this pattern divided, and two lines of tradition were distinguishable. By one of these, the line of prophets was envisioned as continuing, as need and conditions arose, until the final salvation of Israel. According to the other, the dim outline of a Messianic doctrine began to appear. Here we should be cautious, however, and not confuse the original concept with our own popular understanding of the Messianic intercession.

The term *Messiah* comes from the Hebrew word *Mashiah,* which means *anointed.* As used in the Old Testament, it is applied to at least two distinguishable classes of persons. Those appointed to certain specific high offices were consecrated by being anointed with sacred oil. Saul, the first king of Israel, and David were both referred to as *anointed,* and the heathen King Cyrus of Persia was also designated *God's anointed.* This term certainly applied also to a second group, including the prophets of a direct line of spiritual descent, and to the high priests of Israel in their proper succession. Gradually, the meaning of the word was broadened to include figuratively all persons whose lives bore evidence to the presence of God's favors, and to those who had renounced all worldliness in the services of God. This anointing, therefore, implied something of a continuance of spiritual power, perpetuated by sacred rites, much as the Christian doctrine of the Apostolic Succession.

In the Prophetic Books, there is therefore an intimation of the advent of the Messiah-king, whose attributes suggest Plato's idea of the philosopher-king. This mighty one was to arise in Israel and restore the congregation of the Jews. He was to herald in a Golden Age—a blessed time—which was to precede the last judgment and the paradise to come. Gradually this Messiah-king concept came to be associated with David, whose exploits had caused him to be elevated to the level of a culture-hero. David was affirmed a just ruler, and to him the promise had been made that his dynasty should last forever. It naturally followed that the Messianic vision was closely associated with David and the seed of David, until, by the commencement of the Christian era, it was broadly held among the Jews that the Messiah would be an earthly ruler of the House of David, and would come to restore the glory of Israel. We find this thinking in the minds of some of the apostles of Jesus, whom he rebuked by telling them that his kingdom was not of this world. Yet, the genealogies carefully trace the line of descent from David to Jesus, as though the Evangelists considered this a matter of prime importance.

Yemoth Hamashiah, literally the "Days of the Messiah," has come to have increasing meaning in Jewish traditionalism and modern Judaism. It is substantially equivalent to the vision of a Golden Era, an age of peace, security and prosperity, dedicated to wisdom, and ruled over by the love of God. This belief is certainly founded in the prophetic intimations of the early Biblical writers, but it has also been strongly influenced by medieval and even modern thinking. The great Jewish scholar, Rabbi Maimonides, envisioned a Messianic kingdom as restoring the political independence of the Jews and the reconstruction of their nation upon the soil of Palestine. He felt that a happy termination to centuries of exile would enable Israel to re-dedicate itself to the study of the Torah and the cultivation of universal wisdom, thus leading all mankind to the intimate knowledge of God, and to its right and proper share in the everlasting joys of a better world.

It is quite understandable, therefore, that the establishment of the state of Israel as a sovereign political power should be regarded as the fulfillment of ancient prophecy and as an announcement of the coming of the Messianic age. At this stage in the mental unfoldment of an ancient belief, we come again to a parting of the ways. There is distinct difference of opinion as to whether the Messiah is to come as a person *to* his people, or as a power or principle, derived from God, *through* his people as a collective spiritual being. Many mystics, Jewish and non-Jewish, have contemplated the latter alternative. There is an increasing conviction of a world-wide release of truth from within the human heart, and its dissemination through all the sincere and devout people of the world, regardless of race or creed. Naturally, it is unprofitable to take a dogmatic attitude, and it is certainly inconsistent with our policy.

In fairness to all concerned, however, we must point out that there is a considerable group which affirms the story of Israel to be a symbolical account of the vicissitudes of all humanity. Thus, under the guise and figure of one race or nation is set forth the total story of humanity's tribulation. We have all passed from bondage through ignorance and the long desert of uncertainty and hardship, until we have seen the distant vision of a Promised Land. In our hearts and our souls, we all long for peace and security. We build instinctively toward a better world than we have even known. And those who are devoutly religious dream together of the day when the kingdom of heaven shall be established upon the earth.

Most other religions—those of India, China, Japan, and the broad reaches of Moslemism—have voiced their conviction that in one day yet to come there shall be one heaven and one earth, and that the ways of heaven shall prevail upon that earth. Then indeed, swords will be pounded into ploughshares, boundaries of creeds and doctrines will fade away, war and crime shall be no more, poverty and pain shall vanish with the darkness, and the heavenly anointed king, by whatever name we wish to call him, will restore the priesthood and the royal line of God's anointed.

In this connection, we should like to quote a few words from the platform adopted by American liberal rabbis in

1937: "We regard it as our historical task to cooperate with all men in the establishment of the kingdom of God, of universal government, justice, truth, and peace on earth. This is our messianic goal." From this it will be evident that there is no essential difference between this vision and the religious convictions of all men of good spirit. Nor does this vision conflict in any way with the prophetic implications of the Old Testament writers. In fact, the word *prophetic,* as used in the Bible, implies specifically this one grand prophecy of the return of the prodigal son to his father's house.

When we go beyond this broad generality, we fall inevitably into differences of opinion. Efforts have been made to associate the elements of Jewish prophecy with the numerous and complicated political situations of the modern world. Some of these interpretations may best be described as fantastic, but the more valid of them relate to such signs and testimonials as might bear upon the establishment of the Messianic kingdom. Most of the specific prophecies of the older writings were directed against those nations which had persecuted the Jews, and may be said to culminate in Jewish resentment against the Roman empire. Certainly this was the attitude of the Jewish community at the beginning of the Christian era.

It should also be noted that with the medieval emphasis upon Jewish mysticism, as revealed through such works as the *Sepher Yetzirah* and the *Sepher ha Zohar,* there was a broad insistence upon the cultivation of man's latent spiritual and mystical resources. The gradual development of an esoteric science among the Jews followed the pattern exemplified by other and related teachings, notably those of the Essenes, Therapeutae, Johnanites, Gnostics, and Neoplatonists. The works of Philo Judaeus are indicative of the rise of North African transcendentalism in Jewish thought. All historical and symbolical elements of the Bible story were unfolded and restated in the terms of a powerful spiritual impulse toward the regeneration of the human being.

This emphasizes an important aspect of the Messianic vision. The coming of the Messiah depends upon a certain pact or covenant. Man must earn the mystery of his salvation through bearing witness to his devotion by a life of good deeds and personal morality. Heaven rewards the good man, not the bad; but heaven does not demand that all men shall see the light equally. Salvation is not for the few, but for Israel; not for the individual, but for the collective. Man must bear his part of the collective burden, until men of good spirit everywhere and among all faiths rise up and unite their efforts. If this is not a dogma, it is certainly of the mind of the faith, and bestows a new concept of the benefits totally experienced by man if he earns the right to be the servant and teacher of his brother.

In large, then, the Prophetic Books prophesy that the good man shall find his God, and shall come in the end to serenity of spirit. He shall live in a good world, and the lion and the lamb shall lie down together. Sin and death shall be no more, because men in their hearts have chosen righteousness. Then the glory of God shall be made manifest outwardly as well as inwardly. That which was seen and known only to the prophet in his ecstasy shall come to pass in the experience of all men. There are many wonderful details, upon which extensive commentaries have been written, but always for the same purpose. The true believer is invited to seek the substance of the doctrine, mend his ways, and cling to the truth.

THE BOOK OF THE PROPHET EZEKIEL

Ezekiel was one of those who was carried as a captive to Babylonia during the reign of Nebuchadrezzar. Little is known of him other than that he was the son of Buzi the priest. He lived for years at Tel-abib on the banks of a river or canal called the Chebar. He received his call to prophecy in the fifth year of the captivity, about 592 B. C. The name *Ezekiel* means "God will strengthen him," and he was one of the four great prophets. Josephus says he was but a boy at the time of the captivity, but this hardly agrees with the other elements of the story. Origen conceived Ezekiel as a prototype of Christ. Tradition ascribes several miracles to Ezekiel. He walked upon the waters of Chebar and fed the hungry with a miraculous draught of fishes. There is a report that he was murdered in Babylon by a Jewish prince whom he had convicted of idolatry. He seems to have been buried in a tomb on the banks of the Euphrates a few days' journey from Bagdad. Ezekiel makes very few references to himself, and according to the opinions of scholars, he is not quoted in the New Testament directly or indirectly, except for certain parallels in the Apocalypse.

The Book of Ezekiel, which is one of those regarded as controversial, is divided into two major sections. The first deals with the destruction of Jerusalem, and various predictions delivered prior to that event. The second part is concerned principally with the future condition of Israel and the final restoration of the Jewish nation. A parenthetical section, lying between chapters 25 and 32, is concerned with prophecies directed against seven foreign nations. This section appears to be highly symbolical. All the tribulations of the captivity are justified by a new theocratic state under the rulership of the Messianic king. There will be a new temple, not in the Old Jerusalem, but in an ideal city, the name of which is *Jehovah Shemmah* (The Lord is there).

Apart from its prophetic form, which is essentially traditional, the most remarkable and curious parts of the Book of Ezekiel are to be found in the opening chapter and in chapter 10. A vision came to the prophet "in the thirtieth year, in the fourth *month,* in the fifth *day* of the month." Some authorities hold that this date refers to the age of Ezekiel. Metaphysical experiences described in the Bible occur most frequently near water, and Ezekiel was by the River Chebar. In religious symbolism, water signifies the etheric world that extends beyond the physical plane of life. In the Greek Mysteries, the River Styx, across which Charon rows the dead, symbolizes the etheric interval between the physical and superphysical world. Of similar significance is the river Jordan, upon whose farther shore await the souls of the redeemed, according to old Christian belief. The Nile was sacred to Egypt, and the pious Brahmin hopes to die beside the Ganges.

Thus it may be said that Ezekiel received his strange vision on the shores of the stream of etheric memories, or psychic consciousness. The account therefore indicates that the prophet was in a mystical reverie, or was dwelling in a state which bordered on superphysical consciousness. It is ever thus that visions come. Ezekiel beheld a whirlwind rising out of the north, a great cloud filled with fire, in the midst of which appeared the chariot of the Most High. The direction from which the vision came is most significant. In the teachings of the Egyptians, for example, the dark and silent north was regarded as the abode of the great gods. In one secret system, it is clearly set forth that a temple to the gods should have an eastern, a southern, and a western gate, but in the north, there shall be no gate. The ancients devised this belief because to them the sun never appeared in the northern part of the heavens. The north polar mountain of the Egyptians was the abode of the old dark gods, the fathers of the divine kings. The mysterious Mount Meru of the Hindus is the polar mountain, where the gods dwell, and, like the Shamballah of the Buddhists, its ridgepole is the polar axis. As the secret gods dwell in the north, men might not travel there, except in their dreams and visions or in the initiatory rites. The northern part of the temple was without gate or opening, to honor the hidden gods, to signify the unapproachable majesty of divinity and the secret abode of the most venerated masters of the ancient learning. Hence, it was from the north, from the axis mountain of the earth's sacred government, that the whirling vision of Ezekiel came. This seems to indicate beyond reasonable doubt that the prophet Ezekiel was wise in the learning of the Egyptians, and had accepted their concepts of the mystery of the north.

Out of the whirlwind from the northern region, there appeared an extraordinary instrument of power. The Bible does not actually describe this vehicle, but in the commentaries it is called the *Merkabah,* the *Chariot of Majesty.* This Merkabah was so sacred to the old rabbins that it might be spoken of only with the greatest veneration, and only in the presence of, or among, the elders. It is written that the Merkabah shall not be named if there be two and one is not wise. The Merkabah is described as one of the deepest mysteries of Cabalism.

The chariot of righteousness, the seat of the Most High, the mystery of "the wheels that go all ways and are filled with eyes," is thus interpreted by the wisest of the ages. The chariot consisted of four creatures called cherubs, each going a different way, each with four heads, six wings, and the hoofs of a calf. Each of the cherubs bore the face of a man, a bull, a lion, and an eagle, and their wings met at the corners of the Merkabah. These mysterious creatures rode on wheels filled with eyes, and above them was a throne chair, and upon the throne was an awesome presence in white, surrounded by light and power and accompanied by a rainbow. So numerous and complicated are the interpretations of this vision that we can mention only a few of them.

The Merkabah is the world or universe as the body or vehicle of the Creator. It is beneath his feet, for the earth is his footstool. The Merkabah is therefore this footstool, wherein God is manifested only in his lesser parts. We may thus expect to discover an astronomical significance in the form and structure of the Merkabah. The cherubs are the symbols of the four cardinal angels, the equinoxes, and the solstices. It should be remembered that at the time this vision was described, the equinoxes fell, according to popular belief, in Taurus and Scorpio, and the solstices in Aquarius and Leo. These four signs are the bull, the eagle, the man, and the lion respectively. The four fixed signs, as they are called in astro-theology, occur not only in Jewish metaphysics and in the sacred sciences of the Greeks and Egyptians, but reappear in the Christian Mysteries in the forms of the symbols attributed to the four Evangelists, who, as St. Augustine observed, were witnesses unto the four corners of the world. The sarcophagi of medieval European princes and prelates were frequently adorned with the four creatures and they recur consistently in religious architecture.

The cherubim, or living creatures, are the four great guardians of the four corners of the earth or sky. They return in Buddhism as the *Lokapalas,* or the four guardian-kings of the hollow square. They also find parallel in the mythology of the American Indians. Ancient astronomers on the plains of Chaldea established four great stars which appeared in the four constellations—Taurus, Scorpio, Aquarius, and Leo —and called them the guardian angels. Each of the four guardians had six wings, which were said to make up the twenty-four hours of the day. These angels also referred to the zodiacal galaxies of stars, for it is written in the Cabalistic books that the stars are the eyes of the angels, and that the bodies of the angels were full of eyes. In the Apocalypse occurs the account of the four horsemen, representing the four ages, or Hindu Yugas, and these are aspects of the same symbolism. Among the primitive peoples of the three Americas, there were giant chieftains guarding the houses of the four winds.

In the Greek mythology, Phanes, the Logos, ornamented with the heads of birds and animals, burst from the egg of chaos. Thus Phanes is almost identical in description with the cherubim of Ezekiel. Each human body is a Merkabah, a chariot of the law. The four natures, or the four-fold constitution of man, are represented by the four heads of living creatures. The physical body corresponds to the earth, is assigned to Taurus, and is centered in the heart. The next is the watery, or humid body, associated with the sign of Scorpio, the eagle, which has its seat in the human spleen. The third is the fiery, or emotional, body of man, ruled by Leo, with its seat in the liver. The fourth head, that of a human being, corresponds to Aquarius, the principle of mind, and has its seat in the brain. Each of these creatures goes a different way—that is, has its own powers and temperament—yet together they form the chariot, the Merkabah of the spirit.

In the Paracelsian theory, which prevailed in Europe during the medieval period, the compound nature of the earth is composed of four elements: earth, water, fire, and air. They also correspond with the four heads of the cherubim. These elements or substances combine to form bodies, and these, in turn, are chariots or vehicles for the being which inhabits the bodily complex. The hierarchies of the four corners, or fixed signs of the zodiac, are called *the builders,* and they preside over the principle of form because they control the formative processes of Nature. They are identified with the streams of those elemental substances which, pouring through their respective hierarchies, are distributed throughout the corporeal sphere. Thus the cherubim correspond to the four rivers that flow out of Eden to make fertile the world. From their co-mixings are produced the vehicles for the manifestation of life. They are the four white horses that draw the chariot of Abraxas, the Gnostic Pantheos.

It is interesting that four-headed creatures occur in many religions with similar or identical meanings. In India, the lord of the material universe is Shiva, frequently represented with four heads. Brahma, brought into manifestation through the Saivistic principle manifesting in the material universe, is likewise depicted with four heads. He had a fifth head which was cut off during a battle in heaven. The story of the fifth head of Brahma conceals the mystery of the fifth element, the azoth or quintessentia of alchemy. The four heads of Brahma are also symbolized by the four *Vedas,* or Books of the Law. There is also a concealed, or fifth, *Veda,* to correspond with Brahma's missing head. In the Ezekiel account, the four creatures or elements carry in their midst the golden throne, or the fifth element. Paracelsus says there is no greater mystery than that of the hypothetical medium, ether, for it is truly a connective energy binding the material and spiritual worlds, and making possible the action of superphysical principles upon material organisms.

The likeness of a man full of fire, which rode upon the cherubim, is, of course, spirit, whether considered in its universal or individual aspect, which is supported and carried upon the elements and their principles. The "wheels full of eyes" refer to the heavens, the planets, the constellations—particularly the great wheel of the zodiac which surrounds the earth, and in which the cherubim turn. The universe itself is indeed the wheel within wheels. In the midst of all its creatures, sits the Ancient of Days, the Eternal One, the Axis of Law and Life, the Master of the Mysteries.

The Talmud mentions a number of wise and dedicated scholars who have attempted to solve the mysteries of the Merkabah, and there is no doubt from the numerous intimations and allusions that it was regarded as a symbol of the whole esoteric tradition of Israel. We learn from the old lore that when Moses received the vision from the burning bush, the Lord commanded Metatron, the Angel of the Face, to lead Moses into the higher regions of the celestial world. When Moses objected that he was not worthy to see the wonders of heaven, Metatron transformed the eyes of Moses into "Merkabah Wheels." During the same vision, the Lord said unto Moses: "Perchance thou thinkest I have no messengers, hosts, seraphim, ofannim, ministering angels, and Merkabah wheels, to send to Egypt, to bring my children thence . . . " It is also stated in the Talmud (*Sanhedrin* 102a) that Ahija and Jeroboam discussed together the mysteries of the divine throne, these mysteries being the greater secrets of the Torah. It is said that God opened the heavens to Isaac so that he beheld the "chambers of the Merkabah." There is a reference in rabbinical literature that the countenance of Jacob is in the Merkabah, and that it is the face of the being seated upon the divine throne. This being, it is said, therefore represents the human race.

It is written that there was a difference between the revelations of God to the Fathers of Israel and those made to other prophets, for the Fathers are the Merkabah, the bearers of the divine throne, and their lives were a constant revelation of God. There is a legend that, at the request of Ezekiel, God changed the ox of the Merkabah into a cherub so that men should not remember Israel's sin of worshipping the golden calf. Rabbi Immi said: "It is not permitted to impart the mysteries of the Torah except to one who is enlightened." For this reason, it is unlawful to declare the secrets of the Maaseh Merkabah, or the chariot throne.

The Maaseh Merkabah, or the secret work of the chariot throne, is the religious mystical philosophy of Israel, and certain of its teachings have come to be associated with the Cabala. The ancient followers of the Maaseh Merkabah were held in high estimation, and originally they were of the family of Moses. They are believed to have had power to perform miracles, and from them descended the fragments of the *Sod* and the secret learning. From various hints and intimations, it would appear that the concept of the Merkabah was associated with a secret science devoted to the development of the apperceptive powers of human consciousness. Like the meditational disciplines of Yoga and Vedanta, and the mystical experiences of the Sufis and the Dervishes, it led to communion with God and the invisible creatures of the divine world. Seekers after this esoteric doctrine were therefore warned of its dangers and were not permitted to advance such studies unless they were wholly dedicated to truth and had reached forty years of age.

Certain Jewish mystics who sought an internal contact with the Divine Being, called themselves *Yorede Merkabah,* or "Riders on the Divine Chariot." They believed that they could cultivate trances and visions and, like Elijah, they could travel without death into the celestial regions by means of the chariot of ecstasy. Such beliefs, prevalent among Persians and Arabian devotees of mysticism, probably influenced the more devout and transcendentally inclined Jewish thinkers, and gave a new wealth of inner meaning to their religious traditions. All the great faiths of the world have experienced the need for mystical overtones and have developed disciplines of meditation, reflection, concentration, and reminiscence, by which the pious could detach themselves from the limitations of the mortal mind, and transcend the formal structures of their faiths. There is considerable evidence that theurgic arts were cultivated by Jewish religionists at an early date and led ultimately to the integration of Cabalistic philosophy, with its attendant spiritism and demonology. Most of the early Jewish prophets were accredited with the power of inner vision, and some even claimed that they had visited the immortal regions of space, even as Moses had been lifted into the firmament to commune with God. It is known that Egyptian metaphysics and the Mystery cults of Babylon had such teachings, and the Jews had long contact with these peoples.

Ezekiel's description of the new temple which was to come after the punishment of Gog and Magog is obviously an allegorical account with strong mystical implications. In Ezekiel 48:35, the prophet records that the name of the city shall be "The LORD is there" (*Jehovah Shemmah*). The whole prophecy suggests the wonderful city set forth in the Revelation of St. John. Like the Shamballah of the Northern Buddhists, this utopian theocratic state recurs in most mystical literature. It is the wonderful abode of the Dervish saints to which their disciples are occasionally permitted to journey. Like the Paradisio of Dante and the troubadours' court of love, it was the secret dwelling place of the redeemed, ruled over by the Messiah, the grand hierophant of the Mysteries of religion. Obviously, then, it could be a veiled account of the temple of initiation, situated in the invisible sphere to which the soul could travel when it was lifted up from the body in the chariot of ecstasy. Thus, in Ezekiel, we have one of the most powerful statements of esoteric disciplines to be found in the Old Testament.

THE BOOK OF THE PROPHET ISAIAH

The Book of the Prophet Isaiah, generally regarded as the greatest and most important of the Jewish prophetic writings, opens with the words, "The vision of Isaiah the son of Amoz, which he saw concerning Judah and Jerusalem in the days of Uzziah, Jotham, Ahaz, *and* Hezekiah, kings of Judah." According to the scanty biographical material available, sustained by the text of his writings, Isaiah ben Amoz, the first of the major prophets, was called by the will of God to prophesy to the kingdom of Judea about 738 B. C., in the reign of Hezekiah. The name *Isaiah* means "the salvation of Jah" (Jah is a contracted form of Jehovah). There is a legend that Isaiah was born circumcised and was one of those foreordained to be a teacher over the Jews. It is also said that he prophesied in seventy-one languages, and there is an account, held to be common knowledge at an early date, that he suffered martyrdom.

In an apocryphal work of uncertain date entitled " The Ascension of Isaiah," a number of traditional fragments were gathered by an unknown editor. "The Ascension of Isaiah" is divided into three parts. The first covers the martyrdom of the prophet, and is believed to be an authentic Jewish work of about the 1st century. The other divisions of this apocryphal book are regarded as essentially Christian. One is the Testament of Hezekiah, and the other, the Vision of Isaiah. The Testament of Hezekiah deals with prophecies bearing upon the life, death, and resurrection of Jesus, and the Vision of Isaiah is an account of a mystical experience in which the prophet was raised through the seven heavens and brought into the presence of God and Jesus and the redeemed souls of the past. Isaiah sees Enoch in the seventh heaven, which is the residence of the righteous since the time of Adam. This vision parallels in many ways the *Pymander* of Hermes, Mohammed's Night Journey, and the Apocalypse of St. John.

Before attempting a survey of the Book of Isaiah, the problems involved in its authorship must be considered. There are several schools of thought, of which two should be mentioned. Deeply hidden among the ruminations of learned rabbinical commentators is one, attributed to Baba Batra, that is most stimulating. This is to the effect that Hezekiah and his associates wrote the books of Isaiah, Proverbs, Song of Songs, and Ecclesiastes, and that the men of the Great Assembly wrote the books of Ezekiel, the twelve Minor Prophets, Daniel, and the Scroll of Esther. While such a statement is contrary to most contemporary thinking, studies in comparative religion would broadly support such an hypothesis. In the course of time, we shall probably learn that many sacred writings attributed to individuals were actually the productions of groups working under obligations of secrecy and from some central core of knowledge and revelation.

The more conservative Biblical scholars are in general agreement that the book of Isaiah was the work of at least three persons living at different periods. This is sustained not only by the style of the writings, but also by the internal content, which emphasizes widely separated historical incidents. The scope of the book has therefore been described as pre-exilic, exilic, and post-exilic. To meet this situation, three Isaiahs have been distinguished. The first is Isaiah Proper, to whom is ascribed the principal part of chapters 1-39; the second is Deutero-Isaiah, or the Second Isaiah, who has been allotted chapters 40-55; and Trito-Isaiah, or the Third Isaiah, who has been more or less conjured into existence, is accredited with the authorship of chapters 56-66.

The structure of the book suggests that parts thereof may have been circulated separately. Although principally a poetic writing, there is a considerable prose section made up of chapters 36-39. The complete work came into being, therefore, over a period of approximately three centuries. Isaiah Proper is dated betwen 738 and 701 B. C.; the Deutero-Isaiah, about 540 B. C.; and the Trito-Isaiah, about 450 B. C. If Hezekiah is associated with the authorship of the book, his contribution must have covered what we now know as Isaiah Proper; otherwise, Isaiah ben Amoz, or whoever wrote under that name, must be accepted as the author.

Of the Deutero-Isaiah nothing is known historically, but the section attributed to him is evidently the work of a most learned person or persons, and it is believed, from the literary excellence and structure, that it was originally prepared in written form and not as an oral prophecy. The Deutero-Isaiah strongly emphasized an aspect of Jewish doctrine about which only intimations occur in earlier writers; namely, the universality of the Jewish God, and the belief that the God of Israel would ultimately be worshipped throughout the world. The Trito-Isaiah, also an anonymous prophet, has been a subject of considerable scholarly controversy. As the fragments contained in the chapters allotted to this hypothetical scribe relate to circumstances before, during, and even after the exile, there is much to indicate that they could have been the work of several persons.

We have examined the authorship of the book of Isaiah in some detail because it is typical of problems to which the average Bible student has given little thought. Assuming, as we must, that compilations of this kind were prepared with intent and purpose, we are invited to greater thoughtfulness and discrimination in our examination of the Scriptures.

The call of Isaiah, the son of Amoz, to the service of the Lord, is described in the 6th chapter of the book. The Prophet beheld the Supreme One seated upon a throne attended by seraphim. Isaiah was greatly frightened because he considered himself unworthy, but one of the seraphim, holding tongs in his hand, took a coal from the heavenly altar and, approaching the Prophet, laid it upon his lips, saying: "Lo, this hath touched thy lips; and thine iniquity is taken away, and thy sin purged." (6:7). After this, the Lord spoke and instructed Isaiah to go forth according to the divine will. This is followed by prophecies concerning the state of foreign nations, and is climaxed in chapters 13 and 14 by a magnificent ode relating to the downfall of Babylon.

There are two verses in Isaiah which are held to predict the virgin birth of Jesus. Chapter 7:14 reads: "Therefore the Lord himself shall give you a sign; Behold, a virgin shall conceive, and bear a son, and shall call his name Immanuel." It seems that Isaiah's own explanation of his prophetic statement is contained in chapter 8:3. It should be pointed out that in his prophecy concerning Immanuel, Isaiah does not use *bethulah,* the Hebrew term for virgin, but *'almah,* which simply means "a young woman," whether married or unmarried, and conveys no implication of an immaculate conception or a virgin birth. The symbolic name *Immanuel,* meaning "God with us," is applied by the Apostle Matthew to the Messiah born of the Virgin (See, Matthew 1:23). In fact, this verse is obviously borrowed from Isaiah through the Septuagint.

Isaiah 9:6 has also found its way strongly into Christian thinking. "For unto us a child is born, unto us a son is given: and the government shall be upon his shoulder: and his name shall be called Wonderful, Counsellor, The mighty God, The everlasting Father, The Prince of Peace." Compare this with Luke 2:11, John 3:16, and Matthew 28:18.

These obscure allusions associated with the advent of the Messiah have been subjected to a great deal of controversy and interpretation. A modern position suggests that Isaiah, being elevated to a mystical state, spoke ambiguously and probably symbolically about both immediate things and larger events affecting the more distant future. The author of Matthew seems to have directly associated the words of Isaiah with the Christian Mystery, but there is no clear proof that such was the original intent. It cannot be denied, however, that the Messianic concept existed in Israel as early as the time of the prophets.

One of the most significant contributions which Isaiah made to the religious life of his time is the emphasis which he laid upon the holiness of God. The power, wisdom, strength, and righteousness of God, had already been included in the concept of the Divine Nature. It remained for Isaiah to spiritualize the very being of Deity. God kept his own laws. He was the "Holy One," whose very nature was perfect morality and absolute integrity. This truly good God is available to man as an experience of consciousness. To know God, however, man must live in conformity with that benevolence which is forever in the heart of God. The great prophecy, therefore, is that if Israel places itself in the keeping of God, and follows in the way of righteousness which is God's will, the people will be rewarded with everlasting peace. The prophet further emphasizes the spiritual significance of faith. The good man must renounce his own ways and serve God with his whole heart. Only through such a way of life can he abide in the radiance of holiness.

To Isaiah, also, God emerges as a supreme being. He created the universe according to the wisdom resident within his own nature, and he governs all of his creatures by a plan which he alone fully understands. Through this plan, Deity accomplishes his own purposes, in his own way and in his own time. If mortals keep the laws of God, they will be strengthened and enjoy security, but if they depart from these ways through selfishness, violence, or unrighteousness, then they will be punished for their false belief or their unbelief. Like most of the prophets, Isaiah assumes that the Jewish people will ultimately be preserved and will return to God with a full heart and a perfect love. Thus, he seems to speak first to the few who have cultivated internal vison, and second to the many whose inner sight has been darkened by ignorance and ambition. To these latter, he gives stern warning that man stands forever in the need of God much more than God has need of man. Thus it is proper that humanity should restore itself in the sight of God, and re-dedicate its conduct to the service of the "Holy One."

BIBLIOGRAPHY

Bension, Ariel. The Zohar in Moslem and Christian Spain. London: George Routledge and Sons, Ltd., 1932.

Berosus. Chaldean History. Included in Ancient Fragments, by Isaac Preston Corey. London: 1832.

Blavatsky, H. P. Isis Unveiled. Covina, Calif.: Theosophical University Press, 1950. 2 Vols.

Budge, Sir E. Wallis. The Queen of Sheba and Her Only Son Menyelek (I) being the "Book of the Glory of Kings." Translated by Sir E. Wallis Budge. London: Oxford University Press, 1932.

Conway, Moncure, Solomon and Solomonic Literature. Chicago: The Open Court Publishing Co., 1899.

Da Costa, Hippolyto J. Dionysian Artificers. With an Introductory Essay on the Myth of Dionysius by Manly P. Hall. New York: Macoy Publishing and Masonic Supply Co., 1936.

Doane, T. W. Bible Myths and Their Parallels in Other Religions. New York: The Commonwealth Co., 1882.

D'Olivet, Fabre. The Hebraic Tongue Restored. Done into English by Nayan Louise Redfield. New York: G. P. Putnam's Sons, 1921.

Drummond, Sir William. The Oedipus Judaicus. London: A. J. Valpy, 1811.

Dunlap, S. F. Sod, the Mysteries of Adoni. London: Williams and Norgate, 1860.

Faber, George S. A Dissertation on the Mysteries of the Cabiri. Vol. I. Oxford: The University Press, 1803.

Fludd, Robert. Collectio Operum. Oppenhemi: 1617.

Frazer, Sir James. Folk-Lore in the Old Testament. New York: Tudor Publishing Co., 1923.

Freud, Sigmund. Moses and Monotheism. New York: Alfred A. Knopf, 1949.

Fuller, Thomas. Church History of Britain. London: 1655.

Gaffarel, James. Unheard-of Curiosities Concerning the Talismanic Magic of the Persians. London: 1650.

Gesenius. Hebrew and Chaldee Lexicon to the Old Testament Scriptures. Translated by Samuel P. Tregelles. London: Samuel Bagster and Sons, Ltd., 1885.

Ginzberg, Louis. **The Legends of the Jews.** 7 Vols. Philadelphia: The Jewish Publication Society of America, 1909.

Higgins, Godfrey. **Anacalypsis.** 2 Vols. London: Longman, Rees, Orme, Brown, Green, and Longman, 1836.

Josephus, Flavius. **History of the Jews.** Included in **The Works of Flavius Josephus.** Oxford: 1839.

Kircher, Athanasius. **Oedipus Aegyptiacus.** 4 Vols. Rome: Ex Typographia Vitalis Mascardi, 1652.

————— **Turris Babel.** Amsterdam. 1679.

Massey, Gerald. **The Natural Genesis.** 2 Vols. London: Williams and Norgate, 1883.

————— **Ancient Egypt, the Light of the World.** 2 Vols. London: T. Fisher Unwin, 1907.

Montfaucon, Father Bernard de. **L'Antique Expliquee.** London: 1721.

Mueller, Max. **Chips From a German Workshop.** 2 Vols. London: Longmans, Green, and Co., 1867.

Philo Judaeus. **Vita Mosis.** Included in Vol. 3 of **The Works of Philo Judaeus.** Translated from the Greek by C. D. Younge. London: Bohn, 1855.

Priest, Josiah. **American Antiquities.** Albany: Hoffman and White, 1833.

Renan, Ernest. **The Song of Songs.** Translated into English by William M. Thomson. London: Wm. M. Thomson, 1860.

Reuchlin, Johann. **De Arte Cabalistica.** Haguenoae: 1517.

————— **De Verbo Mirifico.** Bardeneis: 1514.

Rosenroth, Knorr von. **Cabala Denudata.** 2 Vols. Frankfurt: Joannis Davidis Zunneri, 1684.

Smith, George. **The Chaldean Account of Genesis.** New York: Scribner, Armstrong and Co., 1876.

Steinthal, H. "The Legend of Samson." An Essay, Appendix to Goldzhier's **Mythology Among the Hebrews.** London: Longmans, Green, and Co., 1877.

Tylor, E. B. **Primitive Culture.** 2 Vols. London: John Murray, 1871.

Zohar, The. Translated by Harry Sperling and Maurice Simon. 5 Vols. London: The Soncino Press, 1931.

INDEX

Aaron, brother of Moses, 62; cast down his rod before Pharaoh, 63; represented the priesthood, 62; upholds the arm of Moses, 72, 73; ref. to, 273

Aaron's rod, budding of, 162, 163; compared with Joseph's rod, 163; compared with Tannhauser, 163; enclosed in Ark of Covenant, 162; meaning of, 63

Abel, as agrarian principle, 120; birth of, 120; offering of, 122

Aben-Ezra, Rabbi, on meaning of Song of Songs, 195

Abraham, ancestor of the Hebrews, 147-148; meaning of name, 151-152; originally Abram, 147,151; patriarch associated with Cabala, 29; see also Abram

Abram, God made covenant with, 151; meaning of name, 151-152; meets Melchizedek, 148; name changed to Abraham, 147, 151

Abraxas, the Gnostic pantheos, 284

Absolute Being, according to Cabala, 34

Adam, body of, 107; body of placed in Noah's ark, 138; body of, re-interred at Golgotha, 138; creation of, 106; falls into sphere of generation, 121; first man not so named, 105; greater than angels, 107; instructed in Cabala, 28; named all creatures, 112; Noah called

the second, 130; resided in paradise, 107; spiritual archetype of humanity, 125; the anthropos, 121; tomb of, 75

Adam Kadmon, and Nebuchadrezzar's dream, 229; man of the red earth, 106

Adept-King, meaning of, 191

Adi Buddha, produces the seven Dhyani-Buddhas, 97

ADM, see Adam

Adonai, name of God, 112, 162

Adonijah, conspiracy of, 169

Adonis, killed by wild boar, 240

Aged, the, comes forth from the Aged of the Aged, 37

Aged of the Aged, the, related to Ain Soph, 37

Ahura Mazda, the Supreme One, 98

Ain, the Boundless, 34; the Triune Divinity, 36

Ain Soph, Boundless Life, 35

Ain Soph Aur, Boundless Light, 35; numerological study of, 35-36

Akasa, subtle ether, 162

Akhenaten and Moses, 52

Akiba, Rabbi, and the *Sepher Yetzirah*, 29; mentioned, 69

Alchemy, and Solomon-Sheba legend, 189; and Song of Songs, 198; and Temple of Solomon, 173

Alexander II, Czar, caused Codex Sinaiticus to be published, 16

Demeter, fertility deity, 117

Dervish saints, mystical abode of, 287

Deutero-Isaiah, 289

Deuteronomy, derivation of name, 83; full revelation of the law in, 88

Dhyani-Buddhas, creative process according to, 99; modes of conditioned consciousness, 97

Diamond Sutra, earliest example of Chinese printing, 19

Diana, Great Goddess of Ephesians, 165, 186; and Shulamite maiden, 198; represented as black, 186

Diaspora, ref. to, 196, 270

D'Olivet, Fabre, on first verses of Genesis, 95; translation of Elohim, 105

Dove, symbolism of, 238; the Holy Spirit, 134

Dragon, symbolism of, 114, 220

Druid, derivation of word, 116; priests called serpents, 114

Dryads, tree-spirits, 117

Earth, inadequate translation of, in Genesis, 95

Ecclesiastes, and Near Eastern thought, 245, 246; discussion of, 245-247; fatalistic tone of, 245; meaning of word, 245; mystical content of, 246

Eden, Garden of, see Garden of Eden

Edom, kings of, 108

Ego, symbolism of, 122

Egypt, a theocracy, 53; learning of, influenced many systems, 54; of the Exodus, not a country, 55

Egyptian, account of creation, 103; Book of the Dead, originally ritual-drama, 118; religion and Moses, 52; teaching of immortality, 252

Ehejeh, "I Am," 38

Eleazar, High Priest of Jerusalem, 14

Elements, fifth, 284; five, symbolized by human body, 161; four, correspond with heads of cherubim, 283

Eleusinian Mysteries, pomegranates used in, 117

Eleusinian rites, 159

Elihu, admonishes Job, 262-263; an Initiate of the Mysteries, 262

Elijah, appeared to Simeon ben Jochai, 29

Elohim, a plural word, 104; descent of, 103; gods of the dawn, 101; reflection of, in the four worlds, 99; related to Saturn, 134; seven creating spirits, 65; shadows of, 99; symbolism of, 98; the formators and builders, 97; translation of word by D'Olivet, 105; word analyzed, 95

Emanationism, taught by Cabalists, 43-44

Enoch, ascension of, 127, 128; father of Methuselah, 127; golden delta of, 128, 129; in modern Masonic symbolism, 129; "Royal Arches" of, 127-129; seen by Isaiah, 288; transformed into Metatron, 128

Equinoxes, in astro-theology, 209

Erda, the Great Mother, 251

Essenes, mentioned, 277; on storehouse of souls, 111

Esther, and Matrona, 226; great heroine of Jewish people, 222; inspired song of, ref. to, 90; meaning of name, 222; symbolizes divine love, 227

Esther, Book of, 222-228; and Feast of Purim, 222

Eternity, Rosicrucian axiom about, 37

Ethiopic version of Solomon and Sheba story, 183

Eucharist, Melchizedek first priest of, 151

Eve, creation of, 112; tomb of, 75

Everlasting House, see Temple of Solomon

OTHER TITLES BY MANLY P. HALL